W9-BCX-041

WANDERER ON MY NATIVE

SIMON AND SCHUSTER · NEW YORK

For Barbara,
who kept faith

CONTENTS

FOREWORD

New York's Gateway National Recreation Area is composed of four former military-surplus parcels of land from New Jersey's Fort Hancock to Brooklyn's Floyd Bennett Field. These 26,000 acres are barely 1 percent of the acreage of our best known and presumably most popular national park, Yellowstone. Yet last year Gateway hosted *four times* as many people as Yellowstone. More than nine million beachcombers, bathers, birders, and fishermen sought recreation on this handful of seaside sites surrounding New York Harbor.

New Yorkers are not unique in their curiosity about and longing for the sea. Last year some 75 million people visited the beaches and bays of the U.S. Atlantic coast—poking through tidal pools in Maine, collecting shells on Cape Cod, catching king mackerel off Cape Hatteras, and photographing rockets and ruddy ducks at Cape Canaveral. If all the people who visited the 28,673 miles of Atlantic shoreline in 1982 had done so in a single day, there would have been over 2600 people standing shoulder to shoulder on every mile of beach, marsh, and mud flat between Key West and the Canadian border!

There are many excellent field guides to identify what people see at the seashore, but few that attempt to answer the hows and whys of life in coastal waters. Identification guides look at distinct categories of life—shells or birds or fishes—as though these creatures existed in laboratories, unconnected with other forms of life, including our own.

While *Wanderer on My Native Shore* is a guide of sorts, it is something less in order that it may be something more. It is about marine ecosystems, but it is also about people, since we are now the dominant ingredient in every marine ecosystem. I want the reader to wonder about what man has wrought as well as to be able to identify many of the sea and coastal plants and animals with which we associate. Since *Wanderer on My Native Shore* is designed for reading rather than a dusty slot on a reference shelf, I have kept statistics, footnotes, and Bibliography to a minimum without, I hope, sacrificing anything in the way of clarity or accuracy.

For readers who want to check the identification of species, there is a Glossary of common and scientific names at the back of the book. There is also an Appendix with further information on selected conservation organizations.

My partner in this enterprise has been Bob Hines who, for thirty-three years, was the principal staff artist for the U.S. Department of the Interior. Bob's work has appeared in dozens of books and periodicals, but he may be best remembered for his collaboration with his friend and former colleague at the Fish and Wildlife Service, Rachel Carson, in her pioneering achievement, *The Edge of the Sea*.

I would like to thank the publishers of *Audubon, Field & Stream, On the Beach*, and *Sea Frontiers* for allowing me to season this present effort with paragraphs from articles I originally wrote for them.

Any amateur marine naturalist who wants to keep up-to-date is better off with subscriptions to a spectrum of scientific periodicals than a library of reference books whose value fades with each new major discovery about the sea. Foremost among such useful magazines, I would list *Oceanus, Oceans, Natural History, National Geographic, Science, Science News*, and *Scientific American*. The latter four publications only now and again publish a sea-science piece, but as the reader of *Wanderer* will discover, one never knows when a new insight on insect behavior or plant distribution might enlarge his or her larger understanding of the sea. *National Fisherman* keeps me abreast of what the working waterman is thinking, especially when such thoughts are reported by a writer as capable as John Frye, whose *The Men All Singing* is the best book on the menhaden fishery since George Brown Goode published his monumental tome in 1880.

As a member of the American Littoral Society and the National Coalition for Marine Conservation, I am kept up-to-date on what marine conservationists are doing in the society's *Underwater Naturalist* and the coalition's *Right Rigger!* And if you're a diver, you already subscribe to *Skin Diver*; a marine recreational angler, to *Salt Water Sportsman*; or a pelagic birder, to *American Birds*. I use the word "or" rather than "and" because one of the pities of people and the sea is that few see it with comprehensive eyes.

Finally, my thanks to Peter Schwed, a superior being as well as editor, for showing infinite patience while I grubbed a living in a dozen different directions; and to John Gottschalk, a man of so many dimensions it would only embarrass him and not convince the reader that such a man was real if I tried to list all his attributes. John kindly read the original manuscript and made many valuable suggestions to improve it. Any remaining flaws are due entirely to my stubbornness and not his lack of perspicacity.

GEORGE REIGER
Seaside Road
Locustville, Virginia

And what if behind me to westward the wall of the
    woods stands high?
The world lies east: How ample, the marsh and the sea
    and the sky!

SIDNEY LANIER

1

OVERTURE

If nature's first green is gold, so, too, is her last, and October is the most beautiful time of year to be alive and in rural New England. School openings have long since drawn the last of the summer crowds back to the suburbs, and Interstate 95—the long green tunnel through Maine—is now deserted and glowing with autumn color.

I took the exit at Lincoln and made my way through Springfield, Carroll, and Topsfield, then turned southeast on U.S. 1 to find Leen's Lodge near Grand Lake Stream. Tourist facilities were mostly shuttered for the winter, but everywhere hunter-orange-hatted men were standing and talking in pairs and foursomes at service stations, hardware stores, and beneath the American flags at post offices.

Before turning onto the gravel road past the Peter Dana Point Indian Reservation, I drove on to find a store where I could buy a hunter-orange hat of my own for the woodcock hunting I planned to do. The old man behind the store's counter put on his glasses to check me out and then tried to identify the license on my car. While I picked out the only cap that fit me, the shopkeeper craned his neck trying to make out the type on the white plates.

"Where'd you say you was from?" he finally asked.

"Virginia."

"Oh." A pause. And then by way of explanation and apology, "I thought you was from Massachusetts. They got white plates, too."

"Don't you like Massachusetts?"

"Got no use for nothing or nobody south of the Kittery bridge! Big business runs the world down there, and if it's not the bosses coming up here to try to change our ways, it's the wives and kids telling us how damned quaint we are!"

He then extracted my change from an old glass cookie jar with as many nuts and washers and arrowheads in it as nickels and dimes.

Xenophobia is endemic to rural areas. In the mountains of Carolina, the scenery is being despoiled, so locals say, by folks from Atlanta. In my own area of the Eastern Shore, Baltimoreans and Washingtonians are considered the greatest threat to the quality of life. And in Maine, the Dark Riders mostly come from Boston.

Yet, so far as conservation is concerned, xenophobia has its uses, for suspicion of outsiders—especially outsiders with profitable schemes incompatible with rural environments—sometimes delays the entrepreneurs long enough to have common sense, law, or time prevail.

Tourism has long been the principal industry of northeastern Maine, but the economic currents that bring visitors to Maine are as fickle as the winds that blow woodcock south or the briny currents that bring young sea herring, alias sardines, to local waters.

At Eastport, some residents hope that a proposed oil refinery will help replace the broken glass in the deserted homes and put the economy on a less whimsical footing. Yet many fishermen in Canada and down the New England coast are distressed that some of their kith and kin in Eastport are willing to sell their birthrights for a few barrels of petrodollars.

The lobster fishermen, sea scallopers, and fin fishermen who run to Jeffreys Ledge and Georges Bank know that the seafood industry has meant useful work and a generally stable economy for the region for four hundred years, whereas even if oil is found in abundance on the Georges Bank, the wells will still run dry in about twenty years— and what may happen to the offshore fisheries in the meantime?

Of course, details of this debate are sometimes lost beneath the roar of petroleum-powered engines carrying fishermen to offshore grounds. There is no question of man's present dependence on oil. The question is only whether he needs to sacrifice the long-term values of the coastal margin for something as temporary as this petroleum interlude in human evolution.

After a successful woodcock hunt, I drove along the St. Croix River to Eastport to discuss the proposed refinery with some of the people in town. I heard a mixture of opinions about the project,*

* The saddest comment ever made on the proposed refinery—sad, even tragic, because it was saturated with unintended irony—was made by city manager

but even the industry's local boosters were worried that oil might change the character of the area. After all, the thinking goes, oil money is largely Sun Belt money, and what do those people know or care about us Yankees?

There are several ironies associated with the possible location of an oil refinery along the Maine coast. The first is that the scions of the greatest of all family fortunes founded on oil—the Rockefellers—have spent much of their money trying to keep the oil industry out of Maine.

Bar Harbor was settled by the Rockefellers and other oil-rich families as a summer retreat from the abuses of the petrochemical revolution they had brought to the rest of the nation. When the "wrong" sort of people began buying into the Acadia region with the hope of generating quick riches from its beauty, the Rockefellers and others turned their holdings over to the National Park Service for tax-free protection.

Another irony resides in the name *Cadillac*. Route 1 south to Acadia National Park skirts Frenchman Bay, offering the motorist several spectacular views across the water to Cadillac Mountain, the highest point along the entire western Atlantic seaboard north of Rio de Janiero. The Sieur de Cadillac first settled here before moving inland and founding the culminating spin-off center for the oil industry: Detroit, Michigan. His name is now a synonym for the ne plus ultra in automotive luxury as well as the conspicuous consumption of petroleum.

Yet the Sieur de Cadillac was a phony whose real name was Antoine Laumet. Everything about Cadillac was fake, including his coat of arms which, surmounted by a make-believe-count's coronet, is still the symbol of the automobile named for him.

However, Cadillac Mountain has a more profound story to tell than that of a poseur. The granite mass of the Mount Desert Range is a souvenir of a time approximately 225 million years ago when North America and Europe were one continent colliding with North Africa and folding up a mountain chain stretching from present-day Alabama through New England to the British Isles and Norway.

Although each geological age has played its part in the formation of the northwest Atlantic coast, the Triassic period, between 225 million and 180 million years ago, was especially important.

Dana Jacobs: "Eastport needs the oil industry to help us finance our pollution-abatement facilities."

During the early part of this period, when North America first began to drift away from North Africa and the American Northwest was growing through volcanic surges, much of the southwestern part of our continent was underwater, working on its sedimentary—and ultimately its petroleum—development.

Toward the end of the Triassic period, the once mighty Appalachians began to wear down, and eroded materials were deposited in downfaulted troughs parallel to the mountains from Nova Scotia to North Carolina. These deposits, unlike the marine-enriched sediments to the west, were mostly inorganic sandstone and conglomerate. But where organic shales prevailed, so, too, did oil, as in the Pennsylvania fields that first made the Rockefellers wealthy.

The young Triassic ocean's floor was hot, and because the covering sea was warm, it occupied a larger volume than does the older, colder Atlantic today. Some areas of the new ocean may have been too warm for certain kinds of life, but where it flooded shallow basins, the warm, mineral-rich seas provided ideal growth conditions for a great variety and quantity of marine algae. Although amphibians were not as numerous as in earlier epochs, a fabulous assortment of fish and shellfish fed on the myriad creatures spawned in this rich coastal broth. The stage was set now for the creation of vast oil and gas fields.

For several decades petroleum experts have felt certain there must be immense reservoirs of oil and gas off the Atlantic coast. However, until the last decade, the cost of drilling was prohibitive. The Atlantic is a more treacherous environment than the Gulf of Mexico, and the risks are many times greater. Yet with the dramatic rise in petroleum prices during the past ten years, the gamble of drilling off the Atlantic coast was finally worth taking because of the potential gains.

Sediment accumulations in the Atlantic greatly exceed those of the Pacific. In fact, it was only the natural release of oil and gas from formations off California and at several Pacific coastal sites (such as the tar pits of La Brea) that first induced drillers to test what seemed like unpromising terrain. In time, some of the lucky speculators reasoned that if the Pacific had proven itself to be so rich in petroleum deposits when the geological odds were apparently against it, then the Atlantic must be practically seething with oil waiting to be extracted!

In the 160 million years since North America and West Africa drifted apart, the sediments off the Atlantic coast have reached a maximum thickness of fifteen kilometers. During that same time frame, the eastern United States has subsided approximately three kilometers, with the rate slowing over the past 40 million years as the Atlantic margin matured and cooled by moving away from the hot, young plate boundary of the midoceanic ridge. Best of all from an oilman's point of view, there is the hint of an ancient buried reef that existed about 130 million years ago running from the Blake Plateau off eastern Florida to the Scotian Shelf off eastern Canada.

And so the drillers got busy. First, due to a scarcity of conservationists in eastern Canada, the oil industry tried the Scotian Shelf. Although the oilmen found suitable thicknesses of sand and shale, the associated organic materials were "thermally immature," meaning there had been insufficient heat in the geologic past to generate oil and gas from plant and animal cells.

Although some natural gas was discovered, the Scotian Shelf drilling was rated as an expensive failure. The oil industry did not want to drill again in the Atlantic until it could drill a sure thing. Although the Georges Bank off Massachusetts and the southeastern Georgian Embayment off Florida and Georgia looked promising, the most certain bet appeared to be the Baltimore Canyon Trough off New Jersey and Delaware.

The Trough's geological profile was remarkably similar to the productive Powder River Basin in Wyoming, and from the standpoint of younger sediment deposits of the Cretaceous period (130 million to 70 million years ago), the Baltimore deposits resembled some of the underlying terrain of southwestern Alberta, Canada, and even the Texas-Louisiana coast. The oil industry was so convinced it would find a bonanza of fossil fuels in the Baltimore Canyon that drilling platform manufacturers and other oil-related industry began acquiring (or trying to acquire) base camps from South Carolina to Maine in anticipation of the boom times ahead.

The focus of attention in the drilling-lease sales for the Baltimore Canyon Trough was a structure called the Great Stone Dome, a hundred miles due east of Atlantic City, New Jersey. Five companies paid $1.13 billion for the right to extract oil from this igneous intrusion that looked in profile like a slender Cadillac Mountain thrust up through nearly fifteen kilometers of sediment.

Five wells were drilled, and all five were dry. Farther east and south, Texaco and Tenneco were having a little better luck. Texaco discovered gas on the seaward edge of the Continental Shelf, but a subsequent well also drilled by Texaco three miles away came up dry. In June 1979, Tenneco struck oil at a production rate of 630 barrels a day—a decidedly unprofitable return for all the billions of dollars spent.

The oil industry is presently at a crossroads regarding the petroleum potential of the Atlantic. Since the available oil seems exorbitantly expensive to find and move, many executives want to cut their losses and use the profits from the sale of petroleum products to acquire non-petroleum-based subsidiaries.

Some executives are pushing the development of systems to extract more oil faster from proven reserves and oil fields. Others feel there are still fortunes to be made from offshore Atlantic oil, and they are currently rolling their dice on the Georges Bank.

This area has some of the characteristics of the oil-and-gas producing edge of the outer Continental Shelf farther south, and its shallower waters and proximity to an oil-starved region of the nation make the gamble of drilling more appealing than in any other comparable area along the coast. The ancient Berriasian Reef lies close to the surface of the sea floor at Georges Bank, and this is the good news. The bad news is that the reef is exposed to the sea at one location on the bank, making it possible that any gas or oil which the reef once contained may have been lost to the sea in ages past.

Although reefs are known for their porosity and ability to serve as petroleum reservoirs, this recently discovered "leak" to the oceanic environment has raised some doubts about oil-producing

prospects all along the Atlantic coast. If the reef was exhumed in the past at other points, the billions of barrels of hydrocarbons it may have once contained may long since have evaporated or dissolved.

Although a costly legal battle was fought over the issue of whether the U.S. Department of the Interior has the right to lease drilling sites on the Georges Bank, it was done as much to establish the boundaries between U.S. and Canadian rights to other resources on the bank as to enable an increasingly reluctant oil industry to begin bidding and drilling.

Only the Eastport refinery proponents remain optimistic, and they have to be. Unless oil is found in commercial quantities on the Georges Bank, there will be no need for a refinery in Maine.

While conservationists were not able to dissuade the U.S. Supreme Court from jeopardizing the long-term fisheries benefits of the bank for its short-term oil potential, the conservationists did win a delaying action on the proposed refinery. Significantly, the legal issue was not tourism and fisheries versus the petrochemical industry, or even traditional values versus change—these were merely what was at stake. Instead, the legal issue was whether the bald eagle should continue to breed in eastern Maine.

When you look at time from a geologist's viewpoint, what does it matter whether we find oil on the Georges Bank, or whether we drive Cadillacs for another fifty years, or whether the bald eagle survives for another thousand years? Any definition of the geological Big Picture must include the fact that few species last more than about twenty million years, and the bald eagle has already been around for most of its allotted span.

The geological Big Picture tells us that Eastport won't be Eastport in a million years, and even Cadillac Mountain will one day subside beneath the sea. The Big Picture's most trite truth is that in the long run, we're all dead.

Yet as I contemplate the purple majesty of Cadillac Mountain, I feel an awe for its origins mingled with wonder for human optimism. On one hand, our capacity for hope has created marvelous machinery for drilling through the sea floor. On the other hand, this same optimism has generated laws to protect the eagles soaring over Cadillac Mountain.

Life may, indeed, be a dream, and the best efforts of all mankind may be nothing more than brief shadows on a granite dome. Yet isn't our persistent stretching for perfection in the face of inevitable death what touches humanity with divinity?

Our greatness lies not in our sense of humor or intelligence, for other creatures besides man exhibit humor and intelligence. Our greatness lies in our knowing that, although we are doomed, we still want to fashion a better arrowhead or drill bit, and that men may devote themselves to preserving a hard, but productive, way of life as well as eagles drifting on the winds of time.

2

DOWN EAST

Marine fishes are the greatest of human resources. Unlike timber, we do not have to wait twenty years to a century to harvest each new generation. Unlike domestic crops, including most freshwater fishes but excepting Pacific salmons, we do not have to cultivate marine fishes, only harvest them when they, more often than not, come inshore or otherwise make themselves available for convenient harvesting.

Unlike oil, coal, and metals, fish are renewable, and the pharmaceuticals, plastics, paints, fertilizer, and dozens of other items we make from their flesh, bones and oil require fewer steps with fewer poisonous by-products than anything the petrochemical industries can provide. Although fishes are not as affectionate as Al Capp's Schmoos, they can be as bountiful, but only so long as we abide by a covenant with nature to keep our rivers and estuaries free flowing and biologically vigorous. In this fundamental charge, we have miserably failed nature and ourselves.

Study a map of Maine. Looking north into the country, you see it as the explorers and early traders saw it sailing "down east" along the coast on prevailing summer breezes. Now turn the map upside down, and you will see Maine as nature created it. This vast wedge of well-watered woods is the source of four large river systems: the Androscoggin, the Kennebec, the Penobscot, and the St. John—the latter includes the Allagash and Aroostock. These watersheds are what Henry David Thoreau wrote about (*The Maine Woods*) and visited in 1846, 1853, and 1857. They are the same woods traversed by Benedict Arnold on his march to Quebec, and by the Jesuits and their native allies in the French and Indian Wars.

For millennia before Europeans appeared, this semisolid interior of sphagnum bogs, crystalline streams, and blackwater lakes was paddled and portaged by red men who hunted moose, trapped beaver, and harvested salmon as far inland as the high yoke formed by the East and West branches of the Penobscot, but which the Indians even then called Ktaadn.

Every summer the rivers of Maine and New Brunswick became a kind of commons for Indians whose cultural differences were sometimes greater than those of the two huge nations presently divided by the St. Croix. The Indians hunted, fished, and foraged along the river shores, and they drifted downstream to the coast where they herded molting waterfowl in the marshes and harpooned harbor porpoise and bluefin tuna close offshore. The earliest evidence we have of people summering along the Maine coast are tuna bones and stone artifacts which date the concept of *rustication* at least six thousand years before our Victorian ancestors invented the word.

If your map describes elevations ashore and depths in the ocean, you will be able to see the handiwork of the periodic ice sheets which carved out the river basins and separated them by what Maine residents call "heights o' land." These heights reach like fingers into the flooded basin of the sea where knuckles bulge above the surface as islands and where the sides of the fingers form the walls of submarine canyons that grope into abysmal depths beyond the edge of the Continental Shelf.

This then is nature's perspective of Maine and one that is more in accordance with its gifts and grandeur than what can be seen from Interstate 95 or Route 1, crossing rivers at right angles and offering only brief glimpses of its geology. The southward trend of Maine's rivers serves to funnel Arctic air to the sea where it is warmed and turned back onto the land as wet snow in winter and fog in summer.

Fog—moisture condensed from cool, damp air lying above warmer water—shades and moderates the changing seasons of New English coasts. On Mount Desert Island, fogs temper the acidic growth of pitch pine, white spruce, black crowberry, and blueberry that creep down to the margins of the licking surf. The misty air drenches tender twigs and drips to roots gripping the lichen-crusted rocks above the spray line.

A struggle goes on within each lichen that is not unlike the sea's conflict with the shore. As early as 1902, a Russian lichenologist, Alexander Elenkin, observed that the fungi which inhabit the algae in each of the more than 20,000 lichen species gradually parasitize the algae. However, the process is controlled and so slow it is not readily apparent to a short-term observer. Until recently, Elenkin's notion was ridiculed by botanical colleagues who accepted the Swiss Simon Schwendener's discovery in 1867 that lichens are associations of fungi and algae but insisted that the association must be of mutual benefit since anything as ancient as lichens could not have survived except in symbiotic partnerships.

However, just as the sea is constantly eroding the shore only to have the shore extend itself elsewhere as a river delta or a rearing tectonic plate, so the lichens' algae hosts evolve subtle defenses to prolong their individual lives by sometimes hundreds of years and their species by aeons. Still, while the phycobiont algae have evolved defenses against mycobiont fungi, neither the phycobionts nor mycobionts have had enough time to evolve comparable defenses against man's toxic chemicals. Lichens are extremely sensitive to pollution, and that Mount Desert Island is losing some of its lichen flora is mute testimony to the contamination of the region's rain and fog which provide the lichens with their moisture.

Coastal fog is slightly brackish to taste. It condenses around tiny drops of seawater shot skyward from the surf or broken wave crests. The height to which such droplets rise depends on their diameter. Although the tiny droplets are rarely thrown more than twenty centimeters above the surrounding sea, this is enough for them to be picked up by slow winds and carried into the atmosphere. If the air is humid—and what seaside environment is not?—fresh water will condense about the saltwater droplets and be carried for many miles.

In 1915, chemist W. K. Knox measured the amount of chlorine deposited by rain and snow during a nine-month period in a small Iowa farming community. He was astonished to discover that nearly thirty-seven pounds of chlorine fell per acre. Although Knox knew that chlorine was a ubiquitous element in the atmosphere, he did not suspect that the sea was Iowa's ultimate source for this essential ingredient to successful plant growth.

Much of North America's chlorine, like most of our weather, comes from the Pacific Ocean. The Scripps Institution of Oceanography's Climate Research Group, which is the nation's first non-governmental climate forecast center, makes long-range weather forecasts, even for Maine, based on sea-surface temperatures at a variety of locations in the Pacific. However, New English apple growers, potato farmers, and berry pickers also depend on chlorine carried into the atmosphere by fog and transported inland by nor'easters blowing across the Gulf of Maine.

Of course, people who inhabit the coast, especially those who make their livings from the sea, are more often victims than beneficiaries of fog's largesse. Ungalvanized nails bleed rust down the sides of seaside homes, and no smart buyer would ever pay top dollar for a secondhand truck or car kept within an easy drive of corrosive sea breezes. However, such problems are only minor nuisances compared to fog's threat to human life. Once while fishing for cod in a fog at the edge of a major shipping lane, my father and I heard the approaching thudding splash of a large ship's propeller. We pulled anchor and ran well inshore, only to find after we stopped the engine that the sound of the ship was even nearer! We barely had time to don life jackets before enormous waves plowed up by the ship crashed over the gunwales, and we could not hear each other shout above the pulsing of the ship's screw. We were nearly swamped, but most frightening of all, we never saw the mystery ship whose own crew had been endangered by running so near the rockbound coast.

Once again it's a foggy morning as I drive to the southernmost headland of Acadia National Park to explore Ship Harbor. The patches of mist that drift across the winding road lend an aura of fantasy to the forthcoming outing—fantasy rather than foreboding, because there is little wind with the fog, and I anticipate calm water around the rocks where I will launch my canoe.

The prehistoric Indians of Maine built boats not very different from the single-paddle model I have with me at the start of my trip down the Atlantic coast. Contrary to the impression made by romantic novels, Indian craft were not all two-man birch-bark affairs. Massachusetts boat designer and kayak instructor Bart Hauthaway stresses that "Indians built an incredible variety of canoes in all shapes and sizes according to materials available and intended use. These ranged from tiny one-man craft to huge cargo carriers capable of hauling a ton or more. The larger Indian canoes were beautifully crafted and finished. But the boats the Indians used most —their everyday knockabout canoes—were single-handers of from nine to twelve feet long."

Governmental regulators insist that single-paddle canoes are too dangerous for use along the Atlantic coast. They presume that no one has the good sense to come off the water when it breezes up. And they certainly don't like the idea of anyone boating by himself. They ignore the facts that an ardent paddler named Nathaniel Bishop took a fourteen-foot canoe from New York to Florida more than a century ago, and that hundreds of solitary paddlers, like writer Carol Storrs—who calls her ten-and-a-half-foot, Hauthaway-designed, Rob Roy canoe, *Dr. Robert, the Psychiatrist*—safely solo coastal coves and tidal rivers from Canada to the Florida Keys.

Maine's Abnaki Indians knew that a lightweight canoe's versatility and safety depend on what inexperienced boaters imagine is its principal defect: its small size. Should I fall over in a light canoe, I would be able to fend off its weight in white water and steer it to shore in calm water, whereas I could be crushed by a heavier craft or forced to allow the currents to carry me wherever they would—so long as I had warmth in my body to hold on at all. Part of the pleasure in paddling across mist-shrouded Ship Harbor is my small canoe's intimacy and appropriateness to its surroundings. I wonder how long it has been since the last person "gunkholed" these placid waters and imagine it must have been a red man.

Ship Harbor is a somewhat ironic name, for two eighteenth-century ships ended their careers here. During the Revolutionary War, an American schooner sought refuge in the shallow bay where a pursuing British warship of deeper draft could not follow. But the British ship didn't need to follow; the American schooner grounded herself and could not be refloated.

Even earlier, in 1739, a British merchant vessel named *Grand Design* piled up on Long Ledge off the mouth of the cove. Most of the crew and passengers, emigrants from Ireland on their way to Pennsylvania, came safely ashore in small boats. Had the castaways been Indians or befriended them, they would have found ample food in the tide pools and ample shelter along the shore. However, with edible land plants, sea plants, and fish and shellfish available merely for the stooping to gather them, the Europeans slowly starved to death.

Although we don't know the precise origins of the Irish passengers, I presume they were peasants rather than watermen, for they starved while one of the best known of all Irish seafoods flourished just below the low-tide mark. *Chondrus crispus* is called Irish moss because it has been collected and eaten by the coastal

Sea Gooseberries (tiny jellyfish) and Irish Moss

folk of that island for at least six hundred years. The active ingredient in this red alga is known as carrageenan and honors County Carragheen on Ireland's southern coast.

The average American uses a product containing carrageenan about fifteen times a day. These range from ice cream to air fresheners to dog food. Several hundred people in Maine once harvested Irish moss with long-handled rakes, supplying this country with about half our needs. But now, as with much else in our economy, the Koreans, Filipinos, Mexicans, and others working for lower wages provide most of the $40 million worldwide market.

A decade ago when clams were $7 per bushel, Irish moss cost Maine wholesalers 4 cents a pound. Now that clams are $25 per bushel, Irish moss is only 5 cents a pound. Formerly, "mossers" worked from boats, but modern waterborne mossers can spend more money on equipment and fuel than they will earn from the sea. There are only about half a dozen old-timers left in Maine who try to make their livings by mossing. Most of what is supplied our market from domestic sources comes from the efforts of a few knowing New Englanders who scavenge the moss from beaches after a storm.

Even today, many American seaweed foragers and sea-urchin divers have never tried the fare they exchange for cash. When I tried to persuade a Boothbay Harbor lobsterman that mussels were as tasty and nutritious as the scorpion's relative he caught for a living, he replied that besides the fact that lobsters were too valuable to eat, he wouldn't touch a mussel after tasting "skunkhead coot," alias surf scoter, at a friend's house.

"Them birds love mussels," he said, "and that's what makes them stink so bad!"

Yet almost nothing in the waters along the Maine coast, including sea ducks, is bad or dangerous to eat unless the waters are industrially or municipally polluted or poisoned by a red tide. This latter phenomenon is misnamed, for it is neither red nor a tide, and although some New Englanders think it is a form of divine retribution for their despoilation of the region's estuaries, red tides are probably as old as life in the seas and hardly confined to New

Surf Scoters, hens and drakes

England. Indeed, because of red tides—which are usually colorless, rarely pink, and almost never* red—the entire coast of Alaska has been closed to the harvest of shellfish since 1943.

A major source of confusion regarding red tides is that there are at least two kinds caused by two distinct types of dinoflagellate. The one exploited by Moses in the seventh chapter of Exodus to turn the color of the Nile's tidal waters bloodred and to cause the fish in the river to die and the river to stink may have been a member of the genus *Gymnodinium* which periodically affects other warm-water areas around the world, including southern U.S. coasts. As many as fifty-seven million of these dinoflagellates can be found in a single quart of seawater, and since they absorb all available oxygen, they kill not only every creature in the vicinity, they end up killing themselves through an excess of procreative zeal. Even people walking along Florida beaches plagued by a red tide are likely to find their noses itching and their throats sore from these half-plant, half-animal life-forms cast into the atmosphere by the breaking waves.

* Never say never. In 1972, the coasts of Maine, New Hampshire, and Massachusetts were closed to shellfishing due to the intensity of red tides which included discernible red patches of water in some areas.

In the summer of 1976, a massive fish kill occurred over three thousand square miles of sea bottom between Montauk Point, Long Island, and Cape May, New Jersey. At first believed to be a red tide, the kill was later traced to the daily dumping of seven hundred tons of sewage sludge in the New York Bight and culminating with an alga bloom of the species *Ceratium tripos* which died, sank and as the bloom decomposed, exhausted available oxygen in this vast oceanic area. The National Sea Clammers Association took a $500 million lawsuit all the way to the U.S. Supreme Court which ruled that fishermen can sue governmental agencies for enforcement of environmental protection laws, but not for damages if the agencies fail to do their jobs.

In Maine and other northern waters, red tides are caused by *Gonyaulax tamarensis* var. *excavata* which is siphoned from the surrounding sea by shellfish in the normal course of their feeding. This dinoflagellate is more benign than its southern relatives, and *Gonyaulax* does not usually harm the bivalves. However, it does become concentrated in sometimes fatal doses for predators, especially mammals, which eat contaminated shellfish. A single milligram of what scientists call *saxitoxin* can kill a human being, while mollusks can sometimes concentrate more than one hundred times that amount without being affected. Dr. Clarice M. Yentsch, a red tides specialist at the National Marine Fisheries Service's West Boothbay Bigelow Laboratory, notes, "We have discovered toxicity so high in the waters off Monhegan Island that eating one healthy-looking mussel would have meant certain death."

The Abnaki Indians knew the hazards of paralytic shellfish poisoning (PSP), and they avoided it by going out the night before they planned to harvest shellfish and stirring the water over their beds. If the water revealed a characteristic phosphorescent glow, the Indians moved to another bay.

Maine waterfowlers use a comparably unscientific, but reliable test for the safe eating of shellfish. So long as the sea ducks they shoot have mussels or other bivalves in their crops, all is well with the shellfish. However, when the eiders and scoters switch to diets of baby green crabs and other non-filter-feeding crustacea, the duck hunters give up their own appetizers of steamed mussels or clams. Unfortunately, this method of ensuring safety in the eating of shellfish is limited to that quarter of the year when waterfowling is legal.

Dr. Clarice M. Yentsch uses mice—as many as 13,000 a year—to test suspected shellfish in Maine. While such laboratory work has helped prevent any PSP-related deaths in Maine for over two decades, Dr. Yentsch is trying to find a cheaper and more convenient test which watermen or shellfish wardens can use. One problem with her research is that the more she learns about *Gonyaulax*, the more complex an organism it becomes. For example, at least seven additional toxins have been discovered in association with saxitoxin. Furthermore, in addition to the familiar mobile or summer stage of development, *Gonyaulax* has a static stage—a resting cyst that is probably a zygote produced in sexual reproduction. These cysts, which sink and overwinter on the bottom, are at least ten times more lethal than mobile phase *Gonyaulax* and possibly, when first formed, a thousand times more toxic. Since the cysts behave as fine silt particles, they are easily stirred up and broadcast by dredging activities, whether by the Army Corps of Engineers maintaining boat channels or by crab or clam dredgers, or even trawlers dragging bottom for flounder or shrimp.

Can we eliminate red tides as we have smallpox and the hazards of many childhood diseases?

"Given the complex interactions that make oceanic systems function," says Dr. Yentsch, "attempts at eradication might prove to be tragic cures that are far worse than the disease."

The ocean is a biological broth inhabited by tens of thousands of species of mircroorganisms, some of which, like *Gonyaulax*, we are not even sure whether the different organisms we call by that name should be regarded as separate species—for example, whether *G. tamarensis* is actually a distinct organism in New England waters known as *G. excavata*—or whether these differences are only a matter of strain, form, or variety.

Gonyaulax is a member of the phytoplanktonic community, which generally means the organism drifts passively with the sea winds and creates chlorophyll as all plants do. However, *Gonyaulax* is a dinoflagellate busily whirling about by means of two whiplike appendages called flagella. Although biology textbooks try to simplify the study of plankton by dividing them into "phyto," or plant forms, and "zoo," or animal forms, some phytoplankton consume zooplankton the way pitcher plants eat insects; and some zooplankton grow chlorophyll the way captive polar bears turn green with algae cultures inside their hollow body hairs. Whether they are animal, vegetable, or bizarre blends of both, many planktons have the capacity to absorb and store endless variations on the industrial and municipal minerals with which we contaminate the sea and which may be working their way back up the food chain to haunt us years from now.

Take the case of the best grades of antifouling paints for boat bottoms. Before the *Great Eastern*, the cable-laying goliath that was five times larger than any other hull afloat when she was launched in 1858, could sail on her fifth and finally successful expedition to make a lasting telegraph connection across the Atlantic, this ship had to be dry-docked so that a two-foot-thick encrustation of barnacles could be stripped from her hull. This scraping and re-painting took several months more than the actual laying of the cable.

When antifouling paint manufacturers began devising organic (carbon and hydrogen-containing) compounds of copper and, more recently, tin, they seemed to be the answer to a sailor's prayer. Although expensive and requiring annual application to be effective, antifouling paints save money in the long run by eliminating barnacle and weed growth which lead to extra weight, loss of speed, and wasted fuel. In the past, working watermen tried to keep their hulls as busy as possible under the supposition that boats under way are less likely to grow barnacles and weeds than boats at rest. Yet it only takes a few moments for barnacle larvae to find the hard substrate of a ship, glue their heads against the hull, and begin extracting lime from the sea to make their crusty, cutting shells. With the newer antifouling paints, no matter how long a boat sits at a dock or remains on a mooring, the organic metals in the paint form a toxic film on the hull that gradually leaches into the surrounding sea and prevents barnacle larvae or algae from developing even if they manage to make initial contact. At the end of a long idle summer, a treated hull may show a slight spotting from the barnacles' aborted attempts to establish themselves, but that is all.

Unfortunately, about the time we began complimenting the chemical industry for a job well done, researchers at the University of Maryland's Chesapeake Bay Solomons Laboratory discovered that many marine microorganisms have the capacity to attach methyl (CH_3) groups to these organic compounds and bring them into the food chain. Although this methylation by microbes was previously known to occur with mercury and lead, in 1982 the Maryland researchers found that the process also occurs on tin, and organic tin compounds—more than 25,000 metric tons per year—are the ones most commonly used in antifouling paints as well as agricultural pesticides which frequently find their way into estuaries and thence to the sea.

The National Bureau of Standards and the Environmental Protection Agency both feel it is "premature" to order industry back to the drawing board on the basis of a single research laboratory's findings. Yet as the tide ebbs from Ship Harbor and exposes the omnipresent zone of barnacles, I contemplate the irony of toxins being converted from water-soluble compounds unable to cross biological membranes into insoluble forms which can by microorganisms that store the toxins and drift with the tide where they become part of a food web which includes being eaten by the very crustacea the compounds were developed to repel.

People cannot see microorganisms, just as they cannot see an increasing range and quantity of man-made contaminants in the sea. Sewage sludge contains a variety of heavy metals and known carcinogenic chemicals. Yet every hour along the Atlantic coast we dump or pump hundreds of tons of sewage directly into the ocean where the material sinks or is diluted. It may be out of sight, and, hence, out of mind, but it is not out of our food chain.

This does not mean people are not worried about pollution. On the contrary, people get quite emotional about the subject, especially pollution they can see or think they see. Every summer along the Maine coast, tourists notice and report black bathtublike stains above the barnacle zone on sea-fronting rocks and cliffs. Many people report these stains as proof there has been a local oil spill. Yet this particular "ring around the collar" is *Calothrix*, a blue-green alga that thrives where it can be periodically bathed by spray. *Calothrix* will die if submerged in the sea, and it will die if extended calms allow it to dry out. A swatch contains many thousands of cellular filaments, and its resemblance to oil extends to its "slippery when wet" condition that has skinned more knees and elbows among people launching their canoes or kayaks over the rocks than any of the more obviously slick rockweeds or bladder wrack.

Some of these slippery weeds are good to eat. I found a frond of dulse where I launched my canoe and have put it under my seat to have with lunch. Dulse is a purplish-red alga with flattened translucent fronds that grows in clusters from a holdfast. It cannot withstand much sea surge so is more prevalent in tidal pools or protected waters like Ship Harbor than on exposed headlands. Asians cultivate this alga and eat it fresh or boiled in soups. Yet American fishermen pick it with repugnance off their lines or nets and throw this good condiment away.

Fishermen are conservative creatures. They are slow to try anything their fathers didn't know or use. Yet coastal water chemistry and global weather trends are more than matters of idle curiosity for fishermen; they are matters of survival.

In the nineteenth century, several warm-water fish species, including the sheepshead and the Spanish mackerel, regularly appeared as far north as Long Island, and the common sea bass was frequently caught off Maine. Today the sheepshead and Spanish mackerel are rare north of the Carolinas and the sea bass is uncommon north of Montauk Point. Are such decreases a result of overfishing, changes in coastal water temperatures and water chemistry (the latter implying pollution), or a combination of all three factors? No one knows, but except for a few oceanographers and ichthyologists, only fishermen are vitally concerned, for such unpredictable trends affect what gear they need from season to season, what additional manpower they hire, if any, and where they fish.

Young Jonah Crab amidst Dulse

Yet even if scientists could measure and forecast global phenomena, what could fishermen do about it? Dams have had a measurably deleterious effect on fisheries, and any forecasts about new dams would have to be adverse so far as fishermen are concerned. Each dam, even those supplied with fish ladders, eliminates at least 10 percent of each anadromous species' spawning run. Large dams without ladders are fatal to the reproduction of many species, and they have even altered local weather patterns. Yet despite the protests of angry fishermen, engineers without any grounding in biology or interest in meteorology are busy planning a host of new dams for New England and eastern Canada culminating with a huge hydroproject that will attempt to regulate the tidal flow of the Bay of Fundy.

The pity is that for a period during the 1960s and 1970s, it looked as though conservationists, fishermen, and others with an interest in free-flowing water were going to succeed in unplugging and cleaning up some of the dammed and dirty rivers of New England. There was even the hope that one day fishermen would again see profitable runs of alewives, shad, smelt, salmon, and even sturgeon.

Oh, you can still catch these fishes in Maine, but their present populations mock their former glories. You can still rent a smelt shack on the lower Kennebec for $5 for each six-hour fishing period following flood tide. If you're lucky, you may catch as many as fifty of the little fish. However, at the turn of the century, one fisherman tending a dozen lines with several hooks on each line expected to do ten times as well.

Or you can take your turn fishing for Atlantic salmon at the Bangor Pool, which is actually on the Brewer side of the Penobscot River. You may be lucky and take a fish with your first cast. Or, more often, you may cast all summer without catching a salmon which were formerly such symbols of Maine's piscatorial bounty that the first fish of the year from the Bangor Pool was sent to the White House for a presidential dinner.

In 1976, the Federal Energy Regulatory Commission reviewed only four applications for preliminary permits to construct dams in New England. Five years later, the total approached one thousand. Under new federal tax incentives, dams, but not fishes, are declared to be "renewable energy resources." (So much for legislators' understanding of the word energy!) A dam builder can depreciate the entire cost of his project over the first five years of power production, although each dam is built to last and produce electricity for at least fifty years. In addition, all interest on Uncle Sam's loans for dams under twenty-five megawatts is tax free. On larger projects, you can take a 21 percent investment tax credit for federal loans, bank loans, or any money of your own you may want to put into the dam. However, the less you spend of your own money, the better off you'll be. Smart dam builders always arrange to use public debt to finance their personal fortunes.

The cost-effectiveness of New England's relatively small hydropower units is based on the cross-flow turbine. Inside this turbine is a spinning, drumlike assembly with vanes so that water hits the blades twice, coming and going. The vanes are self-cleaning, resistant to cavitation, adaptable and efficient across a range of flows—and 99 percent destructive of any size fish trying to pass through. Over fifty preliminary permits have been issued for dams having this type of turbine on New Hampshire's Merrimack River alone, and there is not a river in Maine without at least one of these power projects on the drawing boards.

The justification for this widespread hardening of New England's arteries is that since the region burns four billion barrels of oil annually, the new or restored hydroprojects will give New Englanders that elusive prize, "energy independence"—particularly if such "frills" as fish ladders are eliminated. However, of the four billion barrels burned each year, only seventy-seven million are used to make electricity. If all the dam sites presently being considered are approved and developed, they will reduce New England's dependence on imported oil by only two-tenths of 1 percent. Meanwhile, the loss in recreational and commercial fishing revenues and other intangible benefits associated with the region's abundance of free-flowing waters far outweighs all the alleged savings.

Maine fishermen have been so long without shad in their nets, the few they catch today are sold to lobstermen for bait. Part of the cost of restoring anadromous fisheries, if the dammers and polluters don't prevail in the meantime, will be educating New Englanders to eat fish they haven't seen in three or four generations.

Yet getting people to try shad may be easier if Maine's catch of sea herring continues to decline. Although this fish grows to eighteen inches in length and lives as long as twenty years, it is most desirable as juveniles canned and sold as "sardines." For well over a century, sardines have been Maine's most important seafood export,

Sardines

but the industry peaked eighty years ago, had a brief revival after World War II, and has been decaying ever since.

In the lunch pack slung beneath my canoe's seat, there is a can of Beach Cliff–brand sardines from Prospect Harbor, Maine. The four fish in the can are large, but still not as large as the ten-inch minimum (four years of age) needed for sexual maturity. Over-fishing juveniles craved by the canners has been the downfall of the sardine industry.

In order to maintain optimum sustained yields of herring as well as their economically important predators, including cod, haddock, pollock, halibut, striped bass, bluefish, and bluefin tuna, herring should be allowed a generous reserve in the summer when the predators range through the same 12- to 180-foot depths used by the herring to lay their 20,000 to 40,000 eggs per female on appropriate substrates, including seaweeds. Tragically, instead of managing the beleaguered resource comprehensively, some Maine fishermen are scrounging even further down the food chain by harvesting kelp fronds sticky with herring eggs for the epicurean Asian markets.

My can of sardines cost just 43 cents—roughly ten cents a fish. The soybean-oiled chunks of herring will be put on crackers and covered with strips of dulse. This salty meal will be washed down with a can of beer. Tasty, nutritious, and cheap—yet for the herring to reach me, an aircraft pilot had to spot the school and call the netters who pursed the fish and brought them to the surface where a vacuum pump sucked them aboard a tender that returned to the packing plant where women waited on assembly lines to clip off each fish's head and tail with shears their grandmothers may have used. The fish were packed by hand, but the soybean oil, a pinch of salt, and the lid were added by automation. The cans were stacked into cases, the cases were loaded into trucks, and the trucks eventually distributed the fish to every state of the Union. Yet the total cost to the consumer is less than six minutes' worth of minimum wage earned by one woman on the sorting or packing line.

"Twenty years ago," reminisces Robert Peacock, owner of the Peacock Canning Company in Lubec, across the bay from Eastport, "there were fifty-two sardine plants in Maine. Now there are fourteen. There used to be nine factories in Lubec alone. Only two are left. Just along Front Street, sixty-two buildings—stores, factories, smokehouses, even homes—have been torn down or closed since the 1960s.

"In 1901, more than 456,000 cases of sardines were packed in Lubec. In a good year today, we are lucky to pack less than one-quarter that number. Lubec was the leader in sardine production until the Great Depression, and though we've had some good years since, we've never recovered the leadership. We don't have the schools of fish we used to have, and because we don't have the fish, we can't afford to install the stainless-steel equipment that would make my operation more efficient and marginally more profitable."

Ironically, bountiful herring years can create as many problems as lean seasons. Most of Peacock's workers are old women. Some are over eighty. Up until the 1960s, young mothers with two or three kids in school used to come running when the factory whistle blew, signaling the arrival of a loaded tender. They were the backbone of the coastal canning industry. Today nonworking housewives are scarce anywhere along the Maine coast. Even women with preschool children want full-time jobs, not part-time employment for minimum wages.

Thus, fishermen with full nets who want to empty them so they can get back to fishing before the herring schools move on sometimes have to wait—and wait. Some have to wait as long as two weeks while an understaffed packing plant services the other fishermen in line ahead of them. Sometimes a fisherman can't hold his fish that long. Sometimes a net tears or, if cotton, rots, and the herring escape. Sometimes the fish die, and the fisherman has to sell the lot to a rendering plant or chicken grower. In either case, he doesn't get another chance at the schools which have meanwhile wandered down the coast or out to sea.

Still, fishermen are gamblers and as such, compulsive optimists. Whereas farmers are inclined to complain while driving Cadillacs to the bank, fishermen tend to sing while thumbing rides to the poorhouse. When sardine seining becomes unprofitable, they try shrimp trawling. When green sea urchins attack Irish moss beds, fishermen don wet suits and dive for the sea urchins which are sold to the better-heeled citizens of some of the same nations whose fishermen have made mossing in Maine unprofitable.

In none of their mostly improvised activities do Yankee fishermen make great fortunes or even earn enough for generous retirements. The shrimp and sea urchins may disappear or become unprofitable as precipitously as the sardines and Irish moss before them. As a result, although they are optimistic for themselves, fishermen mostly want something else for their children. Unlike successful farmers whose greatest fear is that their sons will not follow in their footsteps, even successful fishermen pray their children will seek employment ashore. However, the independence offered by life on the water is so far superior to any kind of work the youngsters find on land, generation after generation of young men and increasingly young women thumb rides to poverty, danger, and frequently early death fishing the fogbound and fertile coasts of Maine.

3

SOUTHERN NEW ENGLAND

Like many middle-class kids too young to remember World War II but old enough to enjoy the good times that followed and presume that such bounty would last forever, I was sent to summer camps in New England from the time I was seven until I was old enough to earn summer money by working in a television repair shop and delivering prescriptions on Saturdays for a pharmacy near home.

My camp experiences ranged from a pseudomilitary school in New London, Connecticut, where for punishment—such as when my roommate and I threw water balloons into a tea dance—we had to march for hours around in a circle, carrying Springfield rifles; to a kind of counselors' resort called Monomoy in Massachusetts where for punishment—such as the time three of us short-sheeted all the counselors' beds—we had to carry rocks to grade the camp director's seaplane ramp; to a roughhewn affair deep in the Maine woods where for punishment—such as being late for the daily "polar-bear" swims —we had to dig new privy pits and fill in the old.

Although I learned a little about canoeing at one camp, something about riding at another, and a fair amount about survival at all of them, I was out of sync for all but my last, Tabor Academy in Marion, Massachusetts. By the time I went to Tabor, I was no longer the bewildered little boy who left his mother in New York's Grand Central Station on the first of his perennially dreaded June trips north. I was nearly a teenager (meaning I had turned twelve in April), confident because of that fact and increasingly more curious than frightened of the world around me.

Only the other day I came across the archery pins I won my

first summer at Tabor, and only two years ago did I finally misplace the fishing knife I had won for keeping the neatest room. Proudest of all, I still refer to my copy of Ann Haven Morgan's *Field Book of Ponds and Streams* inscribed "to George W. Reiger, for outstanding achievement in Nature," by Gilbert E. Stokes, Tabor Summer Camp's naturalist.

Among other compliments, Mr. Stokes cited me for my "constant willingness to do the extra details which help make the program function smoothly." That means I was responsible for keeping the camp's captive toads, frogs, salamanders, and mice supplied with earthworms and insects, and our captive snakes and screech owls supplied with amphibians and mice. The owls also ate chipmunks, and these rodents were more abundant than mice, especially under and in Marion's many rock walls. However, I felt there was something rather too fiendish about feeding owls such entertaining fellows as chipmunks rather than the house mice, which chewed up rope and sailcloth to make their smelly nests in the loft above the nature shed.

Still, the feeding of the camp's beasties was never a chore, and I could always count on a small army of volunteers to help round up the food and a larger army of spectators to sigh and cheer with immense satisfaction when the stalking hognose snake finally caught the incredulous toad or the screech owl dropped on the quivering mouse.

Yet for me that summer, the exquisite horrors of predator–prey relationships were best seen among the insects, whether it was watching the hypnotic rocking of a praying mantis (Mantidae)* gauging the distance to a butterfly immersed in a flower, or a restless mud dauber (Pompilidae) expertly constructing clay cuddies for the paralyzed spiders she brought to store with her eggs so her larvae could eat the living spider flesh in seclusion.

There are more than six times as many insect species on earth as there are mammals, birds, fishes, reptiles, and amphibians combined. Contrary to most people's imaginings, insects are not all primitive creatures like the cockroach and mayfly, which date back to the Carboniferous Age when some amphibians were evolving into reptiles. Some orders of insects, like Hymenoptera, including wasps, bees, ants, and sawflies, are noted for their complex social lives

---

* There are two mantids common to Massachusetts: one introduced from Europe and mature at about two inches (*Mantis religiosa*), and another from the Orient that grows four or more inches long (*Tenodera aridifolia*).

Bald-Faced Hornets and their nest

and/or their venom, a sophisticated adaptation for attacking such primitive prey as spiders (arachnids, not insects), crickets and grasshoppers (Orthoptera), or cicadas and aphids (Homoptera).

For the same sort of reasons that copperheads, which inhabit freshwater lowlands behind the coast in the north, and cottonmouths, the same kind of ecosystem in the south, are categorized as highly evolved reptiles, the bald-faced hornet, whose large paper nests are found on deciduous trees and shrubs throughout the coastal plain, is one of the most highly evolved of insects.

Venomous salivary glands, hypodermic fangs, and heat-sensitive facial indentations are intricate adaptations enabling pit vipers to feed on equally highly evolved mammalian prey. By comparison, bald-faced hornets may be even more highly evolved due to their complex social behavior, their ability to distinguish between prey, which they merely paralyze, and adversaries which they sting repeatedly to kill, and in their marvelously swift and maneuverable flight which enables them to capture a spectrum of lesser insects on the wing, paralyze them, and turn them for optimum aerodynamic transport to the nest. If hornets grew as large as vipers or their avian counterparts, accipiters, they would probably be the most fearful predators on earth.

Had I been independently wealthy or endowed by a great institution, I might have spent many arm-waving years contemplating the greenhead fly, an unholy terror of the coastal marshes from Cape Cod to Florida. Although not as large as the black horsefly, like all members of the ferocious Family Tabanidae, greenheads lay their eggs in masses on leaves and stems of plants overhanging damp ground or water. The eggs hatch, the larvae tumble onto the mud and immediately begin tunneling through the soft soil and detritus in a savage search for small invertebrates. The first few days are usually spent devouring their siblings, but even after the brood's ranks are thinned, greenhead fly larvae concentrations may remain as high as seventy to a square yard of salt-marsh muck.

Unlike the horsefly, whose predaceous larval stage lasts two years before the insect pupates into a mammal-biting adult, the greenhead fly matures in twelve months. Only female flies, like female mosquitoes, seek blood meals, but the greenhead fly, unlike most mosquitoes, retains enough plasma protein from its larval life to lay its first eggs without fresh ingestions of blood. This first egg mass is small, usually only a few hundred units, but it is enough to ensure the perpetuation of greenhead flies even if the female is not able to find any cat, dog, horse, cow, deer, or human victims to sustain further procreativity.

If a fly cannot find mammalian flesh to slit with its knifelike mouth parts and from which to suck an uninterrupted blood meal, the fly will weaken and die within a few days of emerging from the salt-marsh sod. However, since the Atlantic coast is crowded with humans from June into September, and this period coincides with the emergence of the adult greenheads, yelps of pain from people and their pets are heard almost daily throughout the summer within a few miles of a coastal marsh. Under ideal conditions, a fertile female greenhead can zip back and forth several times between bloody encounters on a beach or boardwalk and a salt marsh before her capacity to reproduce is exhausted and she dies.

Most would-be controls of the greenhead have gone awry. Up until World War II, ditches were dug in salt marshes to cut down on mosquito production. This was also believed to alleviate the greenhead problem. However, it had just the opposite effect by creating more damp, but not saturated, environments in which the greenhead larvae thrive.

After World War II, DDT (dichloro-diphenyl-trichloro-ethane) was broadcast over coastal marshes to kill mosquitoes and greenhead flies. Unfortunately, mosquitoes gradually evolved spray-resistant forms and greenhead larvae and flies were too large to be much affected by the spray in the first place, except that by their unwittingly storing it, the DDT worked its way up the food chain to do substantial harm to organisms that fed on creatures which fed on greenheads.

In the early 1970s, researchers from Rutgers University and the University of Delaware began looking for a way to control greenheads without adverse side effects. The first thing they discovered was just how intense greenhead attacks can be during the height of the July fly season. At sample stations just a few square feet in area along the New Jersey and Delaware coasts, researchers collected more than a thousand greenhead flies per station per hour, and every fly was hungry for blood! The researchers also discovered—and exploited the fact in designing traps—that greenhead flies search for their blood feasts at an average altitude of twenty-four inches and that the flies are attracted to glossy surfaces, like the perspiration-shiny body of a man, or an enamel-painted surface.

Greenheads have preferred flight paths. We don't understand how these are chosen, but one trap only ten yards from another will frequently catch a thousand more flies a day than the second. The best way to locate a flight path is to sacrifice yourself as a temporary target. When you are no longer able to flail away the assaulting flies with both arms and dancing legs, you have found the perfect location for a greenhead fly trap!

The most popular punishment for wayward campers at Tabor was to send us out into the shallows between the marine railroad and the sail dock to pull the eelgrass up by hand. Either we were more effective than we thought or eelgrass is suffering from another mysterious period of decline, for as eelgrass beds go, so go brant. According to Dr. Wyman Richardson, author of The House on Nauset Marsh, "in 1907 the Nauset Marsh was lush with eelgrass. I can remember too well when I was a boy trying to help my brother-in-law push a boat through the mud-embedded grass. In 1912 it was practically all gone; in 1919 it started coming back, and by 1922 the marsh was full of it. However, in 1928 it began to disappear again, and by 1932 it had completely disappeared. This time it went, not only locally, but from every part of the coast supplied by the North Atlantic Ocean, European as well as American."

In each one of these cycles of eelgrass abundance and scarcity, Atlantic brant flourished and declined accordingly. In the 1930s, years when eelgrass virtually disappeared,* brant populations fell by more than 90 percent. Some ornithologists feared the species would become extinct. Scallops, clams, snails, crabs, and eelgrass-associated fish populations also plummeted.

Dr. Richardson who, by the way, was the uncle of the chief U.S. negotiator at the United Nations Law of the Sea Conferences, Elliot L. Richardson, noted that by 1946 the eelgrass had begun returning to Massachusetts, which was cause for rejoicing among the scallopers at Marion. It was also cause for rejoicing among coastal waterfowlers, for brant numbers increased all through the late 1940s. By 1951, they were plentiful enough again to justify a hunting season throughout their wintering range from southern New England to North Carolina.

On a recent visit to Marion, I noted that the lush jungles of eelgrass by the marine railway and along the seawall are gone. However, the Atlantic brant population continues to be reasonably high, possibly because at last brant are beginning to feed on lawns and winter wheat in coastal fields and are no longer relying on one undependable food source for winter survival.

In the early 1950s, Marion was one of many coastal municipalities that periodically fogged its environs with DDT. Although its primary target was mosquitoes, DDT was also used to eradicate Japanese beetles, a tiny tank of an insect whose metallic green hordes swarmed over the flowers and foliage of rosebushes growing around Tabor's tennis courts. These beetles apparently entered this country before the federal government mandated the inspection of all imported plants starting in 1912.

When the spray trucks appeared, many of Tabor's campers were like spectators at a battle: we enjoyed the risk as well as the show. We stood nearby and inhaled deeply while the organochlorine mists dispelled the early evening clouds of gnats and mosquitoes. We childishly assumed that anything which killed bloodsucking insects could do us no harm and possibly some good. We certainly never

* Cautious marine botanists insist the jury is still out on what caused this catastrophic decline of eelgrass, but some allow as to how it may have been the mycetozoan, *Labyrinthula*.

Osprey and Bald Eagle

imagined anything as farfetched as the fact that this panacea would shortly threaten every osprey community from Boston to New York City.

The osprey is a semisocial raptor that will tolerate the proximity of other nesting ospreys so long as abundant fish supplies encourage such tolerance. Although the birds fish freshwater ponds when they first return from the Gulf of Mexico in the spring—because such shallow, land-bound waters warm up faster than neighboring estuaries—as soon as the sea reaches temperatures suitable to the activities of school fishes, the male ospreys, which supply all the food for nesting females and their young, shift their fishing activities from fresh water to salt. In a study published in the May 1980 issue of *American Birds*, ornithologists Paul Spitzer and Alan Poole found that all known osprey nests in southern New England and New York were within a couple of miles of the coast and 95 percent were within sight of salt water.

In the early 1950s, our nature group at the Tabor Summer Camp made field and collecting trips from New Bedford, where the hotel near the whaling museum on Johnny Cake Hill used to serve whaleburgers for lunch, to the Cape Cod Canal. Anywhere along

Route 6, we took the sight of ospreys for granted. Yet today almost all nesting ospreys in Massachusetts are confined to two areas: the Westport River estuary southwest of New Bedford (about twenty nests) and Martha's Vineyard (less than a dozen). There are no breeding ospreys near Marion or anywhere else in the upper reaches of Buzzards Bay, named for these birds by not-very-scientific explorers.

No one took the time in the early 1950s to count all the ospreys between Boston and New York, because in those days we assumed the birds would be with us in comparable numbers "forever." We knew that bald eagles were shy, fiercely territorial, and that they would continue fading as breeders along the coast as more people took over the birds' breeding areas for their own purposes. However, ospreys are wonderfully tolerant of humans, and insofar as boating activities near channel markers supporting osprey nests help discourage eagles from hounding male ospreys carrying fish and owls from haunting female ospreys tending eggs or young, we assumed man was an asset to the osprey, not a detriment.

Watermen everywhere regard ospreys as emblems of good luck in fishing, and, insofar as ospreys generally build their nests near abundant supplies of fish, they are indeed symbols of a healthy bay or estuary. In the nineteenth century, coastal folk in New England commonly erected old wagon wheels on poles in the marsh for the ospreys to use as nesting platforms in much the way Northern Europeans have traditionally encouraged the nesting of storks on their roofs. Ornithologist John Weske recalls from his teenage years in Rhode Island that it was said you could get away with most anything in that state but the killing of a "fish hawk."

DDT was first sprayed on Long Island in 1948. Within a few years, it was fashionable for community leaders from Cape Cod to Cape May to boast about the number of tons they used annually to make their resort beaches more "bug free" than the next town's. By the late 1950s, some observers began noticing serious declines in a number of raptor species, and in 1960, ornithologists P. L. Ames and G. S. Messereau initiated a study of ospreys nesting in the Connecticut River estuary. By the time their work was published in 1964, only 24 of the area's original 200-plus osprey nests remained, and the species' local population was plummeting at a catastrophic 31 percent annual rate.

In 1956, Dr. James B. DeWitt of the U.S. Fish and Wildlife Service published a study on the "Effects of Chlorinated Hydrocarbon Insecticides upon Quail and Pheasants" (vol. 4 of the

Journal of Agriculture and Food Chemistry). In 1960, Rachel Carson, also with the Fish and Wildlife Service, cited Dr. DeWitt's research in a series of articles for *The New Yorker* magazine and asked why, if DDT and its more powerful cousins, aldrin and dieldrin, were suppressing in some yet unknown way the reproduction of gallinaceous birds like quail and pheasants, would they not have similarly adverse effects on other orders of birds? She expressed particular concern for bald eagle populations in Florida, the Chesapeake, and New Jersey where the species' principal prey was fish. She could just as well have used the osprey of Long Island Sound and Buzzards Bay for her example.

By the time the *New Yorker* articles were published as the book called *Silent Spring* (1962), the evidence was mounting in the Ames and Messereau study that DDT metabolites were playing a significant role in the disappearance of ospreys from the Connecticut River estuary. Amazing quantities of these chlorinated hydrocarbons were showing up in the food fish and eggs of the birds. Using such information, in 1967 the Environmental Defense Fund sued Long Island's Suffolk County Mosquito Control Commission to stop the indiscriminate use of DDT and won a court-ordered ban against further broadcasting of this chemical, the first such legal restraint in the nation.

Since piecemeal protection would obviously be insufficient to solve the problem, a national campaign was mounted to obtain a federal ban of DDT. This came in 1972, but some ornithologists believed it was already too late for some raptors. All through the 1970s, when osprey eggs from the heavily contaminated Long Island Sound region were being exchanged with those from the less contaminated Chesapeake, the Long Island Sound eggs remained infertile and helped depress Chesapeake osprey populations faster than nature would have done. However, Chesapeake eggs which hatched in Long Island Sound nests sustained a core of northern-oriented ospreys during the healing years in which the coastal environment was purging itself of DDT residues.

By 1978, a group of technicians could report in *Science* magazine that since the preban days of the 1960s, there had been a fivefold decrease in DDE (a derivative of DDT) in Connecticut and Long Island osprey eggs, and while PCB (polychlorinated biphenyl) levels remained unchanged and high, this carcinogenic compound apparently has little effect on avian reproduction, since osprey numbers in the region suddenly began escalating in 1976.

The osprey comprises a single genus and species within the Family Pandionidae and is found on every continent except Antarctica. Its population has been increasing wherever suitable nesting structures and adequate fish supplies can be found. Since 1970, nesting populations from Boston to New York have doubled and now number over three hundred birds. On the 3300 acres of Gardiners Island alone, there was until recently an active nest for every ten acres. Still, the New England coastal population is less than one-third of what it was thirty years ago, and a major caveat for the future is found in the Gardiners Island colony. Although some summers this former wellspring of ospreys still manages to produce enough young to offset attrition, most years a majority of the birds starve to death because commercial overfishing has eliminated most surface-schooling fishes in Long Island Sound and Gardiners Bay. Since the South Fork of Long Island is now the nearest area to Gardiners Island where predictable supplies of fish are readily available, the Gardiners males must fly fifty miles round-trip between their nests and Shinnecock Bay, and this does not include sometimes lengthy fishing periods over the bay. In addition, the twenty-five or so males from Gardiners Island must compete with the half-dozen conveniently sited male ospreys from the South Fork region. Furthermore, male ospreys, whether they are successful or not in fishing, spend many "down-time" hours each day resting and preening. Thus, so long as we continue to manage marine resources with only ourselves in mind, ospreys will continue to starve in Gardiners' otherwise idyllic (meaning predator-free) surroundings.

On Saturday evenings at Tabor, and on occasional weekdays after dinner, one of the counselors would lead a fishing expedition into Buzzards Bay, using the big launch to carry a couple dozen campers. Since there were always more boys interested in going than there was room, I wrangled permanent crewman's status by supplying bait.

Our principal prey were porgies, or "scup," as they are called in New England, and large hard-shell clams or quahogs were the best bait. These I'd shuffle up with my feet in the shallows near the marine rails. The scientific name of the quahog is *Mercenaria mercenaria* and refers to the shell's former use in making Indian money beads or wampum. This same clam is sold up and down the coast under a variety of names, depending on size. Littlenecks are the smallest, up to about one and a half inches in diameter. Cherry-stones are next, up to about two and a half inches, and named for a creek on the Eastern Shore of Virginia from which great quantities were shipped after the New York, Philadelphia and Norfolk Railroad was completed in 1884. The larger hard-shells are called chowder clams and they, along with ocean quahogs or black clams and surf clams, are what you find in soups, homemade and canned. Because mollusks toughen with cooking, some seafood gourmets prefer to eat the chowders raw and put the littlenecks in stews. However, since commercial processors dice any and all clams of whatever species, a generalized clam flavor is what most people get in canned soups, not refined distinctions of taste and texture.

The other bait I supplied was also a mollusk, but one that most people cannot believe is related to clams and oysters. The long-finned squid is less desirable as scup bait, but ideal for sea bass. I would go down to the floating dock after dinner with a line and treble hook, find a swarm of baby menhaden, or "pogy" as they are called in New England, snag one of the fish and leave it in the water quivering tantalizingly on the hook and scattering pearlescent scales like tiny sequins. In no time at all, a squid would dart from the deepening shadows beneath the dock, clutch the menhaden with its tentacles, and snag itself on the treble hook.

With most species of seafood increasingly overfished and consequently overpriced, squid may become a familiar meal for more Americans. There are two species of these curious creatures off the Atlantic coast: long-finned squid and boreal, or short-finned, squid. Boreal squid prefer cold offshore waters and are mostly found from Cape Cod to Newfoundland, where they have been taken for centuries at night under lights by cod fishermen who had exhausted their herring supplies and needed fresh bait. Long-finned squid prefer cool inshore waters and thrive from Cape Cod to Cape Hatteras. In the late nineteenth century, they were part of a southern New English pound-net fishery for bait whose principal targets were menhaden, herring and mackerel, but whose fishermen were happy to catch and sell squid which they toughened with salt to make as durable as pork rind.

Long-finned and short-finned squid both winter beyond the edge of the Continental Shelf. In the spring, they migrate toward the coast—long-finned squid to spawn and short-finned squid to feed. Squid stay deep on sunny days and rise toward the surface at night or on overcast days to feed on anything they can catch, including one another. Squid spoil quickly if not kept cold or if their ink sacks are ruptured, and until recently American trawlermen sorted the squid and crabs they caught from the flounder and sea bass they were after and threw the "trash" over the side.

In 1973, Europeans began coming to the edge of our Continental Shelf to trawl specifically for squid. West German fishermen refined depth-sounding equipment to pick up the weak signals returned by the swim-bladderless animals. By working within the shortest possible pulse range of 75 to 200 kilohertz, the Germans were able to find schools that yielded nearly a ton of squid for each hour of trawling. With current dockside prices of a dollar per pound, squid have become profitable for fishermen and still a bargain for the fish buyer since 70 to 80 percent of a squid's body weight is edible, while less than 50 percent of most fish can be eaten.

By night, Japanese and some Canadian and U.S. fishermen are using bright overhead lights (Japanese vessels have lighting capacities of up to 250 kilowatts, but the Canadians and Americans make do with a few 100-watt lamps) to lure squid toward the surface where they hover in the boat's shadow, much like my Tabor squid of yore hid beneath the dock, to dash out at baitfish—and squid jigs— moving at the edge of the light. The most sophisticated squid fishermen use automatic jigging machines and seventy lures per line. Each lure is brightly colored (any hue will do) with rings at either end and two rows of barbless spines at the bottom. The line is dropped and retrieved with a jerking motion at an average speed of two hundred feet per minute. A large jigger in productive waters can catch up to ten tons of squid a night with less fuel expended and with each squid coming over the side in better condition than its trawl-compacted counterpart. Japanese gourmets will not eat trawler-caught squid; consequently jigging is the only method Japanese fishermen employ to take these highly mobile mollusks.

I spent one cool, calm night in June of 1982 aboard the automated squid jigger, *Kiyo Maru*, in approximately thirty fathoms of water south of Block Island. Our catch was small, barely a ton, and composed entirely of short-finned squid over a foot in length, which the Japanese said were small and not as tasty as long-finned squid, but which I found large enough and delicious.

I also found that I could outfish the two machines on either side of me with the only hand-cranked jigger along the port rail. By imparting a more erratic retrieve to the line than the machines could duplicate, I outfished them by better than four to one. However, I was glad to stop after half an hour—which is the point. The ma-

chinery patiently works all night without letup, while people need to be fed, clothed, berthed, and, when they are too old to crank, retired. By contrast, the *Kiyo Maru* can sail anywhere in the Atlantic (after coming through the Panama Canal from Japan) and catch and process over ten tons of squid a night with a captain and crew of twenty-one. If the ship were not so highly automated, she would require three times that number of men to duplicate that high catch and processing rate.

During the night I was aboard, three *Mola*, or ocean sunfish, came around the ship's lights. The National Marine Fisheries Service's observer, Kevin Flanagan, told me that the Japanese would harpoon *Mola* whenever they had a chance to supplement their diets of rice, frozen and preserved foods, and fresh squid and the occasional ling or hake they caught off the fantail. The Japanese also caught spiny dogfish on rod and reel, but much to the disgust of an

Mola and Squid

American commercial fisherman named Bill Stevenson, who was also aboard and who makes his living catching spiny dogfish during the winter, the Japanese said American dogfish were "no good." As if to prove the point, the Japanese tied the tails of two or three dogfish at a time together and threw them back, or they played obscene pranks on one another with the dogfish before smacking them against the deck and tossing them over the side. I detail this not to condemn the Japanese—for people were ever thus with creatures they decide are of no immediate value—but by contrast to show their high regard for *Mola*.

The first two appeared so briefly, the crewmen had little time to get their harpoon gear from the fantail to where the gigantic fish were drifting ghostlike beneath the starkly illuminated surface. However, the last and by far the largest *Mola* of the night obligingly returned to the surface after each futile throw of the harpoon until a new man took over, and the prize was toggled and hauled aboard with the help of an enormous pair of ice tongs and a power winch.

While two men carved out chunks of the thick plastic rind that encloses the animal's flesh and vital organs, others pulled intestines out of the still flopping fish and began cutting them into sections and scraping out the food residues and lining. Other crewmen hacked out the milky white and oily flesh and began separating the bands of muscle fiber. Although *Mola* are mobile reefs for a variety of parasites and other freeloading invertebrates, the interior of the fish seem wonderfully free of anything that is not supposed to be there. The thick, oily rind, sections of which look like oversized but inedible portions of coconut meat, probably prevents many would-be internal parasites from tunneling into the drifting or slowly gliding jellyfish eaters.

After discarding the creature's hull, the Japanese lugged its cleaned intestines and muscle fiber off to the galley in plastic laundry baskets. The meat was marinated for several hours in citric acid and eaten about 6:00 A.M., unfortunately a couple of hours after I finally crawled into a deserted bunk to sleep.

With this incident fresh in mind, when I came across a *Mola* on the Fourth of July swimming slowly at the surface off the coast of Virginia, I decided to tag it with the thought that someday a Japanese squid jigger, long-liner, or another of the many Asian fishermen off our shores might recover it and we might learn a little about the travels of these mysterious fish.

There is a muscular and penetrable hump of flesh below the huge dorsal fin and, like sticking a banderilla into a bull, I jabbed the tag into the *Mola*. The huge sunfish responded like a bull and smashed my NMFS tagging pole into three pieces and took off with both the tag and the stainless-steel tagging lance. Such are the small costs and high adventures of oceanic research!

Tabor Summer Camp featured sailing, and I took the course that would qualify me to take out a Wood Pussy or catboat. The instruction went slowly because the class included several boys who had never been near the sea and at least one who wished he still wasn't. However, I was impatient to get certified because a catboat skippership would make me independent as nothing else offered by the camp could.

I remember the pride and pleasure of slipping the mooring for my first solo run into Buzzards Bay. Boys mark many milestones in their progress toward manhood, but nothing gave me the self-confidence and freedom that sailing did. You *operate* an engine-driven vessel, but you *fly* on the wind, with the wind, and, most miraculous of all, against the wind in a sailboat. Snorkeling or diving with air tanks makes you part of the sea's environment, but sailing makes you its master.

Soon I was teaching boys even younger than myself the glories of catboating. Although my roommate urged me to qualify in the sloop-rigged Zips and Mercurys, I was not interested in racing, which he was, nor did I desire companionship for my explorations of the bay, and camp rules made Zips and Mercurys two-man boats. However, instructing others in catboats meant that for two hours a day I got to poke around Marion harbor or sail out to Bird Island while ostensibly teaching the finer points of seamanship.

Some of my students arrived at the dock with their ditty bags surreptitiously stuffed with comic books and not the lines they were supposed to practice splicing on long downwind reaches when the boat sailed herself. They were at camp under duress, had no interest in sailing, and were, therefore, content to go wherever I wanted to go so long as I left them in peace to read the latest adventures of Batman, Captain Marvel, and Superman.

My own ditty bag was surreptitiously stuffed with fishing lines, leaders, small spoons, and rubber shock cords. As soon as I had tacked clear of the harbor and reached the more open water running away to Bird Island, I put over a fishing line from either side of the stern and trolled for "snapper" bluefish of about a pound. The sail to the island usually took less than an hour, and if there was a favorable breeze blowing for a swift return, I would land and look around a bit before sailing back to the dock to drop my students.

One day I found a dead common tern with a band on one leg which excited me as though I had discovered a note in a stranded bottle. I was filled with hope that this bird might have been ringed, as the British say, in some distant corner of Canada and was consequently disappointed when the letter from the U.S. Fish and Wildlife Service office in Laurel, Maryland, informed me that the bird had only been banded the month before near Yarmouth, Massachusetts, less than twenty-five miles from Bird Island. However, additional information in the letter consoled me with the thought that any band return helps provide data about "migration routes, distribution to wintering and breeding grounds [and] mortality." Certainly my return would help with the latter!

During the past three decades, I have recovered a good many banded birds. Yet each one fills me with the same keen anticipation that the first one did. I recovered in Virginia—and was reimbursed $15 for doing so—a "reward" black duck banded on Prince Edward Island, Canada. I shot a greater scaup on Long Island just a few miles from where it had been banded nine years earlier, and I wondered at the many thousands of miles it must have flown betweeen its breeding grounds in northern Canada and its regular winter home on the Great South Bay.

Most of my band recoveries are made near where the birds were banded. This is because banding efforts are usually concentrated on breeding or wintering grounds or along migratory corridors like Cape Cod's beaches. Naturally the recovery of bands, which involves recreational hunting as well as ornithological research, is done in the same prime areas. Still, as more people develop an interest in non-game-bird species, and as a growing number of these people qualify as birdbanders, banding may become an exotic form of communication between far-flung personalities with similar interests. Shorebirds and songbirds banded in southern New England will generate scientific pen-pal correspondence with mist netters in the Caribbean and South America. This is already going on in a small way, especially among people who band near their backyard feeders. However, the effort recently moved into high gear with the logistical support of the U.S. Navy. Reserve officers on summer duty have begun carrying their banding equipment on ships to band any weary migrants which come aboard. While recovering such birds will delight bird people up and down the migratory pipeline, it continues to baffle scientific administrators who cannot understand how a warbler can be banded several hundred miles at sea!

During my second summer at Tabor, another boy and I took a slick little sloop called an E-boat or, more properly, the Herreshoff 15 (fifteen feet at the waterline; twenty feet overall) through the Cape Cod Canal and across the bay to Provincetown. The only trouble was the camp didn't know about it, and the powers-that-be would not have let us go had they known. However, we had ideal winds and tides and made the journey in less than a day.

That evening, while we wandered through the Provincetown carnival and gawked at the girls wearing the latest in nylon windbreakers with dragons and maps of Korea on their backs, someone at Tabor noticed the E-boat was gone and someone else noticed that we were missing as well. The next morning while we debated whether to return via the canal or cruise around the Cape, visiting Martha's Vineyard and the Elizabeth Islands along the way, an enlisted Coast Guardsman stepped aboard and told us the jig was up. The most humiliating part of our capture was that we were eventually driven back to camp while two counselors got to sail the E-boat home.

At that time, although carnival sideshows had replaced the salt-works at Provincetown of which Henry David Thoreau had taken notice, the town was so little changed that Thoreau would certainly have recognized it. Cats still swarmed everywhere, as Thoreau put it, "like mosquitoes on the summits of [Provincetown's] hills." By sleeping aboard the boat, we avoided the cats and most of the mosquitoes.

Cape Cod was probably more down at the heels in the early 1950s than in Thoreau's time. Although lobsters wholesaled for 30 cents a pound, local lobstermen were making less real money than in 1849 when the anthropods sold for 2 cents each. Furthermore, mackerel were both more abundant and worth a great deal more in the 1850s than in the 1950s. Indeed, a century ago, these fish were the principal support of a large fleet of Cape Cod vessels and the many families who tended the men who tended the vessels. Sometime between Thoreau's first tour, when he saw lobsters caught in the shallows with nets much the way crabs are still caught elsewhere, and his 1857 visit, when he was sufficiently intrigued by the innovation to draw in his diary a slat-sided trap made in Vermont and costing a dollar, lobster potting was introduced to Cape Cod and necessarily increased the price of these creatures to three cents each. In those days, lobsters were hardly the rage they are now and were often used for bait to catch something more desirable like striped bass or bluefish.

Although Thoreau is best remembered for his praises of solitude, he was not totally averse to what the nineteenth century called "improvement" and what we call "development." He concluded his book, *Cape Cod*, with this prediction: "The time must come when this coast will be a place of resort for those New-Englanders who really wish to visit the seaside. At present it is wholly unknown to the fashionable world, and probably it will never be agreeable to them. If it is merely a ten-pin alley, or a circular railway [today Thoreau might have used miniature golf course or water slide], or an ocean of mint-julep, that the visitor is in search of—if he thinks more of the wine than the brine, as I suspect some do at

Newport [Rhode Island]—I trust that for a long time he will be disappointed here.

"But this shore will never be more attractive than it is now. Such beaches as are fashionable are here made and unmade in a day, I may almost say, by the sea shifting its sands. Lynn and Nantasket! [then popular beach resorts lying on either side of Boston harbor], this bare and bended arm it is that makes the bay in which they lie so snugly. What are springs and waterfalls? Here is the spring of springs, the waterfall of waterfalls. A storm in the fall or winter is the time to visit it; a light-house or a fisherman's hut the true hotel. A man may stand there and put all America behind him."

After the refinement of steam power brought an end to the Cape's sailing-ship-building industry; after the construction of the Cape railway led to the importation of inexpensive farm products and the suffocation of local agricultural effort (all except cranberries); and after this same railway took away the best and brightest of the young people to the cities, the towns of Cape Cod began their transformation from being the utilitarian workplaces within wild surroundings that Thoreau admired to merely being picturesque.

Middle-class shopkeepers and factory owners from Boston were the people who came to Cape Cod to rusticate. The "right people" still went to Newport or Mount Desert Island in Maine for their recreation. After it became clear that the Cape's brand of development was out of control, there could be no meeting of a few powerful families to set things straight. There were only more waves of prosperous burghers from Boston whose recreational ideals clashed with the work ethic of the down-at-the-heels Yankees who still controlled the townships.

Thoreau was mildly contemptuous of the Cape's Puritan heritage and those Yankee traditions which put down the role of his French ancestors in the founding of the New World. His original manuscript for *Cape Cod* included a lengthy history in which he ridiculed the parochial prejudices of the Anglo-Americans who had inherited northeastern North America after the French had done all the pioneering work.

I share Thoreau's view of biased New English historians who have taught several generations of American schoolchildren to despise French contributions to the history and culture of this continent. And I go further than Thoreau in speculating whether racism would have been such a pervasive ingredient in American history had the French prevailed over their English adversaries for control of the Eastern seaboard.

In the seventeenth century, the French quickly outpaced their Dutch (New York and northern New Jersey), Swedish (Delaware), and English (everywhere else) rivals in fur commerce because, unlike the northern Europeans who established trading posts and waited for the Indians to come to them with their furs, the French went out with the Indians on their traplines and exchanged children with red families so that French boys could learn the native dialects and Indian lads could learn French. Furthermore, French Catholic policy encouraged intermarriage with the Indians, while English, Dutch, and Swedish Protestantism disapproved of conjugal relations between white men and "savages." As late as the 1820s, the Franco-American bird painter and naturalist, John James Audubon, could scandalize the proper people of London and Edinburgh by publicly wearing buckskins and moccasins. By contrast, the more cosmopolitan people of Paris barely gave Audubon a second glance.

Yet for all their empathy with the wilderness, it may be best the French did not prevail in North America. Posterity seems content with the fact that after Samuel de Champlain took more than three years to map every bay and headland between Massachusetts and Nova Scotia, he neglected to stake a claim to this vast region. Given the unavoidable decline of the coastal wilderness, there is little in French laissez-faire traditions that would have enabled townships, states, and eventually the federal government to protect undeveloped portions of a chaotically manipulated seashore.

The effort to save Cape Cod began with those intransient Yankees of Eastham, Wellfleet, Truro, and Provincetown who refused to sell their dunes and beaches to developers from Boston and New York. In some cases, the local people could not sell, because the lands had been tied up in public trusts since 1714. Although these trusts were periodically challenged in the courts, such challenges tended to strengthen the laws protecting the beaches and dunes, particularly after Massachusetts became a state. In 1854, for example, a Province Lands Preserve of 3800 acres was formally declared by an Act of the General Court even though colonial proclamation had reserved these lands for the public more than a century earlier.

In the early 1800s, a Commonwealth Harbors and Lands Commission recommended that a strip five hundred feet wide above the high-water mark be reserved for public use along the bayside between

Truro and Jeremy Point and along all the Cape's oceanfront from Provincetown to Monomoy. Although state bills based on this recommendation failed to become law, most of the Cape's towns subsequently established municipal beaches and landings. In addition, the "foreshore"—meaning the intertidal zone—was declared to be public as well as any ponds ten acres or more in size.

However, these efforts to ensure public access did as much to whet the appetites of developers as to discourage them. After all, a cottage could now be sold anywhere on Cape Cod with the assurance that the buyer would have ample access to the beaches and bay.

The Harbors and Lands Commission never anticipated that would be a problem because it never anticipated the population and recreation boom in the latter half of the twentieth century. The commission had been thinking only about the landing rights of fishermen and the salvage rights of wreckers. Certainly, nineteenth-century planners would have laughed at the notion that the vulnerability of beach-nesting seabirds gave them legal rights superior to those of people's pets which, if allowed, will run through the nesting colonies, gobbling down eggs, chicks, and adult birds.

People's pets and toys, like off-road vehicles, are still problems at the Cape Cod National Seashore which has only enlarged and federalized the jurisdiction of those lands the Commonwealth of Massachusetts sought to protect 180 years ago. Only the political game plan has changed. Where formerly every politician from the eastern half of the state kept a wet finger in the wind to determine whether he was for "saving the Cape" today or "bringing prosperity through economic development" tomorrow, state and local politicians now take credit for anything that goes well and blame the feds for anything that goes wrong. Consequently, weekend traffic jams, unsatisfactory camping regulations, declining fish populations— these are all the federal government's fault. A good nesting season for Arctic terns, a sunset seen from Herring Cove Beach, and a quiet Sunday evening at Provincetown after the crowds have left— these are blessings brought to you compliments of the commonwealth.

Since the federal government was going to be abused no matter what it did, it's too bad the Park Service was not allowed to buy its share of Cape Cod when it first proposed a national seashore there in 1939. It could have had over 30,000 acres for about $10 an acre. By the time the former senator from Massachusetts and then president, John Fitzgerald Kennedy, signed the Cape Cod National Seashore into law in 1961, the American taxpayer had anted up over $700 per acre for just 26,666 acres.

Although the mobs on a summer Saturday can make a visit more like a nightmare than a holiday, I remind myself how much worse conditions would have been without Puritan foresight. Indeed, except for the fact that the Park Service does not permit visitors to sleep overnight on the beach, modern beachcombers can take the same route used by Henry David Thoreau and his companion, William Ellery Channing, in October 1849. The beachscape appears largely unchanged, and only by reference to old charts and contemporary erosion rates (approximately three feet per year) will you discover that the sands which Thoreau and Channing walked over are now four hundred feet out in the Atlantic.

Instead of a partner, you may prefer to take three books for company: Thoreau's *Cape Cod*, of course, as well as Dr. Richardson's *The House on Nauset Marsh* and Henry Beston's *The Outermost House*. Beston's book (1928) is the more sensitive of the latter two; Richardson's (1955), the more sensible. Beston's book might also be more poetic; Richardson's, more personal. However, the real difference may lie in the fact that Richardson was a participant in the life of the Cape, while Beston, like Thoreau, was more of a spectator.

Although both modern writers were well aware of Thoreau's pioneering visits, only Beston makes the barest mention of one of them. It is as though the two twentieth-century authors were apprentices striving for their places in the philosophers' guild and reluctant to accept help—or give credit—to their master. Yet for all their Yankee pride and, perhaps, prejudice, these two books complement Thoreau in the same way his friend, Channing, did. For just as Channing, according to Thoreau, was a genius lacking talent, *The Outermost House* and *The House on Nauset Marsh* are works of immense talent lacking genius.

• Thoreau and Channing averaged ten miles a day, which allowed ample time to explore the rest. That is still a good pace.

• Thoreau wore a hat fitted with a special shelf for botanical specimens. Today the Park Service encourages you to look but not to pick.

• Thoreau carried a basket with partitions for his books, sewing materials, hooks and line, and food staples including a "junk of heavy cake" with plums in it. Fishing and food are still allowed on national seashore beaches, but the Park Service begs consumers of plastic-wrapped cakes and bottled and canned beverages to bring out, not bury, the shards of their good living.

As Thoreau and Channing began their walk, battling the October wind and rain with their umbrellas, they soon learned there are only two "roads," as Thoreau called them, down the Cape: the dune ridge and the hard-packed sand of the lower beach. Although the weather is fickle and often raw in October, this is still a better month to duplicate Thoreau's walk than any during the summer when you will have to zigzag through mobs of sunbathers, surfers and lifeguards. Furthermore, along the so-called Free Beach near Truro, you will stroll among nude bathers who seem defensive about their nudity and inclined to harass you if you chose to keep your clothes on.

In October, fishermen and their off-road vehicles will still be using the beach, and even a few wet-suited surfers and swimmers will be seen. But with the crowds gone, these beach users are pleasant company and in keeping with what the Park Service originally had in mind when it created the national seashore. Furthermore, in October you will have to worry less about maintaining a schedule in order to keep hotel reservations. Like Thoreau, you can plan each day according to the weather and what discoveries you make along the way.

Remember Thoreau's advice:

"Most persons visit the seaside in warm weather, when fogs are frequent, and the atmosphere is wont to be thick, and the charm of the sea is to some extent lost. But I suspect that the fall is the best season, for then the atmosphere is more transparent, and it is a greater pleasure to look out over the sea. . . . In October, when the weather is not intolerably cold, and the landscape wears its autumnal tints, such as, methinks, only a Cape Cod landscape ever wears, especially if you have a storm during your stay—that I am convinced is the best time to visit this shore. In autumn . . . the thoughtful days begin, and we can walk anywhere with profit. . . ."

4

THE NEW YORK BIGHT

It's not your imagination: Winter arrives later than it did when we were young. This does not mean that it is less intense once it is here—only that the hundreds of relict sleighs and sleds now stored in barns and sheds from Virginia north through New England were out on the roads often before Thanksgiving in the 1800s, while today in Virginia, even a white Christmas is becoming rare.

Although meteorologists use wandering jet streams to explain why some parts of the earth are getting colder while the overall global trend is toward warmer weather, they don't always mention the impact of the sea, perhaps because it is difficult to ascertain whether the rising sea contributes to the warming trend or is a result of it. Probably a little of both. The sea has been rising along the western Atlantic coast for many thousands of years at an average rate of five inches per century. It claims a little more land with each tick of the geological clock, and, thereby, moderates regional climate to that infinitesimal degree.

However, the sea is not rising everywhere at the same rate. The tectonic plate on which we sit is shifting west and our coastal plain is subsiding, but the softer, sandier zones are sinking more rapidly than the firmer granite ones. Some areas of the mid-Atlantic region are subsiding almost perceptibly. The backside of upper Long Beach Island, New Jersey, for example, is sinking so fast that residents must be protected from the bay by double-thickness, creosoted lumber sea walls where only a generation ago, they strolled down through a now-vanished marsh to reach the water's edge.

But let us look back even further in time. It is spectacular to contemplate that the entire northeastern coast of the United States stood roughly a mile higher a million years ago. Most mammals, including man, who was evolving in Africa and Asia, had assumed forms much like their modern relatives. Some creatures were much larger than their descendants; the extinct giant beaver and ground sloth, for example, were both as large or larger than the people who would one day hunt them. Although man had yet to achieve his maximum brain size, he walked erect and doubtlessly communicated with speech and hand signals as he hunted and scavenged in family groups. So far as we know, human beings had not yet visited the New World, but even had some bold adventurers made the journey, they would have eventually been annihilated by the tremendous geological and climatic forces that compressed the Atlantic plain beneath ice sheets and pushed the coast out an average of thirty miles from its present perimeter.

In what is today New York, New England, and southeastern Canada, two great river systems drained the region and deeply scarred the edge of the Continental Shelf. Smaller rivers, including Maine's Kennebec and Penobscot, contributed their annual spates to the sea through long fertile valleys, but the faint signatures they left at the edge of the shelf attest to the minor roles they played in comparison with the canyons scoured by the mighty Hudson and the St. Lawrence.

In those dim days, the Hudson drained not only its present valley, but many larger watersheds to the north as well. Four great ice sheets eventually moved down from the Arctic Circle, and the greatest of these stopped at Manhattan and towered a mile high over Red Bank, New Jersey. An immense moraine of rock and rubble melted from the glacier to form the backbone of Long Island west from Montauk and Orient points—where the ice sheet later paused in its retreat for a thousand years to lay down the forks of Great Peconic and Gardiners bays—to Staten Island and New Jersey. Throughout this time the Hudson continued to cut its way to the sea at the Verrazano Narrows, after which it still had to run for another forty-five miles before cascading into the shrunken sea.

When a major glacier melts, oceanic volumes of water carry mountains of silt and stone that grind out channels possibly as profound as the Colorado's Grand Canyon. At one point during the Pleistocene, the Jersey Palisades were four times higher than they are today, and the Hudson River had cataracts beyond the daring of even the most intrepid white-water rafters. These cold, but mineral-rich waters surged into warmer, equatorially driven currents offshore to produce unbelievably fertile interfaces in which vast clouds of plankton and countless millions of other, more complex life-forms flourished.

Since Long Island Sound was not yet a sound, the Connecticut and Housatonic rivers flowed to a confluence with the roaring Hudson where the East River presently merges with New York Harbor. From the west, the Passaic and Hackensack rivers added their then considerable volumes to the flood and bent the Hudson southeast for its final rush across the coastal plain before it roared into the sea in a waterfall greater than any that mankind can atavistically recall.

Nearly a mile wide, the first drop was a third of a mile high. Within four miles, the cataract fell another 2600 feet. By comparison, the highest waterfall in the United States today, Yosemite, drops just 2425 feet in two tiers. Angel Falls in Venezuela drops a total of 3212 feet, including an initial 2648-foot leap into space. However, both Yosemite and Angel Falls combined spill less water annually than the Hudson River dropped within a few minutes at the peak of its canyon-cutting capability.

One way to gain some sense of the former majesty of the now drowned and docile Hudson is to visit Angel Falls and imagine its comparative trickle compounded to Amazonian proportions. Another, more subtle way is to probe the Hudson Canyon's depths with special fishing gear and feel the vibrations of life from abysmal creatures that float up after they are hooked when the gases in their bodies expand as the compressing weight of tons of water per square inch is reduced to mere pounds. These denizens of the deep sometimes arrive at the surface, grotesquely distended or even exploded, sooner than you can draw up the slack in the line that holds them.

You drift placidly over the edge of the canyon on a calm spring day while angling for tilefish, a codlike creature more closely related to burrow-dwelling sculpins than the cusk or hake they resemble. In 1882, tilefish mysteriously died throughout the New York Bight in such sea-covering numbers (an estimated 500 million) that scientists believed for more than a decade afterward the species had become extinct. Today a sizable offshore recreational fishery for tilefish exists between Nantucket and Delaware Bay, with the most numbers and largest fish (up to 50 pounds) caught in the Bight at depths ranging between 270 and 1200 feet. Suddenly your sash-weight sinker drops from a bottom only 400 feet below into a chasm 2800 feet deep. In horizontal distance, you have drifted less than 200 yards.

This is the continental edge where broadbill swordfish feed on cusk and small tilefish down to depths of several thousand feet, and where great mako sharks stalk the swordfish, incapacitate them by biting through their powerful caudal muscles and the tail artery, and then turn again and again upon the helplessly churning prey, devouring it until only the bony head and tail are left to angle into eternal darkness like parts of a flack-torn aircraft in the night.

On the bottom of the canyon, hagfish, eyeless and jawless creatures which burrow into their food to consume it from the inside out, and grenadiers, blind scavengers which tiptoe about on modified pectoral fins, locate the few fleshy shards and recycle them into further life. Meanwhile, several giant bluefin tuna pulse overhead, sensing the canyon's wall and using it as a guide to other drowned lands to the north, ever to the north.

As an impoundment rises and begins to inundate the surrounding lands, the resulting release of nutrients from the flooded forests and soils enhance feeding opportunities for every inhabitant of the impoundment. This is as true of a new farm pond as it was of the Atlantic creeping over the edge of the Continental Shelf thousands of years ago.

The Atlantic rose rapidly, creating islands of elevated landscape like the Georges Bank off Cape Cod and Browns Bank off Nova Scotia. Trapped on these islands and eventually drowned by the rising waters were mastodons and mammoths, giant elk and musk-oxen.

At first, marine mammals did quite well by the rising sea. They had flourished before, but now and for the next several thousand years, their populations bloomed. Walrus spread north from Florida where they had retreated during the different Ice Ages after crossing the submerged Central American isthmus from the Pacific where

Swordfish and Mako Sharks

they evolved. Barrier islands that are now undersea ridges ten to thirty miles offshore Long Island and New Jersey were used as hauling-out sites for vast herds of walrus whose tusks and skulls are recovered nearly every week by sea clammers exploiting the same beds that once provided the walruses with the bulk of their diets.

Gray seals and harbor seals fed on the abundant near-shore fishes, and gray whales used the newly formed lagoons as summer calving grounds. However, something upset this aquatic paradise, and marine mammals in the mid-Atlantic coastal region began to decline a few thousand years ago. Some scientists feel that the blubber-thick animals could no longer tolerate the warming air and waters; others see parallels between the eutrophication of reservoirs and the aging of the Atlantic shelf—that is, just as flooded shallows in new lakes often produce more microscopic life than can be absorbed into the food chain so that the very element of being, oxygen, is locally exhausted, something was altered in coastal water chemistry to disrupt vital links in the marine mammals' food chains.

Yet presently the most fashionable thesis to explain the twilight of large mammals in the Pleistocene is that tribes of hunting humans exterminated them. It is true that man is forever profligate with nature's bounty, and just as Victorian hunters killed tens of thousands more bison than they needed, early Atlantic coastal settlers may have helped reduce some marine mammals to those relict populations, for example, of walrus in Nova Scotia and gray seals on Long Island that European colonists found and finished in the seventeenth and eighteenth centuries. The last Atlantic gray whale died early in the 1600s, but whether at the hands of white men, red men, or a whim of nature will never be known.

However, hungry people still have to be fed, and that is bad news for many other marine species which must now fill the breech— and more than a *billion* additional human mouths—since the time when the conservation of whales first became an issue. Every possible fishing technology from huge purse seiners to primitive harpoons are being used to strip the seas of their lucrative protein, and of all the species presently being harvested to the verge of commercial extinction, none is more valuable than the bluefin tuna.

In April and May—more than 1500 miles to the south—bluefin tuna begin arriving in the purple depths east of the Lesser Antilles. Some come from Venezuela, Brazil, and, perhaps, as far south as Uruguay. Others pass through the Yucatán Channel from the Gulf of Mexico and swim the length of the Caribbean Sea before joining their comrades east of Barbuda and the Virgin Islands. There is no congregating at a particular depot for the departure for northern waters—only pods of torpedo-sized fish funneling through the passes of the Leeward Islands and bending north to the Bahamas on a trek older than the islands themselves.

In the Bahamas or farther north—off Cape Hatteras or Cape May—these bluefin will be joined by others. Most will come directly up the Straits of Florida from spawning zones in the Gulf of Mexico, particularly the area just west of the Dry Tortugas. A few will have crossed the wide Atlantic from Portugal and the Bay of Biscay. While there are feeding grounds in the eastern Atlantic and Mediterranean Sea, an unknown number of tuna born on the other side of the Atlantic make the transoceanic crossing each year, frequently showing up in July off Manasquan, New Jersey, or Montauk, Long Island, after their nonstop trip from Spain or France. Feeding voraciously on shoals of smaller fish and squid, the bluefin linger in the rich waters of the New York Bight—in July, the smaller 25- to 150-pound fish; in August and September, giants up to 1000 pounds. The Bight is the only area along the coast where all the different year-groups of bluefin dependably appear—dependably, that is, until the past two decades when incredible fishing pressure has drawn a dark veil over the species' future.

The bluefin tuna is a great pelagic wanderer, and because the largest of its kind are more than thirty years old, these fish see as much of the Atlantic's undersea shelves and ridges as weathered freighter skippers see of its inconstant surface and shorelines. The tuna is wonderfully designed by nature to accomplish its epic journeys. Rather than being fusiform, like other, less well traveled members of the mackerel family, the tuna's mass is concentrated in its head and shoulders, and its body tapers to an iron-hard crescent that drives the brute at underwater speeds up to fifty-five miles per hour, faster than most any other fish but the largest swordfish and marlins. Even with occasional forays onto the Continental Shelf to feed, some giant tuna make the trip from Cuba to the Hudson Canyon in less than three days.

Some days the schools travel deep, so deep the life-forms they consume are unknown to the scientists who stand by to analyze stomach contents as the tuna are hauled thumping and shivering— and in the spring, desperately shedding milt and eggs in a dying de-

Bluefin Tuna

sire to propagate—onto the decks of commercial fishing boats. They
are immediately gutted and headed, but their tails are left on as
convenient hoist handles for offloading at the dock.

Other days, some sense compels the great fish to rise through
the azure depths until they find themselves beneath shoals of smaller
fish. A rain squall appears to sweep the surface as hundreds, then
tens of thousands, of bait take to the air ahead of the boiling bluefin.
If it is a school of flying fish, the tuna follow those individuals that
keep to the same general course they're already on. Doggedly they
pursue their prey, swerving when it swerves, surging forward whenever the prey's tail begins to droop and flutter at the surface. When
the flying fish can no longer sustain flight and plops in, there's an
explosion of water—and the tuna presses on.

Like most pelagic fishes, bluefin tuna are nonselective in their
feeding. Any prey easily seized is quickly converted to fuel by these
workhorse mackerel whose recorded weights reach 1600 pounds. (One
14-footer taken off New Jersey in the nineteenth century weighed
this much.) Their jaws have a curious double hinge which swings the

mouth cavity out as well as open. Unlike the sedentary anglerfish, which can expand its open mouth twelve times the volume of its closed mouth and, hence, suck in prey rather than lunging after it, a giant tuna draws prey from the periphery of its feeding attack and can swallow several herring or squid at the same time, although only one may have been targeted. One spring, the stomachs of bluefin tuna barreling through the Bahamian passes were chock full of small porcupine fishes, filefishes, and other weed and bottom dwellers which the tuna had engulfed with locked-open jaws the way their filter-feeding cousins, the Atlantic mackerel, consume plankton.

Few creatures are more prisoner of their own supreme adaptation than the bluefin tuna. It can roll its eyes but little and its finlets above and below the rigid caudal fin can be twisted only slightly and in unison, like the miniature rudders they are. The dorsal and pectoral fins fit into depressions within the body the way landing gear is raised within the fuselage of an aircraft. And there is a soft area on top of the tuna's head—a window through the skull for the reception of light which the tuna uses in navigation—that cannot be detected except by running your hand over the fish's smooth brow. Yet this supreme oceanic organism is helpless once its tail has been lifted from the water and it can no longer assert its hydrodynamic dominance. Then its stolid appearance and frantic demeanor help depersonalize the creature for those who must kill it to make their livings from the sea.

In the nineteenth century, giant tuna were valued only for their oil. A thousand-pounder was rendered into approximately twenty-four gallons, and if a gentleman naturalist wanted a specimen for his science club—as did Dr. Joseph B. Holder in 1856 for the Lynn (Massachusetts) Natural History Society—he had to pay the fishermen for their time and trouble as well as the unrendered oil. Dr. Holder's son, Charles Frederick, recalled that almost every professional fisherman along that part of the coast "had the crescent-shaped tail of the tuna nailed to his roof." Inspired by the sight of these huge fish, Charles Holder fished for them off Ogunquit, Maine, in 1875, and although "I fished with patience, trolling and anchored, tried all kinds of bait from mossbunkers to live pollock, I could never lure the Atlantic tuna . . ."

Giant tuna still swim near the upper New England coast. They move mostly alone through the dark water, with barely perceptible pulsations of their powerful tails. Sometimes an individual will circle an island, less with the erratic movement of a feeding fish than as part of a dream in which the age of the island and the age of the tuna seem to merge so that there is no surprise in the sudden, fog-shrouded appearance of men in a boat, one of whom stands with a spear, as the boat draws near the sickle-fin slicing the sea's surface.

The Carthaginians and later the Romans developed a shore-based system of nets with various corridors and pens into which migrating schools of bluefin tuna moved of their own volition and where they were ultimately raised to the surface and butchered. Beginning more than 2300 years ago and continuing into the present century, detailed records for several of these traps on the North African coast reveal a remarkably consistent yield that only began dwindling after World War II when increasing numbers of fishermen started to pursue the tuna far from shore the year around, rather than wait for them to visit the traps on their annual migration.

Purse seining quickly became the most effective means at sea for capturing entire schools of immature bluefin. After a school is located by men in a crow's nest or in spotter planes high overhead, the end of a deep net, buoyed along one edge and weighted along the other to hang from the surface like a curtain, is cast overboard, and the ship or, more often today, an auxiliary speedboat, moves swiftly to encircle the school. Once the fish are enclosed, the net is pursed at the bottom the way a laundry bag's drawstring closes the mouth of the bag, and the tuna are brought to the surface for transfer to the hold of the ship.

Medium-sized bluefin, ranging up to 270 pounds and nine years of age, travel in smaller schools than their younger kin. Hence, they are less vulnerable to the economics that made tuna purse seining the most profitable form of fishing in the world until rising fuel prices and declining fish populations began suffocating profits in the early 1980s. American canners must now charge so much money per case that canned tuna has become a glut on the market. Financially pressed shoppers balk at paying $2 for a six-and-a-half-ounce serving of preserved tuna when fresh fish of several other species can still be bought for less than $2 per pound.

However, seiner skippers once earned $250,000 for six months' work, and even able-bodied crewmen took home up to $50,000 each —and a great deal more when they opted to teach Senegalese crews under French flags the tricks they learned under the Stars and Stripes. Yet large tuna, which have sold for nearly $7000 each,* are normally beyond the ken of purse seiners. By the time a tuna reaches three hundred and fifty pounds, he is often a loner and only associates with numbers of his peers on breeding grounds or choice feeding grounds. Purse seiners rarely harm such fish, but fuel-efficient long-liners take up where the netters leave off.

A longline involves tens of thousands of short lines and baited hooks hanging off a master line stretching up to sixty miles across the ocean. The master line is buoyed at either end and at several points in between, and radio transmitters and radar reflectors keep the fishermen tuned in to the line's precise location while they steam over the horizon to set a second line. Every day or two, the lines are alternately hauled and the drowned tuna retrieved—unless they have been eaten by sharks not caught elsewhere along the line. The effectiveness of this technique in quite literally combing the seas of large pelagic fishes is demonstrated by the fact that Japanese long-liners alone account for more tagged tuna, marlin, and shark returns than any other method of recovery. Biologist Michael J. A.

* On January 1, 1982, a 352-pound bluefin tuna was sold in Tokyo for 1,500,000 yen. Under the existing exchange rate, this sale price was equivalent to $6818.18 (U.S.).

Butler in the August 1982 issue of *National Geographic* calculates that in a single year, "Japanese fishermen set and reset 12 million nautical miles of longline—enough to girdle the globe more than 500 times."

With each passing summer, there are fewer tuna in the waters over the Hudson Canyon. In the cloud-darkened depths, the bluefin move like shadows within a world of shadow. They do not behave as they once did—leaping forward at the surface and forming exploding lines from horizon to horizon to drive all smaller fishes before them. Today they stay deep or cruise over the Continental Shelf with little fanfare. They seem to understand they are more the hunted than the hunters.

The effort to save these fish is now being fought on two fronts. The strategic, or long-term, effort is directed toward closing the tuna loophole in the Fishery Conservation and Management Act. Before this law could be passed in 1976, the California-based tuna industry, which has been poaching the sovereign seas of other nations for decades and been regularly apprehended by foreign navies and bailed out with U.S. funds, insisted that tunas must be declared creatures of the high seas and exempt from unilateral management by the United States. Although the industry has many politically powerful friends in high office, an American Tuna Action Committee (ATAC) of the highly respected National Coalition for Marine Conservation has managed to get legislation introduced in both houses of Congress to put an end to this unique exception to the nation's fisheries management plans.

Tactical efforts to save the bluefin are made at meetings of the International Convention for the Conservation of Atlantic Tunas (ICCAT). In the past, such meetings were studies in frustration, partly because some other member nations' delegations refused to admit that the bluefin was in trouble, and partly because some past American delegations were embarrassed by the fact that the best data on bluefin growth and migrations have been accumulated over the past half century by an obsessive genius named Frank J. Mather III, who not only is not a member of the cozy club of federal resource managers, he is not even a marine biologist. Yet, perhaps because Mather is an outsider straining to have his information accepted by people he mostly despises—Frank feels the most insulting thing he can call anyone is "an administrator"—Mather's statistics and record keeping are impeccable, and his views have finally been accepted by most people in the community of North Atlantic fishery scientists. For the first time in 1982, the beleagured bluefin received some relief from regulations promulgated by ICCAT.

The bluefin tuna is not the only important food and game species of the New York Bight to be dangerously overfished. The striped bass was once the capital marine resource of the littoral or nearshore waters of Long Island and northern New Jersey, but today the striper, like the bluefin tuna, exhibits all the unhealthy signs of a species nearing exploitive extinction.

First, the average size of the fish increases dramatically. In the case of the tuna, the definition of what constitutes a giant rose from 300 pounds in the 1950s to 700 pounds today. In the case of the striper, a huge female or "cow" once weighed 50 pounds; in the past few years, the 70-pound mark has been broken several times.

Next, fisheries scientists are no longer able to suggest meaningful regulations because they are inevitably working with year-old data which are as good as ancient history in dealing with a rapidly depressed resource. Quotas or expected catches for both striped bass and bluefin tuna have gone unfilled for the past four years despite increased fishing pressure.

Finally, few small tuna or stripers are seen in their respective fisheries. And those that are present are quickly caught out. Few youngsters are surviving to reach sexual maturity, which means that when the present stocks of spawners are gone, the very existence of wild striped bass and Atlantic bluefin tuna will be in jeopardy.

Striped bass reproduce well in hatcheries, so in that sense, their situation is less desperate than the bluefins. Furthermore, stripers do not have to be as old to spawn: four years for female stripers, five for tuna. And the current decline in the striper is not its first. In the 1880s, intensive commercial fishing all along the Atlantic coast clobbered striper stocks. Characteristically, as fish numbers declined, more giants were caught. In 1891 at Edenton, North Carolina, the largest striper of all time was landed. It weighed 125 pounds and was at least 30 years old and possibly much older.

The pity of killing such large fish is that any striped bass over 35 pounds is bound to be a female. Such a fish is 12 years or older and will lay nearly 5 million eggs. By contrast, a 4-year-old striper can lay no more than 65,000 eggs. Obviously, the potential for one big cow with an escort of smaller males to make a contribution to

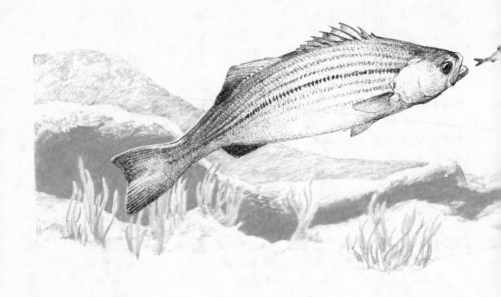

restoring her kind is considerable. However, only the state of Maryland protects such large fish during the spawning season. Sadly, too, every fishing contest along the coast places a premium on the biggest striped bass landed. As in the case of bluefin tuna, anglers in New York, New Jersey, and Massachusetts are presently vying over who will have the dubious distinction of killing the largest of the fertile giants. Such competition is analagous to foresters searching the woods for champion trees and cutting them down and bringing them in to prove they once existed.

In one important respect, the striper's prognosis is more dire than the tuna's, because we don't know what all ails the striped bass, and we do know what is wrong with the bluefin. It is being over-fished, period. Once this pressure is alleviated, the bluefin should restore itself, because its pelagic habitat is still reasonably wholesome. However, overfishing is just one of the problems confronting the striped bass. According to lure manufacturer Bob Pond, who—like his tuna-researching counterpart, Frank Mather—has been waging a lonely battle against established scientific and commercial interests for many years, striped bass are being depleted on their principal breeding grounds by a variety of man-made chemicals that do not allow the stripers' eggs and larvae to develop normally. Bob has spent much of his own money supervising research to prove this

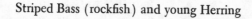

Striped Bass (rockfish) and young Herring

thesis. His noninstitutional approach has alienated many fishery scientists, but it and writer John N. Cole's book *Striper* have reinforced the thinking of some politicians who know that the striped bass is the most popular coastal game fish among their many angling constituents. In 1980, Senator John H. Chaffee of Rhode Island managed to pry $2.3 million out of the U.S. Congress for distribution among the various Atlantic state and federal fish and wildlife agencies to find out what is happening to the striped bass.

Such political largesse comes more than 340 years after the settlers of the Massachusetts Bay Colony passed our first striped-bass conservation law. Surplus stripers taken on hook and line or in pound nets were supposed to be released rather than used as fertilizer on farm fields. Previous to 1639, fishermen had viewed the striper as an illimitable resource, the way John Smith did in his *New England's Trials* (1620): "There are such multitudes [of basse] that I have seene stopped in the river close adjoining to my house with a sande at one tyde so many as will loade a ship of 100 tonnes. I myself, at the turning of the tyde have seene such multitudes passe out of a pounde that it seemed to me that one mighte go over their backs drishod."

Today the striper is finally having its day in court. In April 1982, Federal District Court Judge Thomas P. Griesa enjoined the

U.S. government from paying $90 million to New York City for a proposed landfill of the interpier areas along the Lower West Side of Manhattan as part of the controversial Westway highway project. The reason for the court order was that this ersatz section of broken-backed piers and crumbling bulkheads is possibly the most important wintering ground for juvenile striped bass in the New York Bight. Anywhere between fifteen to a hundred times as many young stripers can be found here in December as anywhere else in the region. Sample trawls also discovered significant concentrations of half a dozen other littoral fishes.

Although the Chesapeake Bay and its tributaries are the most important spawning ground and nursery for Atlantic stripers, the Hudson River provides between 18 and 32 percent of the fish caught in the New York Bight and Long Island Sound. New York's commercial landings have averaged 550,000 pounds over the past several years with a dockside value of over $1 million. The recreational catch is nearly three times greater with an annual value equivalent to what Judge Griesa enjoined the federal government from paying the city if you determine value by the minimal amount recreational fishermen would be willing to accept to give up their sport.

Preserving the piers for stripers was an idea used by many opponents of Westway as a desperate ploy to stop the project so that more attention, and hopefully more money, could be focused on the city's impoverished mass transit system. A similar tactic by opponents of Tennessee's Tellico Dam turned a tiny perch known as the snail darter into a cause célèbre. However, proponents of the Tennessee Valley Authority's power project were successful in getting their dam on line by belittling the snail darter as having little or no economic worth. Westway may yet be built, but it won't be because the project's proponents will be able to belittle the striper's value to society.

The striper has had many generations of influential friends. Following the Civil War, marine recreational angling became all the rage for triumphant industrialist-sportsmen, and striped bass were placed on a pedestal with the Atlantic salmon as the ne plus ultra of angling achievement. Striped-bass fishing clubs were established on Long Island and New Jersey, but the most exclusive clubs were situated on Pasque and Cuttyhunk islands in the Elizabeth chain lying between Buzzards Bay and Martha's Vineyard Sound and on West Island east of New Bedford. By 1886, membership in the West Island Club was limited to thirty fishermen, each of whom paid a $1000 initiation fee plus annual dues. That same year, Atlantic coastal anglers, who had been feeling sorry for their exiled Pacific brethren, shipped several hundred fingerling striped bass seined from New Jersey's Navesink River to San Francisco where their descendants still offer Bay Area residents fine sport and excellent meals.

Although Pacific stripers, which now range from Los Angeles to the Columbia River, have cycles of abundance and scarcity, their cycles are not so extreme as those experienced in the Atlantic, possibly because for many decades the striped bass has been classified as a recreational resource on the West Coast and can only be kept by a commercial fisherman if he plans to eat the fish himself or give it to friends. By contrast, only a few states along the Atlantic coast —and invariably not those which play the most significant role in this species' life history—have made the striper a game fish. Some states have classified the striper as both a game fish and a commercial fish, which means that unlicensed anglers must abide by conservation measures while those who pay the state a nominal tax can catch all they like to sell.

After the striper was overfished at the end of the last century, commercial fishermen turned their attention to other species. Today there are no other littoral species that are not already being pursued to the brink of unsustainable yield, and the rising price per pound for striped bass continues to make the two or three fish caught per outing nearly as profitable as the boxful caught twenty years ago. The first step toward striped bass conservation, therefore, is cooperation among all the states which share this resource. The highest purpose of the federal striper fund may be that it forces state legislatures to acknowledge that there is no such thing as a "North Carolina striper," a "New York striper" or a "Maine striper."

The people who made these designations ridiculous belong to an organization called the American Littoral Society. In 1962, a group of scuba (self-contained underwater breathing apparatus) divers and photographers asked biologists at the U.S. Bureau of Sport Fisheries and Wildlife's Sandy Hook Marine Laboratory if there was something they could do on weekend expeditions to help the lab. Then assistant director, John Clark, who in 1967 would sound the first widely heard alarms regarding continued development of our coastal marshes in his book, *Fish & Man*, was eager to involve amateur naturalists in marine science, and he assigned the divers duty at various inlets and jetties censusing fish. These observations eventually helped establish reliable timetables for the annual appearance and disappearance in northern New Jersey of nearly ninety species of littoral fishes, including the striper. Catch records were invariably less complete because fishermen are not interested in all the species that interest biologists.

In 1963, a vice-president for the Prudential Life Insurance Company came to the fledgling Littoral Society with a problem: he liked to fish for sharks, but he knew no one else who did, and he knew no one who could tell him much about the creatures. In fact, after he entered a huge shark in a Cape May Chamber of Commerce fishing tournament, a nervous tournament committee gave him a citation for the catch but noted on the citation that such sharks are "rare" off Cape May—even though no one on the committee knew or cared what species of shark it was!

Graham Macmillan's curiosity about sharks was well timed. Not only did he find that members of the American Littoral Society shared his curiosity, there was a bright and energetic young biologist working at the Sandy Hook lab, where the society soon had office space, who was on the verge of publishing his *Anglers' Guide to Sharks of the Northeastern United States* (Bureau of Sport Fisheries and Wildlife Circular No. 179). Over the past two decades, John G. Casey's booklet has become a veritable best seller among sport fishermen and coastal naturalists.

By 1964, Graham Macmillan had persuaded the American Littoral Society to take up tagging as a means of learning more about shark migrations. The membership broadened the idea to include all fishes, and Stanley Maselbas of New Britain, Connecticut, helped provide national publicity for the program when he tagged five bluefish off Nantucket Island. Four of the fish were recovered in 1966 from widely separated points along the Atlantic seaboard, and the wire services treated the story as a significant news item. Soon the society was being deluged with tag requests from all over the country.

Although every conceivable sort of fish from eels to oyster toads have been marked with ALS tags, the striped bass quickly became the featured fish. Five years after he slipped his first tag into a striper, John Wells of Stratford, Connecticut, had tagged nearly 1000 of these fish and had received information on 165 of them recaptured from Massachusetts to Virginia. In time, a separate breeding population of striped bass was confirmed for the Hudson River estuary by ALS tags. This race strays as far north as Canada and some begin their odyssey via the East River rather than swim the length of Long

A tagged Sandbar Shark

Island. Although Graham Macmillan would prefer greater emphasis on shark tagging because he feels these creatures are every bit as beleaguered and less well known than striped bass, he is naturally proud of the achievements of the society's tagging program which he supervised for twenty years:

"Some marine scientists don't respect what we've done and mutter about amateurs doing professionals' work. They say we tag too many species indiscriminately. Yet in the great unknown of the sea, every iota of information counts. Our program—however untargeted—is the difference between zero and plus one, or thousands, if you're talking about striped bass tag returns. If we had sat around, like the professionals do, waiting to get sufficient inspiration at the public trough, we would only now be starting to do what we've been doing for two decades. If the professionals were willing to approach our records with a little humility for the millions of man-hours of honest research they represent, they could save the taxpayers a lot of money and themselves a lot of trouble."

The American Littoral Society is presently administered by Dery Bennett who joined the organization in 1968 after a stint of teaching, studying marine geology, and diving with the U.S. Navy. A little less than half the society's five thousand members are divers, but that half are the most active and make the greatest effort to coordinate holidays with a variety of research projects so that seaside vacations will be something more satisfying than lying in the sun and cultivating skin cancer. Society members help protect nesting sea turtles in Georgia, analyze water quality in Delaware Bay, collate data on municipal sewage and industrial toxic waste dumping in the New York Bight, organize beach walks on Cape Cod, and, of course, study the striped bass everywhere in this range.

Bennett keeps office hours in one of the imposing but weather-worn buildings which were formerly part of Fort Hancock. Named for the general (Winfield Scott Hancock) who defended the key flank position (July 2, 1863) and center (July 3) at the Battle of Gettysburg, this facility was developed in 1875 as a proving ground for all U.S. military ordnance. Sandy Hook's seven miles of "waste" dunes and beaches just twenty-five straight-line miles from Times Square were once considered "close enough but remote enough" for testing weapons and playing war games. During the Spanish-American War, enormous guns were emplaced near the end of the Hook to protect the southern approaches of New York Harbor. These guns were reoiled and remanned during World Wars I and II, and in the 1950s, the Nike missile was developed and first test-fired at Sandy Hook.

Gradually, however, the Hook's proximity to Manhattan became more of a risk than a convenience for military officers craving greater security and fewer restraints on their more explosive activities. Since development of missiles like the Nike had made the rifled barrels of Fort Hancock's big guns obsolete, the Pentagon packed up and left about the time the American Littoral Society was getting emplaced.

However, the Army's occupation of this pivotal piece of real estate during the decades of northern New Jersey's most frenetic growth saved this peninsula from a fate that can be seen most everywhere else along the neighboring coast. Although a sunny June day will bring more than 50,000 bathers to the Hook's seaside beaches, horseshoe crabs, identical to their arachnoid ancestors which steered with their telson tail spikes between the feet of wading dinosaurs, spawn on the peninsula's bayside flats while gulls and shorebirds crowd around to gobble the greenish eggs. In the fall, monarch butterflies pause on their migration to Mexico to feed on seaside goldenrod blooming in the dunes, while sharp-shinned and Cooper's hawks hunt robins in a three-hundred-year-old holly grove just north of Spermaceti Cove—named in 1668 after a sperm whale stranded and was salvaged there.

In winter, as many as 50,000 greater scaup may take shelter on the bayside not far from the American Littoral Society's office while storms erode the sand-starved foot of Sandy Hook. Since 1762 when a lighthouse was built at the tip of the peninsula, the tip has drifted a mile and a half to the northwest. Modern mariners from more stable shores must wonder why this facility—oldest lighthouse still in service on the Atlantic coast—was located so far from the point of greatest danger. (By contrast, as Montauk Point keeps eroding, its lighthouse must be moved west periodically to keep it from falling into the sea.)

When the Sandy Hook lighthouse was first built, there was an inlet south of it at the confluence of the Navesink and Shrewsbury rivers. Sandy Hook was still a peninsula, but it curved east from the Highlands of Navesink across a sandy isthmus where the highway bridge now spans the boat channel. Shrewsbury Inlet existed from 1756 to 1778 and again from 1810 to 1832. When Lieutenant General William Howe retreated after the battle of Monmouth by way of the Navesink Road, this inlet caused him some inconve-

Sperm Whale with Bluefin Tuna

nience, for he had to span the cut with a boat-bridge to get his troops over to what Lord Howe mistakenly called "Sandy Hook Island."

However, Sandy Hook was an island earlier in the eighteenth century and at least twice in the nineteenth century. Storms cut and tides maintained an inlet just south of the lighthouse between the ocean and Raritan Bay from 1837 to 1848. The site was briefly reopened by a hurricane in September 1889. Massive groins and jetties have been built by the Army Corps of Engineers along the seaward base of Sandy Hook and south along the coast beyond where another inlet broke through into the Shrewsbury River the year that the one Howe crossed silted in. This so-called New Inlet lasted until 1807, just three years before Shrewsbury Inlet to the north reopened. Nature appears determined to keep the Navesink and Shrewsbury rivers flowing east to the sea just as they did throughout the Pleistocene. The corps may have won in the short run, and indeed, it has no choice but to try to protect the many hundreds of millions of dollars recklessly invested along this fickle shore, but in the long run, Sandy Hook will rejoin the Highlands or become an island before subsiding into the sea.

So crucial to safe shipping is the lighthouse of Sandy Hook that during the Revolution, when an American major named Malcom was ordered to destroy the light, he only hid its lamps. When the British finally left New York, they kept the light burning since they imagined they would soon be back.

On a clear day the bustle of Brooklyn is clearly perceivable to someone on the lighthouse's upper level. Yet the job of keeper must have been a lonely one. The proximity of so many people, yet separated from them by an expanse of water, undoubtedly intensified the keeper's sense of isolation.

In an early attempt to bring the various portions of the New York Bight closer together, Samuel F. B. Morse spanned the harbor with a copper wire soaked in tar and pitch and surrounded by a layer of India rubber and sent his first message to New Jersey from Manhattan in 1842. This was two years before the telegraph line between Washington and Baltimore was finished and the famous message, "What hath God wrought!" sent. By the end of the decade, Sandy Hook was wired into the Battery, and when a pilot from the Hook went out to a newly arrived ship, he took with him a carrier pigeon from the Hook's telegraph station. Once aboard, the pilot recorded the latest news from Europe on tissue paper which was then attached to the bird's leg. The pigeon flew back to his cote on the telegraph tower where an operator was standing by.

More often than not, there ensued a scene familiar to anyone who has worked with carrier pigeons or owned a canine retriever. As George Houghton described in the September 1879 issue of *Scribner's Monthly*, the pigeon "was sometimes obstinate, recognizing his importance very exasperatingly by evading the waiting hand and walking around the tower just out of reach. Now he drew near and looked propitious, 'Come, Dickie, come, that's a dear,' whispered the telegraph man coaxingly. Now Dickie cooed, as if to say, 'What's the hurry! what's the hurry!' and continued to sidle away to the very verge of the roof. And so it sometimes happened that all America, yearning for news from the Old World, waited upon the caprices of Dickie, the carrier pigeon."

The importance of Dickie and Sandy Hook as conduits for America's information on the doings of the rest of the world was diminished in 1858 when the first transatlantic cable was laid between Newfoundland and Ireland. Dickie's fate was sealed after the Civil War when more sophisticated cables were strung between the Old and New Worlds and plugged into coastal cables already running from St. John's, Newfoundland, and St. John, New Brunswick, to Portland, Boston, New York, and Philadelphia.

Cyrus W. Field, the Atlantic cable concept's staunchest promoter, often spoke of "anchoring" Europe and North America with strands of copper. Unfortunately, nothing inanimate—including massive boulders and reinforced concrete—has ever succeeded in "anchoring" the margins of the western Atlantic. The best approximate material are the roots of plants that hold the line so long as the line can be held. When dunes inexorably march west or storms breach the beach, the roots yield to these indomitable forces while their flowers reseed the new dunes and beachheads to start holding the line all over again.

Sandy Hook's dunes are anchored by a variety of plants including an alien called dusty miller, whose primary source of water is the brackish dew condensed on its white-woolly and deeply lobed leaves. The native prickly pear has also adapted to life on the Hook where this typically prostrate cactus secretes a herbicide from its roots to corner all available nutrients and water in the salty and porous soil.

Sandy Hook is now part of the Gateway National Recreation Area created in 1972 by a Congress looking for the most politically attractive way to dispose of the several military reservations whose guns and airfields once guarded New York City's Lower Bay. Gateway is administered from Floyd Bennett Field, which was New York City's first municipal airport before becoming a naval air station. This airfield lies on the north side of Rockaway Inlet and looks east across the Jamaica Bay National Wildlife Refuge toward John F. Kennedy International Airport, once called Idlewild. I was born not far from this area, and whether it—or another—was the first salt-marsh estuary I ever saw, my early experience imprinted me with love for such gentle mergings of sea and shore and their subtle gold and emerald shadings of cordgrass. My soul pulses with the movement of tides soughing over sand flats and sod islands. Profound beauty can cause men pain, and my heart aches when I see sunlight reflected from a flooding marsh.

My childhood was fortunate, for I spent much of it aboard boats in places with names like Montauk and Manasquan. Sadly, I also watched the metronome movement of machines converting the marshes and dunes into marinas and playlands where everything died but man's sense of his own importance. I did not yet understand that bulkheads and pilings can inspire atrophy as well as prosperity. Today, the last tribal ghosts have fled these once mysterious places, and the Indians' immortality resides in road signs and maps.

Blue Crab

On July 6, 1827, the *New York Commercial Advertiser* reported that a man and his son went fishing in Jamaica Bay and caught 472 king whiting or northern kingfish in five and a half hours. One hundred and twenty years later, my father and his sons went fishing in Jamaica Bay and caught great quantities of kingfish, winter flounder, porgy, and blue crabs. There were days we doubtless caught and kept too many, but when you're young, excess is easily confused with enough.

As it turned out, overfishing was the least of Jamaica Bay's problems. Some years fish were small or few in number, but the tidal creeks and bays always provided recreation and food. Then one day a dragline clanked onto the western end of the marsh at low tide, and the delicate balance between life in the city and life in the sea was broken. As youngsters we liked the name Idlewild. It was suggestive of travel and foreign places. Only later did we appreciate the irony of a major urban airport sprawling across a once fertile salt marsh called "idle" and "wild."

Today as you speed along the Beltway from Sheepshead Bay (named for *Archosargus probatocephalus*, a warm-water fish that once flourished there) toward the boulevard bisecting Jamaica Bay, you pass on your left ranks of high-rise apartments, a form of warehousing for people, where little streams once meandered through woods and wetlands. On your right, you see park benches along an old bicycle path that formerly fringed the marshlands of Jamaica Bay. There are places to pull off, but there is little to see—only clouds of gulls circling and crying over the mountains of garbage that block the view. The largest hill is thirty acres in area and as excellent a testimonial to our disposable society as the pyramids of ancient Egypt were to another kind of human bondage. Perhaps in some thousands of years, modern man's descendants will mine the coal that is now the peat that was the marsh that sits below the megatons of garbage along the northern shores of Jamaica Bay.

If only modern man had a little more sense, he could begin benefiting from this dump in a matter of months, not millennia. The 8000 tons of garbage bulldozed into this corner of Gateway National Recreation Area every 24 hours contains approximately 10 million cubic feet of methane gas. If this methane could be burned by Consolidated Edison to light homes and power industry in Brooklyn, it would save the local utility between 400,000 and 600,000 barrels of oil annually. Methane burns cleaner than oil. Furthermore, cost-effective technology for extracting the gas already exists. What's lacking is the willingness of several administrators to work with other administrators or yield some of their authority.

Municipal land-use policies which designate dumps as the highest and best use of New York's coastal marshlands are mocked by statistics which show that more people visit the various portions of the Gateway National Recreation Area every year than visit Yosemite and Yellowstone national parks *combined*. People are starved for recreation in its original sense: re-creation. Leisure is not a luxury, but essential to the workings of our souls. Businessmen and politicians tend to measure prosperity in dollars, but what price can possibly be placed on the value of Gateway's open spaces for millions of people whose aesthetic muscles have become cramped after occupying narrow boxes all week long?

I'm pessimistic, not because I think Armageddon is pending, but precisely for the opposite reason: because people seem to be adjusting to the blight we've put on our lives in how we earn our bread, raise our children, and accept a diminished future.

Variety—an ecologist would say, diversity—is more than the spice of life; it offers our only clue to the meaning of life. Flatten it, and you are left with questions about survival, not the quality of life. Our National Park Service is charged with protecting natural diversity in every corner of America. Yet where the service has had the most variety to work with, it has often sacrificed that variety in competition or collusion with the tourist industry.

Perhaps the best thing about Gateway is its stepchild relationship to other parks within our national system. Gateway does not receive the funding and publicity of a Yellowstone or Yosemite, and you will never find a politician espousing the manifold benefits of the great outdoors from one of the runways at Floyd Bennett Field. And although National Park Service brochures would have it that 350 bird species—"more birds than have ever been seen in all the British Isles"—can be found on the four parcels of land (including Fort Tilden on Rockaway Beach and Miller Field on Staten Island) that constitute Gateway, the brochures are describing ancient history. Industrialization and suburbanization have ruled the shores of the New York Bight for over half a century, and a group of busy Gateway birders is lucky today to turn up 200 species.

Still, that is more than three times as many species as one is likely to find anywhere else in New York City. And so what if a portion of Gateway has become the city's dump, and if its few public facilities are littered or broken? You don't visit Gateway to use its toilets. You visit these open spaces because your soul craves contrast, and you are surprised to find you enjoy the visit precisely because this hodgepodge park is out of the mainstream of institutionalized notions of beauty and recreation. Much to your delight, you discover that unglamorous Gateway is one of the best features of a still noble city.

5

SOUTH JERSEY
AND A LITTLE BEYOND

Atlantic City is an astonishing sight. From the air it looks like an outpost of civilization in an alien world, as though 60,000 people were gathered at one spot on another planet uncertain whether they should revel in their isolation or feel abandoned.

From the causeways coming into the city at night, billboards advertising the hotel-casinos ripple with light and color, and in the distance the newer buildings glow like understudies for the Emerald City of Oz. From close up at dawn, however, the downtown district has a bombed-out appearance. A pair of black prostitutes clickety-clack through the deserted streets in high-heeled ruby slippers.

Atlantic City is where boardwalks were popularized in 1884, when rolling chairs first carried visitors over eight miles of herring-bone-design planks past saltwater taffy and hand-painted felt banner booths to one of several amusement piers where young men threw baseballs at stacked milk bottles to impress their girlfriends or together they watched a horse climb a steep stair to be jumped into a vat of seawater forty feet below.

Yet Atlantic City's greatest glory has practically nothing to do with the city except to offer a surreal view of it across 20,000 acres of upland woods, salt meadows, and marsh. The Brigantine National Wildlife Refuge is situated eleven miles north of the town and bisected by the Intracoastal Waterway running to Atlantic City, but for all the regular social intercourse between the refuge and the town, Brigantine could be located in Canada.

Atlantic City's largest hotel-casinos are designed so that a visitor can choose from a dozen different restaurants, theaters, and other entertainments and never leave the air-conditioned comfort of the interconnecting buildings. The casino operators, of course, don't want visitors to stray far from their gaming tables and roulette wheels, so there is little advertising in most hotels of angling opportunities because the inlet marina lies too close to a competitive hotel's slot machines, and no advertising of a national wildlife refuge where the tourists cannot spend money unless they have lunch at Oceanville, one mile west of the refuge headquarters, or up Route 9 at Smithville, a restored South Jersey village. As a result, few Atlantic City visitors ever rent cars or drive their own for the easy twenty-minute trip to the Brigantine refuge where they can take an hour and a half, self-guided auto tour that is frequently more spectacular than anything they can see in a hotel-casino. No matter; the city and the refuge cater to different clienteles. During the summer months when the boardwalk is clamorous with people, the heavy air of the refuge is etched only by the buzz of locusts or the sweet tea-kettle-tea-kettle-tea-kettle-tea of a Carolina wren. During the winter, however, when only wastepaper whispers through the early morning streets of Atlantic City, the refuge is clamorous with the honks, quacks, whistles, and murmurings of more than 150,000 visiting waterfowl.

Brigantine National Wildlife Refuge was established in 1939 for all species of ducks and geese, but especially for the beleaguered greater snow goose, which in those days numbered only about 10,000 individuals. Thanks to half a century of complete protection and the advent of a chain of refuges from Bylot Island well within the Arctic Circle to Pea Island on the Outer Banks of North Carolina, the greater snow goose has rallied, and some fall flights include nearly 200,000 birds. This species has now been restored to the Atlantic Flyway game lists, and the Fish and Wildlife Service even allows snow geese to be hunted on some portions of the Brigantine refuge. However, the snow geese, like the continuously hunted Canada geese and black ducks, have learned which are the dangerous areas of the marsh and which offer undisturbed rest and relaxation.

Although waterfowl were the bird species emphasized while establishing national wildlife refuges in the 1930s, some 230 non-game bird species regularly use the Brigantine refuge and 85 non-game bird species nest there. None of these birds seem disturbed by the fact that for a few weeks each fall and winter, game birds are hunted on a few areas within the refuge by people whose license fees and self-imposed taxes made the refuge possible in the first place. Of the eight bird species rated as common or abundant at Brigantine every week of the year, three of these, the Canada goose, black duck, and mourning dove, are among the most heavily hunted game birds in the Atlantic Flyway. Ironically, however, the mourning dove is legally a songbird, not a game bird, in New Jersey, and the many dove produced on the Brigantine refuge each spring and summer join· their cousins from other Northern states to funnel south each fall where some forty to fifty *million* mourning dove are shot without any decrease in their amazing abundance. Rather the opposite is true. Mourning dove have increased over the past twenty years due to the compulsion of farmers to convert even more acres of woodland—of little use to dove— to soybean, corn, and wheat fields ideal for fattening the two and three annual broods of two squab each produced by a pair of mourning dove.

A disturbing fact about Brigantine's eight-most-common-birds list is that three species—the introduced English or house sparrow, the herring gull, and the redwinged blackbird—have become so abundant everywhere along the coast that they are considered to be pests by state conservation agencies, some of which allow their residents to destroy house sparrows and blackbirds without special permits, but none of which allow gulls to be killed because state agency biologists know most people cannot distinguish gull species and valuable or rare gulls would be destroyed along with the obnoxious herring gulls.

Ironically, however, even game species can become a pest. Ten wing-clipped Canada geese were released in 1957 to establish a nesting population at Brigantine National Widlife Refuge. Today, annual production at this one refuge alone exceeds six hundred goslings. Canada geese have become so abundant in the Atlantic Flyway, they annually cost coastal farmers hundreds of thousands of dollars in overgrazed winter wheat and rye, and the geese have even become nuisances in many suburban communities. Yet rather than allow biologists to increase the daily hunting limit of three birds to four or more in Maryland, where sometimes half a million Canada geese winter, Maryland guides, hunters, and state officials voted to keep the limit at three a day to ensure that the geese would continue concentrating on the Eastern Shore in such numbers to "ultimatize" (a word from a bureaucratic lexicon) each hunter's opportunity. Let farmers, golfers, and municipal leaders elsewhere in the flyway worry about the overpopulation of Canada goose. So far as Maryland businessmen are concerned, single species management emphasizing geese is a wonderful biological concept.

By contrast, the black duck is increasingly scarce. Once the crown prince of the Atlantic Flyway, the black duck's sagacity made it the most rewarding duck to hunt along the Atlantic coast, and its love of salt marshes made it uniquely ours. Although once found in fair numbers in the Mississippi Flyway, the blackie was always uncommon in the Central and Pacific flyways. The black duck and the woodcock were the only two migratory game birds that sportsmen had to come east to hunt. For decades, well over a million black ducks were shot each season in the Atlantic Flyway. Today, thanks to habitat destruction and, increasingly to overshooting as the resource declines, there are not one million black ducks in existence.

Until 1969, the black duck headed the harvest list for waterfowl in the Atlantic Flyway. That year it was replaced by the mallard and has now fallen even below the wood duck, a species so rare at the turn of the century that the eminent ornithologist and outdoorsman George Bird Grinnell predicted its extinction. Today precise harvest ratios are difficult to determine between black ducks and mallards because so many of the birds being shot are hybrids. Despite the fact they are different species, such hybrid offspring are fertile. Thanks to the stocking of hundreds of thousands of pen-raised birds by the state of Maryland, mallards saturate mid-Atlantic wintering grounds once dominated by coastal-loving black ducks, consequently competing with the black ducks for food and mates, since pair bonds are established well before the ducks move north to breed.

Why should Atlantic coastal hunters, beyond a certain sentimental interest, care about black ducks when there are so many more easier-to-fool mallards? The answer lies in the fact that a mallard's brood is far more susceptible to mortality from a parasite called a leucocytzoan than the black duck. The intermediate host for the leucocytzoan is the blackfly, and the prevalence of this insect in New England and eastern Canada may have played a vital role in the evolution of the blackie nearly four million years ago—about the same time, in fact, that our species was getting started. If we continue to dilute black-duck blood with domestic mallard strains, we could end up with neither black ducks nor mallards once Maryland legislators find some more essential use for the money currently being used to stock farm ponds and roadside ditches with mallard ducklings.

At Brigantine National Wildlife Refuge, increasing numbers of mallards share the freshwater and brackish West and East Pools with black ducks. However, whereas pairs of black ducks will frequently rise on a brisk northwest breeze to sheer away downwind to salty Turtle Cove or to wing farther out over Reeds Bay to rest on the ocean, the mallards rarely leave the proximity of fresh water. It is ironic that at the time the 16,000 acres of salt marsh and bays in the refuge were obtained by the federal government for the protection of the snow goose, the black duck was one of the most abundant game birds in North America. Today, Brigantine is the winter home for over 70,000 blackies—which is roughly one-fifth of all the black ducks in the world.

Although birds are synonymous with Brigantine, no bird there thrives without the association of particular plants. Black ducks and snow geese, for example, depend on *Spartina alterniflora*—the former on its seeds, the latter on its roots. The cardinal and the song sparrow, two of the eight most common birds at Brigantine, depend on the food, shelter, and even water found in the refuge's hedgerows of greenbriar, honeysuckle, wild cherry, persimmon, and poison ivy.

Poison Ivy (left) and Virginia Creeper (right)

This latter vine or shrub is often found in close association with Virginia creeper or woodbine, and the berries of both plants are eaten, fertilized, and broadcast by the cardinals and sparrows. These two plants are distinguished by the five shiny but harmless leaves of the woodbine and the three equally shiny but highly toxic leaves, stems, roots, fruits, and flowers of poison ivy.

No ubiquitous hazard to man is more shrouded in myth and supposition than that of poison ivy. Yet the facts about p.i. are even stranger than the fiction. For one thing, apparently every person is born with an immunity to the poison which in about half the population seems good for life. However, this may represent nothing more than continued avoidance of the plant, for repeated exposure erodes, rather than builds resistance, and your fifth rash is always more severe than your first.

The poisonous substance is a nonvolatile and nearly indestructible phenolic or oil called *urushiol*. It is a saplike substance found in every part of the plant but its pollen. Once urushiol impregnates clothing fibers, repeated washings are necessary to dilute the compound. In an experiment reported in the *Missouri Conservationist* (March 1982), "a canvas glove was used to collect poison ivy, then put away in a closet for ten months. It was then washed in hot soap and water, dried and ironed. After all of that, the glove still caused dermatitis in a volunteer who handled it." Almost anything that touches the bruised leaves or cut runners of poison ivy can transmit urushiol; one of the most violent cases I've seen occurred after Keith Gardner, the editor of *Fishing World* magazine, fondled our family's golden retriever who had apparently found some poison ivy to roll in. Keith dubbed the animal "poison dog" and now never pets unknown quantities.

While you cannot get a rash from merely looking at the plant or standing downwind of it, as was once commonly believed, you can get a horrible case by coming into contact with the smoke of burning poison ivy. As woodstoves have come back into vogue, more rashes are being reported by woodcutters who unwittingly handle anonymous vines grown into the fissures of logs, by people with faulty woodstoves that do not draft all the smoke up the chimneys, and by sweeps who become coated with urushiol-saturated soot and sometimes are hospitalized as a result.

Only humans seem susceptible to poison ivy, for in addition to the dozens of bird species which flourish on the fruit, squirrels and voles eat it, and deer browse the leaves and stems. Since there is no way to be rid of poison ivy, it is best to consider all the creatures which benefit from it—while avoiding personal contact with the plant or with any material that has already had contact. By the way, since urushiol and skin proteins produce an immediate reaction, washing with an alkali soap and water will only reduce, not prevent, your forthcoming rash by diluting excess oil. However, the psychological satisfaction of scouring the "damn'd spot" is enormous!

With the exception of honeysuckle—a nineteenth-century introduction whose berries are eaten by birds and whose leaves and stems are enjoyed by rabbits and deer, but which tends to overwhelm still more desirable native plants—the hedgerows on the high ground overlooking the marshes at Brigantine were typical of the hedgerows separating the fields and meadows throughout eastern rural North America until the advent of tractor flails and herbicides in the 1950s. Farmers and their families once utilized a good many of these plants and their products, yet much of the cultural knowledge as to which plants are useful and for what has been lost in the single human generation since the hedgerows and the woods have been cleared for highways, suburban housing, and shopping centers. Today books and magazines dispense information about once-common practices—how to make tea, for instance, from the roots of *Sassafras albidum*—as though such activities were occult mysteries performed by the ancients instead of our grandmothers.

On the People's Trail at Brigantine you will find highbush blueberry, which generations of local birds, bears, and man had all to themselves until one summer a woman passed out cards with holes punched in them to anyone who would sell to her all the larger berries that would not pass through the holes. She in turn sold these berries to wholesalers who began to market blueberries throughout the region from New York to Washington, D.C. Today the bears are mostly gone from southern New Jersey and only a few local people still run the gauntlet of chiggers and mosquitoes to pick their own blueberries. For the rest of us, it is easier to buy them at the local supermarket.

Along the fringe of the marsh you will see many red cedar. The bark of this tree is used by squirrels for bedding. It not only makes a soft fibrous lining, its sweet-smelling and pesticidal values help control the vermin inherent in any nest. Cedar, also known as juniper, berries are eaten by many birds, especially swarms of waxwings, which disperse the seeds across the countryside and help make red cedar one of the pioneers of meadows and abandoned fields where farmers used to cut them for aromatic firewood and mothproof blanket chests.

Bayberry is another marsh-fringing plant whose fragrant leaves were once used to make Christmas wreaths and whose greenish waxy berries were converted into candles—those berries, that is, that escaped the attention of yellow-rumped warblers. These birds were formerly called myrtle warblers in recognition of their fall and winter dependence on the berries of wax myrtles, alias bayberry. Today both red cedar and bayberry are classified as "trash plants" by nurserymen, who succeed in persuading many new coastal homeowners to buy such exotic evergreens as Norfolk Island pine or Japanese yew to replace the beautiful native cedar and bayberry cleared by the bulldozer that prepared their homesites.

One native tree which sometimes happily survives the busy bulldozer is the American holly. Delaware's legislature has made it illegal to abuse holly by designating it the state tree. While not as darkly lustrous as English hollies, the American holly is hardier, especially in sandy soils and salty air. Its berries are eaten by many birds, and because the seeds develop very slowly and take up to eighteen months after the berries ripen to germinate, birds help distribute this shade-tolerant species throughout the coastal plains. In the old days, specimen American hollies were used for superior cabinetmaking, but today both the unavailability of huge holly and a decline in the market for fine furniture has all but stopped this use. A few coastal residents still use the berry-enriched boughs of the female trees to make Christmas wreaths and other decorations.

Station eight of the Brigantine People's Trail features arrowwood, a tall (up to ten feet) but rather undistinguished shrub with white flowers and clustered berries, which the birds enjoy, and straight, old-growth shafts in the plant's center, which the Indians once used to make arrows. Another locally abundant plant associated with red men is the Indian pipe. This ghostly white and seemingly chlorophyll-less plant looks and lives more like a fungus than the relative of the azaela and the blueberry that it is. Indian pipe feeds on dead or dying vegetation and eerily resembles the white clay pipes Indians made from coastal clays and introduced to the Dutch and English colonists, who immortalized the pipe's design in seventeenth-century illustrations of prosperous European merchants smoking another American Indian contribution to global culture: tobacco.

The twisted needles and stunted appearance of pitch pine are characteristic of the coastal plain from Maine through the mid-Atlantic. While not as valuable as the loblolly, whose southward range to Florida begins at Brigantine, pitch pine seeds are eaten by a number of birds as well as squirrels and rabbits, and in olden days, as the name implies, the resin of pitch pine was extracted to make turpentine, tar, pitch, and medicinal oils. The Swedes and Germans still use the needles of a comparable coastal pine to make "forest wool" for clothing, cushions, and blankets. The needles are treated to remove the resin and loosen the fibers, and many Scandinavians feel that the result is as warm and more durable than eiderdown, which they export to the rest of the world for personal, but high-priced insulation.

By contrast, the loblolly is an important lumber tree, although most coastal specimens, which are not as robust as those found farther inland, end up as creosoted pilings or telephone poles. Once, however, magnificent 200-year-old loblollies were abundant near the coast, and the resinous heartwood from these pines made superb flooring and paneling so hard it had to be drilled before it could be nailed. Such wood can still be found in the floors and mantels of many older South Jersey homes. The doors and window frames are frequently constructed of weather- and insect-resistant bald cypress, once found as far north as the swamps of southern New Jersey, where a good many were sawed at Millville. Even after New Jersey exhausted its bald cypress stocks, rafts of this wood cut on the Delmarva Peninsula across Delaware Bay were sailed to the mouth of the Maurice River, knocked apart, and carried up to Millville for finishing.

Shagbark hickory, from which deep-sea fishing rods were made at the turn of the century, were never common in the coastal plain, but pignut hickory were and still are abundant, their wood making the best of all fires for smoking meat and fish. On Brigantine's People's Trail, you will find numerous specimens of pignut hickory in conjunction with white oak, Spanish oak, and red oak, where these long-lived hardwoods, once and now again so desirable to people who heat their homes with wood, have shaded out the wild grape and nonpoisonous sumac, which pioneered the sandy soil for the pitch pine and cherry that followed and which still lean out into the sunlight along the edges of the deeper woods.

In the forest understory, you will hopefully find shadbush—"hopefully," because its small, applelike fruits are delicious in jams, jellies, and pies. However, heavy crops are rare, because nearly every creature in the woods eats the fruit, including the eastern box turtle, which is sometimes lucky enough to find some of the fruits growing near the ground. Of course, box turtles will scavenge fruit on the ground but between the birds and climbing squirrels, opossums, and raccoons, turtles rarely find fallen fruit. Incidentally, the sexes of box turtles cannot be distinguished by shell color, which is variable regardless of sex, but by the fact male turtles sometimes have reddish eyes, long front claws, and slightly indented bottom shells, while female turtles normally have brown eyes, shorter claws, and slightly bulged bottom shells. American Indians revered the box turtle and used their shells for a variety of totemistic rituals. Many modern children revere box turtles as pets, but they are becoming scarce in most areas along the coast and should be left to go their way.

The drooping white flower clusters of the shadbush or coastal juneberry develop before the leaves, and it was this event each spring that informed people all along the coast from southern New Jersey to northern Florida that it was time to ready their gill nets or sport-fishing tackle for the annual spawning run of American shad. If the nets' mesh was small enough, blueback herring and alewife were also taken. While the roe sacks of these smaller fish are not as large as those of the American shad, they are as delicious, and the many Y-shaped floating bones characteristic of all herring dissolve readily in a pickling solution or are simply less noticeable in smaller fish, especially when the alewives are salted or canned and sold as "river herring."

The scales of alewives were once valued by jewelers and display industries as "pearl essence," and before fly fishing became tainted with snobbery, early-season anglers enjoyed fishing for blueback herring in brackish water where they spawn, or for alewife far up freshwater streams where they spawn. Although all herring are plankton feeders, both the blueback and alewife aggressively attack small artificial lures, especially after spawning—unlike the shad, which takes streamer flies, spinners, and shad darts most eagerly before spawning.

Like most oceanic fishes whose reproduction occurs in or near coastal streams, anadromous herring are declining everywhere in their range. What is particularly disturbing about the shad's decline is that this species is less sensitive to pollution than similarly anadromous salmonids. Furthermore, unlike the Atlantic salmon, which needs to procreate in the stream where it was hatched, shad readily adopt any reasonable facsimile within a hundred or more miles of its natal

Shad

creek. Damming, pollution, overfishing, and possible other causes not yet identified have greatly diminished American shad everywhere along the coast. From once mighty runs up Florida's St. Johns River to the Delaware River and Hudson River invasions, where fish must do the piscine equivalent of holding their breath while charging through the chemically violent effluents of Philadelphia and Trenton, Newark and New York, shad are no longer significant harbingers of spring. Where once blooming juneberries foretold of the first fresh fish of the year for people living all along the Atlantic coast, today their city-bound sons and daughters know winter has gone only after the weather bureau announces that air temperatures at the beach are warmer than sea temperatures.

Yet while the American shad may be the most glamorous of all herrings, *Brevoortia tyrannus*—the menhaden, fatback, or, as fishermen call them in South Jersey, the mossbunker—has probably earned more money for more people over the past century than any other North American fish.

Mannawahatteaug or, simplified, menhaden—like poghaden, the root for the Down Easters' nickname for this fish, "pogy"*—meant

---

* This nickname should not confuse menhaden with "porgy" or "scup" of the genus *Stenotomus*. Both these other names are derived from the Narragansett

"fertilizer" in coastal Indian dialects, and prior to the Civil War fertilizer was its principal use besides fishing bait. As George Brown Goode notes in his comprehensive *History of the Menhaden* published in 1880, "Large quantities were plowed into the soil of the farms along the shores, stimulating the crops for a time, but in the end filling the soil with oil, parching it, and making it unfit for tillage."

While European colonists probably learned from the Indians* the trick of planting one menhaden with each kernel of corn, they did not adopt all methods of Indian farming which included "trekking," a tradition in which cleared land is abandoned to lie fallow for sometimes as many years as it was farmed and cultivated all over again when a new band of Indians move into the area or when the former farmers return from other, now abandoned lands. In their own regional way, Eastern woodland Indians were as nomadic as their brethren who moved out across the Western plains once the Spanish reintroduction of the horse to North America made such wide-range trekking possible.

The Indians of South Jersey and Delaware caught menhaden in the same gill nets and weirs stretched across tidal rivers and streams, or pound nets erected along the bay shores, that they used to catch shad and herring.† The red men probably first began using their incidental menhaden catch for fertilizer very soon after their arrival along the Atlantic when they realized it was food fit only for dogs and slaves. Although G. Brown Goode imagined that menhaden might one day be used to feed a major portion of our population, I

Indian word for *Stenotomus: mishcuppauog.* Ichthyologist George Brown Goode sought to alleviate this confusion in the last century by insisting that porgy everywhere be called *scuppaug* and the menhaden, just that. Needless to say, it is easier to persuade people to give up bad habits than to get popular nomenclature changed.

* An article in the April 1975 issue of *Science* suggests that Tisquantum or Squanto learned about fertilizing fields in England or Newfoundland, where he spent some years before greeting the "agriculturally illiterate" Pilgrims at Plymouth.

† In demonstrating the Indians' reliance on fish and some of the techniques used to take them, the Hagley Museum on Brandywine Creek in Delaware uses a diorama showing red men catching carp as they move into shallow tributaries to breed in the spring. However, carp did not appear in the Eastern United States until 1876 when the U.S. Fish Commission ordered 345 fish from Germany. These fish were kept for a while as curiosities at Druid Hill Park in Baltimore before they and their progeny were ultimately established in every state but Alaska. The Indians might have enjoyed carp had they been available, but what the red men caught and dried or smoked were shad and herring.

suspect his view was analogous to Thomas Jefferson's opinion that it was preferable for our lower classes to drink beer than gin. Striped bass and white wines would be reserved for more sensitive palates such as those belonging to Messrs. Jefferson and Goode.

However, Goode was accurate in his prediction that "as a food for domestic animals, in the shape of 'fish meal,' there seems . . . to be a broad opening" for menhaden. Today the retail price of chicken frequently fluctuates according to the dockside price of menhaden. Goode also noted that "as a source of oil the menhaden is more important than any other marine animal: its annual yield usually exceeds that of the whale (from American fisheries) by about 20,000 gallons, in 1874 not falling far short of the aggregate of all the whale, seal, and cod oil made in America." Today, oil production from menhaden greatly exceeds that of all other marine animals on a worldwide basis. Its oil is used to make paints, pharmaceuticals, pesticides, perfumes, and dozens of other protein-based products, and fishermen still buy great quantities of whole fish to grind up and cast into the sea, where the scraps attract a great variety of marine game fish. When a vast fleet of Jersey sportfishing boats are chumming menhaden over an offshore ridge on a blustery day, the combined oil slicks made it appear as though the boats were anchored in the eye of a storm.

Menhaden fishing has likewise survived by changing character and locality. Despite a spring and fall spawning schedule that greatly enhances the species' odds of producing bumper yields every year, possible water chemistry changes along the coast, water temperature fluctuations, and overfishing from New England through the mid-Atlantic have caused the center of the industry to shift farther south with each passing decade until now hope for its future hinges on the Gulf of Mexico fishery for the closely related Brevoortia patronus. Whereas pogy and 'bunker fishermen once took their catch into dozens of rendering plants from Gloucester, Massachusetts, to Wildwood, New Jersey, and Reedville, Virginia, only a few such plants from New England to the mid-Atlantic still exist, including the operations at Gloucester, Wildwood, and Reedville.

Some of these rendering plants died as a result of the shoaling of already treacherous inlets. That is one reason the facility just inside Little Egg Inlet up the coast from Brigantine eventually threw in the towel. In other cases, such as with the plant at Atlantic City, the local tourism industry objected to the smell. However, most plants close because the resource is "improperly managed," meaning not managed at all.

The menhaden is only one of nearly two dozen fish species that are year-around residents of South Jersey's bays and estuaries. In a study by Dennis M. Allen, Jay P. Clymer III, and Sidney S. Herman of the *Fishes of the Hereford Inlet Estuary*, for Lehigh University and The Wetlands Institute, the researchers discovered that over a hundred fish species are found at one season or another in this tidal complex just north of Cape May, and that more than ninety of these species are represented by larvae or juveniles. Although most of the fishes taken during the study were of species one would expect to find in such latitudes, there were a remarkable number of nominally tropical or even pelagic species. For example, seine hauls or hook-and-line catches accounted for such Florida-reef-type fishes as gag grouper, snowy grouper, and mangrove or gray snapper. Seine hauls at Stone Harbor Bridge brought up such subtropical members of the jack family as jack crevalle, lookdown, and permit. But most wonderful of all at the Stone Harbor station was an immature dolphin-fish, a species that rarely strays far from the sargasso weed lines of the Gulf Stream more than 100 miles offshore.

Such exotic finds aside, the researchers estimate, as a result of their study, that as much as 75 percent of the total seafood harvest taken by American fishermen depends upon such marsh and estuarine ecosystems as those found along the Jersey coast. What is especially noteworthy about the Hereford Inlet research is that this particular estuary, unlike Great Egg Harbor Inlet to the north and Delaware Bay to the south, has no major tributaries. Furthermore, since the maximum depth over the sandbars in Hereford Inlet is only about nine feet, "the tidal exchanges between the embayment and ocean are primarily restricted to the surface waters." Thus, this estuary's brine and temperature ranges cannot be as great, nor its fauna as diverse, as in deeper estuaries into which flow freshwater rivers of some size.

Yet marine life in the Hereford Inlet area is wonderfully diverse, and although only about seven of the estuary's year-round species can be construed as having human food value, almost all the residents are prey species for larger fishes and other creatures higher in the food chain, making the smaller fishes of great indirect value to mankind. For example, the sheepshead minnow was one of the small coastal fishes dependably taken every month of the year in seines at the upper end of a small tributary stream flowing into Scotch Bonnet Creek. Almost every fish and crab larger than the sheepshead minnow will try to eat one, and for this reason it often inhabits areas where temperatures range over 70 degrees on the Fahrenheit scale and where extreme variability in salinity and turbidity are weekly events. Although such environments make them somewhat safer from fish predators, a broad spectrum of bird and mammalian predators still manage to find them. Yet this stubby and pugnacious minnow, with breeding hues of metallic green, blue, and salmon, flourishes on dense algal mats that grow in warm-water pools and buries itself in soft mud when pursued by a predator or when winter temperatures make further foraging uneconomical. Such hardiness is no surprise to taxonomists who recognize that the sheepshead minnow's closest relatives are several species of pupfish which hang on in warm springs and desert sinkholes. These fish are the last living reminders of a time when vast inland seas covered much of California, Nevada, and Texas.

Several other killifishes in the Family Cyprinodontidae are abundant in South Jersey estuaries, but none so important to fishermen as the mummichog. This fish is caught by the dozens in wire-mesh minnow traps and used as bait, live or dead, but always whole, for a variety of saltwater game fishes. Stored in a moist container, mummichogs can be kept alive for several days in a refrigerator, and due to their tolerance of fresh water, they are used as live bait to catch largemouth bass and yellow perch in nearby Jersey ponds. The most popular way to use mummichogs along the coast is to hook a fish through both lips to keep it swimming naturally into the current and to prevent drowning—which occurs when you hook the fish through only one lip or the tail. Bluefish, weakfish, but especially fluke or summer flounder adore the green-and-yellow-spotted and silvery-barred fish wriggling on a hook exactly the way unhooked mummichogs wrestle with a bit of food larger than their mouths. Smart fishermen add a strip of peeled white squid to give their ruse greater credibility, visibility, and smell.

Although one may debate the humaneness of using live bait, one may as well debate the humaneness of recreational fishing, which derives its greatest pleasure from prolonging the panic and struggle of one's prey with light tackle. Experience has taught me that if fish feel pain, their threshold for it is so much higher than any mammal's that my conscience is little affected. I have recaught on hook and line black sea bass and northern puffers which I had just tagged and released, and I have watched a black angelfish in Florida browsing on a reef while grunts and little wrasses fed on its intestines streaming from a gaping wound in its side. One cannot imagine that pain has much evolutionary value in an environment where mutilation and death are so prevalent—where clever bluefish habitually bite off most of a lip-hooked mummichog's body, leaving only its head still breathing on your line.

Thirty years ago, my father and I tried always to have a supply of live mummichogs when we anchored and chummed for bluefin tuna off the Jersey coast. Some days the great fish were finicky and would not touch the choicest butterfish, 'bunker hearts, or even hairnets full of fresh chum. So we put two live mummichogs on the same small, but stout hook, and as they drifted down into the slick, they looked as though they were struggling over the same piece of food. I never felt remorse for our apparent cruelty, only exultation when the deception proved irresistible to a 200-pound tuna.

Another important group of baitfish and year-round residents of the Hereford Inlet estuary are the silversides. Of all the family, the most abundant is the Atlantic silverside. Although not at all related to the smelt, which it closely resembles even to the greenish back, light belly, and metallic silver stripe running down its side, *Menidia*, including the tidewater species *beryllina*, are delicious and marketed fresh as "whitebait" for people to eat, when they are not sold in frozen packages as fishing bait. The most popular bait size is five to six inches, but the most popular size for human consumption is three inches. The fish are fried crisp and consumed whole, although some fastidious diners hold the whitebait by its head and leave that part on their plates.

A decade ago, during a major oil spill in the Chesapeake that killed tens of thousands of marine birds, Dottie Valentine of Accomac, Virginia, managed to save several common loons and sea ducks by triggering their feeding instinct with live food. Since the oil spill occurred in February and March, the only live fish locally available were eels for the loons and mummichogs for the sea ducks and grebes, all of which latter birds she lost. Dottie is a registered nurse whose husband is a physician, and they learned that mummichogs are loaded with an enzyme, thiaminase, that destroys thiamin, alias vitamin B_1. Since thiamin is essential to normal metabolism and nerve function in most plants and animals, Dottie mainly used the live mummichogs to restore the birds' wills to live. She did this by putting several of the small fish into shallow pans set before the grebes and sea ducks confined in cardboard boxes with holes cut so the birds could stab at the fish but not reach back to preen their oily feathers and ingest the poison. The survivors of this therapy were fed thawed silversides laced with vitamin B_1 extract to neutralize any of the ill effects generated by an unadulterated diet of mummichogs. The B_1 additions were also insurance in case the silversides contained thiaminase. This enzyme is broken down by cooking and so cannot harm anyone eating whitebait even if the fish carries thiaminase. But its presence in a variety of small prey-type fishes raises the question of whether this unusual enzyme evolved as a way of discouraging predators who might try to make an exclusive diet of mummichogs or silversides. And its presence explains why winterbound herons feeding on mummichogs massed in ice-free holes in tidal streams will often convulse and die within several days of the onslaught of such conditions. The cold is not killing them; the mummichogs are.

Of all the year-round residents of the Hereford Inlet area, none brings back fonder memories than the sticklebacks. When I taught at the U.S. Naval Academy in the late 1960s, my enthusiasm for aquariums was as contagious as another officer's enthusiasm for coin collecting, and the second floor of the bachelor officers' quarters regularly reverberated with announcements to the effect that, "I got a 1950-D nickel in change today!" or "I've just had babies!"

All of us enjoyed seining the tidal Severn River and bringing back specimens for our many aquariums, but especially one huge model we had dubbed the "pond." Over the course of two years, and occasionally at the same time, we kept eels, striped bass, white perch, yellow perch, redfin pickerel, sheepshead minnows, mummichogs, carp, hogchoker flounder, northern pipefish, four-spine sticklebacks, and three-spine sticklebacks in the big tank. Yet even after carefully determining who might try to eat whom and trying to match species and size accordingly, we often made mistakes and had to return to the Severn to replenish the depleted tank.

A big surprise were the sticklebacks. Although the four-spine variety rarely grows two and a half inches, and the three-spine reaches only four inches, they were among the most aggressive fish we kept. Woe to the eight-inch striper which strayed into the territory of a breeding stickleback male! The best way to keep them, we found, was to separate the sexes (this had to be done by behavioral guesstimate since both sexes look alike) and keep one male to a tank. A gravid female was put in with a male after he had finished building his barrel-shaped nest from scraps of vegetation bound together with sticky threads secreted from his kidneys. The nest is weighted down with small stones, and it was important to keep a supply of this building material in the aquarium. Otherwise the male would tear up the tank in his frustrated search for a substitute.

As soon as a receptive female is lured into the nest and lays about a hundred eggs, she is driven away by the male, and another female is sought to lay still more eggs. Naturally this nesting procedure always took place in the midst of a busy schedule of classes when none of us were available to watch the fish and remove the spent female so she would not be killed by her erstwhile lover, and, if possible, to replace her with yet another gravid female. We once encouraged a Filipino steward to take on the job, but he took out the male by mistake, and the fish destroyed his nest when he was later returned to the aquarium.

Normally, the males will guard their nest for six to ten days, by which time the eggs have hatched. The guardian then destroys the nest but continues to look after the young until they are able to fend for themselves. People find sticklebacks more interesting than most other fishes because their reproductive strategy is similar to our own. Compared to shad, whose large females broadcast over 150,000 eggs, even the most aggressively amorous male stickleback ends up with only 300 eggs to watch. Yet by tending the nest and supervising the young until they are well able to make their own way, stickleback males assure a much higher survival ratio for their progeny per spawning effort than that of the most fecund shad or menhaden.

Still, nature needs only two of each pair of any species to survive to reproduce to survive, ad infinitum. The stickleback may be more attentive to its young than is true of most fishes, but nature is not the least bit interested in such behavior from a sentimental point of view. Nature respects only the fact that shad are as successful at propagating themselves as sticklebacks. And even from a sentimental viewpoint, it might be argued that shad and the other herrings are less "selfish" than sticklebacks, since the surplus eggs from their spawning sustains not only themselves but hundreds of other creatures, including man.

Our last stop in South Jersey is at Graham Macmillan's home in Avalon where my wife and I board his twenty-six-foot sportfishing boat, *Graybell*, for the run through the Cape May Canal into Delaware Bay for a morning of shark fishing.

I have done my share of shark fishing elsewhere along the coast, but I was unprepared for the behavior of Graham's quarry. Shark fishing may be an eighty-pound test Dacron line struck so hard it snaps like cotton thread, or it is the pickup and steady pull of an irresistible force, more suggestive of mechanical power than the hooked brute it becomes. But shark fishing never begins with mere nibbles and tiny tugs. Or, at least that is what I had supposed before our Delaware Bay trip. There I learned that two hundred pounds of *Carcharias taurus* telegraphs its intentions and lunging fight to follow with little bites and taps more suited to a sea bass than to the "bull" or "tiger" of the sand shark tribe.

"There're sharks all over this bay," Graham told us as we headed out from Cape May. "Delaware Bay seems to be the sand tiger's chief pupping ground in the western Atlantic. They come in here by the thousands to bear their young alive which, by the way, are nearly three feet long at birth. Then both parents and pups turn their attention to the abundant weakfish, fluke, and other bottom-hugging species in the bay. Doubtless quite a number of young sharks are also eaten by the adults."

Three miles from shore, Graham slowed the boat, turned on his depth indicator, and continued to cruise slowly ahead, looking for the first of several favorite holes.

"There's no secret about these spots," Graham told us. "The sharks just congregate in the deepest water they can find, and since the bay averages twenty to forty feet deep, anytime you find an area deeper than that, you're in shark country. Earlier this season I took out a group from the New York Aquarium on what has become an almost annual pilgrimage. We finally quit after they'd caught forty-three sharks from fifty to two hundred pounds. You'll hear a lot of snobbish talk against shark fishing, but I've never yet met the angler who would turn down action like that!"

The flashing red line on the depth indicator dropped from thirty-five to forty, then to forty-five feet, and Graham announced, "This is it." Within minutes we were anchored, and he was trickling over the stern menhaden oil he buys from a processing plant not far from his home.

"It's the 'bunker smell that attracts the sharks, and rather than fool around with messy cans or fruit sacks full of ground-up fish, I prefer buying these jugs of fish oil. The oil sets up a good slick and will frequently bring in small fish and birds behind the boat even without the extra inducement of fish bits."

Graham took from his combination footstool and tackle box the hooks, leaders, and sinkers we'd need. When he first started shark fishing, he used the most expensive terminal gear available. Now, since he releases almost all the fish he catches, he keeps his hooks on the cheap side and finds they work just as well.

Our baits were chunks of whole menhaden fished directly on bottom. We used two rods, and Graham attached a balloon to one line to float it some distance behind the boat in order to keep it from tangling the other line.

Then we waited.

"What other kinds of sharks do you catch here?" my wife, Barbara, asked.

"The sandbar or brown shark—*Carchahinus milberti*," Graham replied. "They only grow about seven and a half feet long, while the sand tiger reaches eleven feet. However, the sandbars fight harder. Unfortunately, our ratio is about one sandbar shark to every ten sand tigers."

I was holding one of the lines to determine whether it was still on bottom when I felt a small twitch at the other end.

"Are you ever bothered by crabs or sea robins?" I asked.

"Sometimes crabs. But not sea robins. Our baits are too large for them. Why?"

"Oh, I thought I felt something like a little bite," I said.

"Well, strike, man! Strike!"

Bewildered, I hauled up and felt a solid weight. Then the line suddenly whipped from my hand. However, before I could get the rod out of the holder, the fish was gone.

"That was a shark?" I asked.

"Sure was! And you lost it because you didn't get the hook into him. Rather than use your hand, get the rod out of the holder next time and lay it into the critter half a dozen times with all you've got! The only thing that's tougher to hook is a tarpon."

We fished another fifteen minutes without a "bite." Graham then announced we'd better move:

"Shark fishing in some other areas can be pretty slow sport. But if a half hour passes in Delaware Bay without a fish, you're simply in the wrong spot. We should have had two or three sharks by now."

We pulled anchor and cruised west until the indicator light flashed sixty feet—probably the deepest hole in that corner of the bay.

"We'll get 'em now," Graham announced.

Our second line wasn't even out when the first line went

strangely slack. Barbara took the rod and swung up so fiercely several times I wondered if she had me—and not the shark—in mind! But she hooked the creature and was soon seated and working on it.

Unlike many bottom-hugging fishes that appear to give up once you raise them a certain distance from the bottom, this sand tiger shark wrestled and lunged all the way to the surface. If anything, the shark's initial fight was sluggish and picked up dramatically once the creature realized it was being hauled away from familiar haunts. Even on the surface, the shark seemed to have a few last twists and turns and a flurry in reserve.

This boatside flourish is what makes shark tagging as exciting as shark catching. Graham brought out a boat hook rigged with a miniature harpoon shaft and a metal dart to pierce the shark's hide and then hold the plastic streamer tag in place. As Barbara brought the fish close to the boat, Graham leaned out, much like a matador's assistant in bullfighting, and punched the dart into taurus's back aft of the first dorsal fin.

The shark went berserk, dashing wildly about in circles. Barbara finally brought the fish back to the boat, and I leaned over and clipped the wire leader close to the shark's snaggle-toothed mouth. (But not too close!) Graham took the card that had come with the tag and filled in an estimate of the shark's length and weight, its sex—a male, indicated by the pencil-shaped pair of claspers trailing off the pelvic fins—as well as its species, date, and where the shark was caught. This information goes into the American Littoral Society's master file, as well as a file maintained by the National Marine Fisheries Service research laboratory at Narragansett, Rhode Island, against the day the shark is recaptured.

In all the years of the society's members' efforts, only three sharks—all of them sand tigers—have been recaptured. Thousands of tagged striped bass have been recaptured, and the society's overall ratio for tags sold and tags returned is nearly ten to one. This is especially remarkable when one learns that of the 140,000 tags sold over the years, executive director Dery Bennett estimates that only about half of them have been used.

"In some cases, earnest taggers carry a large stock of tags with them wherever they go," says Bennett, "and these tags will eventually find their way into fish. But in other cases, good intentions have overreached opportunity, and the tags will become collectors' items when they are rediscovered sometime late in the next century."

With the exception of the heavily fished and, therefore, more frequently recaught blue shark, even NMFS's biologists have found that there are relatively few sharks recaptured each year compared to the thousands they and their cooperators manage to tag. Yet because some sharks live so much longer than most any other order of marine life, the only shadow over a fisherman's hope that the shark he tags today can be recaptured and recognized decades from now is the failure of the tag itself.

In September 1980, a sandbar shark was recaptured off Block Island, Rhode Island, after being at liberty more than fifteen years. The tag was barely legible. Yet data from the recovery indicated the shark had grown only about 1.3 inches per year and was still sexually immature at 6½ feet in length and more than 20 years of age. Another sandbar shark tagged off Virginia in 1965 turned up off Vera Cruz, Mexico, seventeen years later. Since sharks as a group are slow-growing and long-lived and produce relatively few young, they are easily depleted by intensive fishing, despite the U.S. Commerce Department's assertion that they are an "underutilized resource."

In just two hours of fishing with Graham in Delaware Bay, my wife and I caught, tagged, and released seven sand tiger sharks, lost four, and had strikes (or rather, bites) from half a dozen others. All around us on the horizon we watched fishermen who were seeking bluefish, weakfish, or fluke drift listlessly—and fishlessly—while we had had almost continual action. True, we brought in no fish for lunch, but neither apparently did all those other fishermen. And we brought in something more substantial: memories—and the possibility that sometime in our dotage, another angler will haul up an old mossbacked sand tiger shark with a tag and its numbers still showing in the shark's back.

6

THE CHESAPEAKE

Something was wrong with the rhythm of the work. Each time the skipper revved the donkey engine to alert the winders that the dredges were ready to come up, the starboard crew was finished culling the previous load of oysters while the port crew was still at work.

Wade Murphy said nothing, but he was angry. Each delay cost money. He brought the *Sigsbee* about for another run downwind of the marker he had thrown over at first light and closely watched the activities of the port crew to see where the problem lay. Suddenly he gave me the wheel, rushed forward, and shoved one of the cullers aside. Then Murphy began to pick twice as many legal oysters from the pile of debris as the displaced man had been doing.

By the time the dredges were again full and ready to come up, the portside work area had been clear a full minute longer than the starboard side. The captain used this interval to cuss the lazy crewman so that even his ancestors would have disowned such shiftless spawn. The man stood downcast, not resentful, for nobody could say that Wade Murphy was a do-as-I-say, not a do-as-I-do, kind of waterman.

The pressure was on because fishing was good. Several other skipjack captains had seen Murphy's full dredges and now crowded him and his marker close on all sides. A spectator ashore would have only noted a panorama of skipjacks on the winter-darkened Choptank River and flocks of old squaw ducks and white-winged scoters kept in flight by the continually turning boats.

Aboard the *Sigsbee*, however, the crew members saw nothing but oysters. They perspired beneath oilskins, yet gloved hands were

Oldsquaw Ducks flying above a Skipjack

stiff with cold. Their minds were numb with the pace, and anything that wasn't a legal-length oyster was tumbled over the side; debris included old ballast stones and a cannonball that might have been sold ashore.

When another skipjack rushed past the *Sigsbee* less than thirty feet away, Murphy called across and asked the other captain whether he was trying to take oysters out of the *Sigsbee*'s dredge to make up for the lack of oysters on his own deck. Skipjacking may be romantic stuff to tourists visiting Maryland. Yet for the men aboard these boats, it is rigorous, highly competitive, and rarely lucrative work.

Less than eighty years ago, there were more than three thousand skipjacks dredging oysters in the Chesapeake Bay and its major tributaries. Today, there are fewer than thirty, but good oyster prices and rising fuel costs have made the wind-powered boats more attractive to young watermen who want to be their own bosses, and several new or rebuilt skipjacks are coming down the ways each season.

According to a nineteenth-century shipwright's formula, a skipjack is any beamy, shallow-draft, centerboard sloop whose raking mast is precisely as high as the boat is long, plus her beam. Thus, the *Sigsbee*, built in 1901 on Deal Island, is 47 feet long, 16 feet wide, and carries a mast 63 feet high. If anything happens to this mast or even the *Sigsbee*'s 47-foot boom, Wade Murphy would have difficulty replacing it, and, like all skipjack skippers, he fears his boat might end up being a rich man's toy.

Most skipjackers have been working their craft a long time. Wade Murphy's father owned one, and his father's father was a skipjack captain before that. However, like farming, few young men can consider entering the business today, because few have the money to get started. Tax laws and banks cater to rich men with toys, not working sailors, and the young crewmen aboard these boats by and large say they are only there "until something better comes along."

Despite the hardships, there is something fascinating about the skipjack that goes beyond the boat's competent good looks and the fact that oyster dredging represents the last regular use of working sail anywhere in the United States. Perhaps, it is because any activity associated with human bloodshed intrigues people, and the nineteenth-century war between the state of Maryland and piratical dredgers qualifies the Chesapeake oyster for a bloodstained footnote in American history.

When British colonists arrived in the New World, they did not eat oysters at first. In fact, one of them complained that "the oyster bankes do barre out the bigger ships." In Europe, oysters were eaten, of course, but large fin fishes were so abundant and easily caught in American coastal waters, the colonists left shellfish for the Indians to eat, much the way slaveowners left rabbits for their slaves.

However, within a generation this cavalier attitude began to change. American oysters are so much larger and more succulent than their European counterparts that once local Indians were driven away from the coast, the colonists began making their own additions to the fabulous mounds of discarded shells left by the recently departed red men.

The notorious seventeenth-century Indian killer and "peacemaker" during Bacon's Rebellion, Colonel Edmund Scarburgh, had such delicate taste buds that he won considerable tracts of land in wagers when he could distinguish Nanticoke oysters from Occohanocks and Chincoteagues while blindfolded. By the time William Makepeace Thackeray visited this country in the 1850s, oysters had become a festive treat, and the ones eaten by Thackeray were so large he said he thought he had swallowed a baby!

Oysters spawn in warm weather when each female produces approximately 300 million eggs—100 times more than the less well known soft-shelled clams, which helps explain why, unlike the nationally consumed oyster, soft-shells are primarily a regional dish from Maine to the Chesapeake. For centuries the British have protected oyster beds by prohibiting the taking of these shellfish in months without an *r* in their names. The practical reason for this tradition is that British oysters lay their eggs inside their shells, and in the process, adversely affect their flavor. American oysters, however, pump their spawn directly into the surrounding waters, and except for a more flaccid appearance, American oysters in June taste no different than dormant oysters in December. Yet because of a lack of refrigeration in the early days, and because the colonists were long bound by British law, there is still no market today for summer-harvested American oysters.

This may be just as well, for oysters have a difficult enough time reaching three and four years of age, at which time most are eaten, without further pressure from us. Because oysters have become a popular seafood even in distant inland cities, and because oysters have so many other enemies like the oyster drill, the sea star, and

Soft-shelled Clams

An Oyster Drill with Barnacles on one Oyster, a Starfish attacking
another Oyster, and a Hermit Crab

various burrowing sponges, not to mention a long list of diseases and
parasites, very few oysters live to ten years and reach the slipper
sizes familiar to our forefathers.

Maryland passed a law during the Civil War restricting the
harvest of most oyster beds to licensed tongers. This was done more
for military reasons than for conservation because tonging is done
from an anchored boat and a smaller one than dredgers use. Smug-
gling was lucrative enough for enterprising Marylanders without
making their jobs any easier by allowing a fleet of alleged oyster
dredgers to operate out of every river on the Eastern Shore.

After the war, the price of oysters rose rapidly in the victorious
cities of the North, but the wartime law stayed in the books because
it has always been easier to write laws than to eradicate them. Since
an oyster dredge can take in five minutes with a great deal less effort
what a set of tongs might harvest in an hour, the clandestine use of
dredges soon became a major enterprise involving dozens of boats
and eventually thousands of watermen.

In 1868, Maryland commissioned an "oyster navy" and outfitted
a steamer and several fast sloops and schooners with cannons and

small arms in order to protect the tongers and their grounds. However, since this police force was mostly composed of friends and relatives of the dredgers, the infrequent raids resulted in a great deal of fireworks but few arrests.

In January 1894, a *Harper's Weekly* editorial complained that "In the 30 years of oyster wars only about 50 men have been killed, and the wounded would not reach 50 more." Since the dredge skippers had possibly killed that many people themselves to avoid paying crewmen or having the boat owners' or their own identities revealed, *Harper's Weekly* seemed to feel that Maryland's oyster navy should be playing a larger role in the murder and mayhem.

When oyster culture was introduced to the Chesapeake shortly before the turn of the century, it quickly crippled the black market in illicitly dredged oysters. State authorities drove the final wedge between the big-city syndicates which bought the illegal oysters and the majority of watermen by legalizing oyster dredging on many prime beds which were then refurbished annually through aquaculture.

Today, dockside prices for prime Choptank oysters vary between $7.50 and $11.50 per bushel. However, state conservation laws restrict each skipjack to a maximum of 150 bushels a day. Further-

Tonging for Oysters

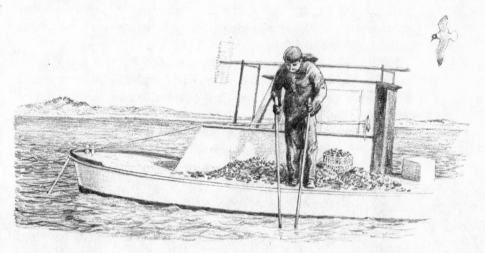

more, each boat must pay 50 cents tax for each bushel she lands, money which Maryland uses to restock oysters in depleted waters.

Thus, while it is possible to gross as much as $1650 on a good day, by the time boat maintenance, crew's wages, and other expenses are deducted—minus those frequent days when it is too rough to sail or the skipper can only find 30 bushels of $7.50 oysters—you have to love working on the bay more than wealth to stick by skipjacking.

The Chesapeake Bay was created nearly 15,000 years ago. In the beginning, the Susquehanna River was born from the melt of the Wisconsin glaciation as that vast ice sheet retreated from Pennsylvania and New York. Fingers of frigid, debris-laden waters trickled into a single stream which assumed a burden of tributaries as it moved to the sea.

Pennsylvania's West Branch of the Susquehanna and the Juniata; Maryland's Potomac, Patuxent, Choptank, Nanticoke, and Pocomoke; Virginia's Rappahannock, Pamaunkee (York) and Powhatan (James) added their winter rains and summer silts to the main flow. By the time the torrent reached the sea more than a hundred miles east of the present Virginia capes, the Susquehanna had scoured a channel a hundred feet deep and surged far offshore to push out the northward flowing warm-water current we call the Gulf Stream.

As glaciers throughout the Northern Hemisphere melted and moved back toward the pole, the seas rose and the Susquehanna's lower flood plains were inundated by tidal waters. Barrier islands were formed twenty and thirty miles off the present coast, where enormous herds of walrus and smaller gatherings of gray and harbor seals hauled out to rest or breed.

The seas continued to rise even as they are still rising today, and marshlands and mud flats were born on ridges where spruce and fir trees had once stood. Striped bass adapted to these new conditions and followed warming waters north along the coast, colonizing newly created bays and estuaries from New Jersey into Canada. However, striped bass south of the Chesapeake maintained more homely traditions and today still stay close to the mouths of the rivers in which they breed.

As the seas rose, great whales, including the now extinct Atlantic gray, entered the lagoons of the nascent Chesapeake to feed and breed even as their Miocene ancestors, the Cetethere, had done in previous drownings of the region. The shallow warm waters of the bay, whose average depth is only twenty-eight feet, may once have been a major calving ground for more than one whale species.

Today, stray whales still penetrate the sonar barrier formed from the many pilings and four artificial islands of the Chesapeake Bay Bridge-Tunnel. Some wander up the bay as far as the 174-foot depression off Bloody Point on the south end of Kent Island, the deepest hole in the Chesapeake. Others, perhaps more atavistic, mill about off Cedar Point at the mouth of the Patuxent where a baleen whale skull more than eleven million years old was found.

Having found their way into the bay over the top of one of the two tunnels comprising the underwater links of Route 13, the whales cannot always find their way out again. On July 28, 1977, a minke whale was discovered floundering about in the shallows of Onancock Creek on the Eastern Shore, nearly fifty miles as the whale swims, inside the Chesapeake Bay. Engineers and bankers never considered the needs of marine mammals when they designed and built the bridge-tunnel. The minke finally died of exposure and was hauled to the local landfill.

Minke Whales

Flint Arrowhead beside a Deer Trail

Man has relatively fragile bones, and probably for this reason, no fossil remains have been dredged up from the Continental Shelf to confirm the scientific surmise that Clovis man (or a related culture) was hunting mammoths and musk-oxen there between 11,000 and 6000 years ago. Such men and their prey gradually withdrew to the mainland as the seas rose, and both became extinct long before a new culture of men came from the west to recolonize the altered ecosystem of the Chesapeake. Arrowhead collectors note that Clovis-type points are rare finds in the area, but Bill Belote of Pungoteague, Virginia, found one close to Chesconnessex Creek. And another was located by Burton Randall on Maryland's western shore.

When that family of red men speaking Algonquian dialects first arrived on the shores of the newly formed Chesapeake, the region offered the happiest kind of hunting, fishing, and farming grounds. Although the great beasts of the Pleistocene were gone, and smaller beavers had replaced the extinct giant beaver even as deer had replaced the vanished moose, more individuals of such smaller animal varieties enabled the Indians to form more or less permanent settlements where crops could be raised and meat could be brought in from the surrounding forest instead of having to range as far as the Clovis hunters had done.

Oysters, blue crabs, eels, white perch, and sturgeon were plentiful in the innumerable brackish-water coves and guts that fashion life along the fringes of the bay. In the spring, shad and herring swarmed into every river and tributary stream to spawn. The Indians used weirs to catch them, often in great quantities, and the surplus was smoked, and thereby saved for weeks or months.

In the lower, saltier portions of the Chesapeake, Sciaenids such as channel bass, black drum, weakfish, spotted sea trout, croaker, and spot swarmed in season to provide substantial catches in the pound nets the Indians made with cedar poles, hickory strips, and vines. Since the Sciaenid family was of great importance to the red man, but is considered of less importance today—except by recreational anglers—the Indians may have known more about the habits of these fishes than many of the marine scientists studying the bay in the Virginia Institute of Marine Science at Gloucester Point.

While many thousands of dollars are spent annually on repetitive examinations of the overstudied oyster, the Indian legend that the boom-voiced and bewhiskered black drum is an ancestor of man is about as good information as we still have concerning this mysterious fish. We certainly have little idea where the 40- to 120-pound adults are during that half of the year when they are not spawning in the Chesapeake and Delaware bays or feeding offshore the barrier beaches that run between these two estuaries.

In the fall, myriads of waterfowl visited the Chesapeake, and while there probably were not as many Canada geese in centuries past as there are now, enormous numbers of ducks, particularly canvasbacks and redheads, provided the Indians with food and recreation throughout the winter months. The birds were sometimes netted and trapped, but they were also lured within bow range by facsimile birds the European settlers eventually called "decoys."

It is ironic that Indian names survive in a region where no Indian survives. And it is curious that Algonquian names for several marine resources persist elsewhere, but not in the Chesapeake. For example, *mummichog* is still heard in New York and New Jersey for the small fish Virginians call "bull minnow," and *quahog* is used throughout New England for what Chesapeake watermen call the "hard-shell clam." Even the word *roanoke*, the name of a Virginia city, is largely forgotten in its original meaning of the disk-shaped beads made from quahog shells. About the only Indian names that survive among Chesapeake fishes are *tautog* for a bottom-dwelling member of the wrasse family, and *menhaden* for the oily herring that moves along the coast and into the bay in dense schools.

There is tangible evidence of Indian culture still hidden in the marshes and forests of the Chesapeake region, and oyster tongers will sometimes pull up a stone projectile point from bay waters many hundreds of yards from the nearest shore. Not long ago a physician friend found a beautifully wrought stone axhead among the eroded roots of a tree on Cedar Island, one of Virginia's barrier chain. However, since such finds are entirely providential, amateur archaeologists usually confine their searches to plowed fields following a heavy rain.

There are few moments more rewarding than the discovery of an arrowhead. Even before the worked stone is picked from the ground, a thrill—like a flash of recognition—electrifies the mind, and you reach back through a dimension of time—perhaps thousands of years—to receive a fragment of an extinguished life and a craftsman's soul.

No matter whether the tip is missing or the form crudely wrought from difficult rock, each newly found projectile point offers a mystery. It is not so much that Indian artifacts are abundant in the loamy fields bordering the Chesapeake as that such rock-free soil simplifies your search. Almost any broken stone more than a few inches in length was probably imported and worked by an ancient artisan.

Half the pleasure of discovery is in speculating how the relict came to be there. You stand and fondle a point's still-sharp edge or the well-worn channel of a shaft smoother and try to imagine the human history behind the fragment. Once I found a rough, but beautifully veined, rose quartz arrowhead in the high corner of a field that jutted into a tidal marsh. The point lay mere inches from the track of a deer in the freshly washed earth.

On subsequent visits to the same spot, I found additional points, including a rose-colored mate to my original find. And always there were fresh deer tracks. Since no oyster or clam midden told of a time when Indians gathered to relax, to smoke their red and white clay pipes, and to work hides into clothing and stone into art, these arrowheads were probably lost during ancient hunts when red men crouched behind shrubs and trees to await the deer that crossed the high ground between the broad swards of marsh even as their descendants do today. Only the forest that once hid the hunted and the hunters are gone.

Although Indians living in the mid-Atlantic coastal plain had little choice in the kinds of stone they used, they fashioned lovely tools from the flint and chert brought down from Pennsylvania or, after the war-loving Iroquois and Delawares had closed the Susquehanna to trade, overland from the Western mountains.

Quartz was much used, and modern jewelers marvel at the quality of craftsmanship achieved merely by using other stone tools. The oldest point in my collection is a scalloped-edged and beautifully polished piece of amber quartzite found on the Virginia peninsula in a field midway between the Chesapeake and the sea. According to style dating, this arrowhead was chipped from its maternal nugget more than three thousand years ago.

Large birds provided the Indians with feathers to make their arrows. The bay was once blessed with immense breeding populations of ospreys, and in pre-Colonial times, there may have been more than a thousand bald eagle nests scattered along the 7300 miles of Chesapeake tidal shoreline. The warm shallows of the bay provided easy fishing, and whenever the eagles were not up to catching their own meals, there were always the ospreys to rob.

All eagles seem to be half-vulture. Although as ornithologist Alexander Sprunt, Jr., points out in his *North American Birds of Prey*, "eagles can attain considerable speed when the necessity arises—certainly enough to capture some of the ducks," bald eagles prefer picking off sick or crippled waterfowl rather than chasing down healthy birds. One December afternoon not many years ago, retired Fish and Wildlife Service director John Gottschalk, artist Ned Smith, and I watched a pair of bald eagles hunt a Virginia marsh for crippled black ducks when there were pods of healthy diving ducks in the open channels around the marsh. During several decades of eagle watching, Alexander Sprunt saw a bald eagle take only one uninjured game bird—a hen mallard—besides an occasional coot, which normally fly like they are crippled!

During the Civil War, Virginia posted a bounty on eagles for the pathetic reason they were a symbol of the Union enemy. And although the bald eagle was selected as our national bird by Congress in 1782, this species was not protected in the lower forty-eight states until 1940 and in Alaska until 1952. Until a decade ago when the National Wildlife Federation began publicizing that it would pay substantial rewards for information leading to the conviction of eagle killers, casual shooting of the birds was not uncommon with young boys and watermen needing no better rationale than "the birds are big targets" or "eagles eat my fish."

Logging and land development remain the greatest enemy of

the eagle, both because they fell the huge trees necessary to support an eagle's massive nest and because, inevitably, more permanent homes for humans mean fewer permanent homes for eagles. Unlike ospreys and their Alaskan kin, the southern bald eagle, which winters in Florida but nests as far north as the Canadian Maritime Provinces, has little tolerance for water skiers or amateur photographers. It has learned that its survival depends on keeping a country mile away from man.

Yet as late as 1936, an Audubon Society survey indicated there were at least 250 active eagle nests in the Chesapeake area. Today that number has dwindled to approximately 95. However, that figure is actually up from a low of only several dozen during the peak of DDT use in the bay area in the 1950s. Best of all, the number of nestlings rose to 96 in 1981 (3 in Delaware, 53 in Maryland, and 40 in Virginia). At the same time, there has been a steady decline in the number of abandoned nests from 85 percent in 1962 to only 36 percent last year. Clearly, the banning of insidious chemicals has greatly improved the health of all fish-eating predators, including ourselves.

Although the Chesapeake still produces an average annual yield of 125 pounds of seafood per acre, every day approximately 400 million gallons of municipal sewage are dumped into it. And although more than 200 species of fish feed and spawn in the bay and nearly 75 species of waterfowl and waders winter on the Chesapeake, an average of 800 tanker oil spills occur each year, and deleterious chemicals from dozens of nonpoint sources increasingly infiltrate the bay's ecosystem.

Because the bay is divided between two state governments that rarely see eye to eye on any issue, and because the bay is further divided culturally between its city-based white-collar populations and its rural-based farmers and fishermen, the Chesapeake offers special problems in resource management quite unlike those found in any other section of the nation.

There is much talk about "mutual cooperation," but state governments—like the people they represent—are stronger with words than deeds. Conferences are periodically held involving representatives from both Maryland and Virginia, and such gatherings may give the ordinary voter the impression that something is being done to save the bay. However, there are so many conflicting opinions expressed by public officials as to what uses the bay should be put that indecision and recrimination, not cooperation, mark the pathways of political and economic change in the Chesapeake.

The agony of the bay is that too many people are trying to make it serve too many perspectives:

• Merchants see the Chesapeake and its navigable tributaries as transportation corridors thrusting toward markets throughout the mid-Atlantic.

• Industrialists and power company executives view the Chesapeake as a limitless source of cooling and processing waters, as a sink for treated wastes, and its people as a pool of relatively cheap labor whose independent working traditions will resist unionization.

• The military sees the Chesapeake as an excellent training ground for various kinds of warfare. (Nearly 10 percent of the total employment in the bay area is connected with the armed forces.) At the upper end of the bay, heavy weapons are tested not far from where young captive-bred peregrines are "hacked" to fend for themselves in the wild; halfway down the bay, Naval Academy midshipmen train with YP (Yard Patrol) boats amid anchored oil tankers and rafts of wintering waterfowl; in the lower reaches of the bay and along the barrier islands fronting the Atlantic, Navy and Air Force jets practice low-level attacks over islands of colonial nesting birds where chicks are tumbled in pathetic confusion by the roar and concussion of the manned missiles overhead.

• Recreationists view the bay as a playground. However, sailors must vie for boating space with fishermen, and Christmas-counting birders must endure the thunder of hunters' guns. Meanwhile, everyone curses the interstate traffic jams on Memorial and Labor Day weekends.

• Scientists see the bay as a living laboratory of undiscovered or insufficiently tested theories. Sociologists see it as a vortex of conflicting cultures and ethnic groups. Writers are fascinated by its history and legends.

• Architects think of the Chesapeake in terms of old homes. Snobs think of it in terms of old families. Corporate accountants and Internal Revenue agents think of it in terms of estates for entertaining clients.

• Farmers want land prices along the Chesapeake to be stabilized so they can continue to make a profit from the soil. Developers want land prices to escalate so they can make a profit from people's dreams.

Most everyone takes the bay for granted, and many think the

Chesapeake will remain the same for generations to come. However, there is no way for that to be. The bay itself is always changing, and so many points of view exist about the value and uses of the bay that conflicting human activities will and have accelerated or retarded natural alterations.

Two unrelated facts dramatize this point: (a) During the past century, an average of 450 acres of land *per year* have disappeared beneath the waters of the Chesapeake. (b) The discharge system for the Calvert Cliffs atomic power plant in Maryland now represents, in terms of water volume, the fifth largest tributary of the bay.

A logical first step toward preserving the most essential features of the bay would be to declare the entire ecosystem an estuarine sanctuary. Such action would put a significant burden of proof on developers and industry which see only water when they see the Chesapeake. At the same time such a declaration would not interrupt or interfere with traditional uses, be they transportation, commercial fishing and farming, or recreation.

There are lessons to be learned elsewhere. From the first arrival of white settlers to the beginning of this century, the lower Hudson, Newark Bay, and the New York Bight supplied most all the seafood needs for the burgeoning population of the mid-Atlantic region. That is why New York's Fulton Fish Market is still the hub of commerce for all fishes caught between Maine and North Carolina.

Today, however, the New York area represents the largest market for Chesapeake Bay crabs, oysters, clams, and other seafoods that New York's and New Jersey's contaminated waters can no longer provide. One wonders what a Baltimore-to-Norfolk megalopolis will do to Chesapeake crab and oyster stocks by the year 2000.

A philosopher might take the long view. This benign-weather interlude we have been enjoying since the first colonists came to the New World may be coming to an end. Perhaps, in another thousand years, climate patterns will be so altered, the Susquehanna will have reverted to its primeval course and surge into the Atlantic many miles east of the present Virginia capes; or, contrariwise, there may be no Virginia capes when a rising sea drowns the coastal plain.

Will our descendants have the diversity of life that inspired such great variety in Algonquian culture? What will recreation be like on a less salubrious and species-poor planet? Will the requirements of survival be so compelling that most people will work with their heads down, oblivious to the world around them, like oyster cullers aboard the *Sigsbee*?

7

BARRIER ISLAND BIRDS

"Hurry!" called John Weske as he trotted close by. "We don't have much time today. It's going to be a scorcher!"

Even as our group spread out and slowly began herding flightless baby terns down the beach through the overwash area behind the low dunes and toward the distant figure of John Buckalew by the holding pen, the sun's ball levitated from the sea and struck us with the brutal force of its radiant heat. A southerly breeze sprung up, but we knew it would offer us and the seabirds scant relief if we didn't have them all banded and released by ten o'clock.

A gang of about eighty terns tried to run through a break in the line two hundred yards away. I dashed over to close the gap. Perspiration soon formed in my eyebrows and dripped onto my glasses, and the glasses began sliding off my nose. I signaled to the flank woman to move out and cover my former zone down by the surf. She couldn't hear me for the roll of the water, and I couldn't hear her for the screaming of adult terns diving close overhead, but she finally grasped the meaning of my frantic arm motions.

Wildlife research is glamorous stuff to read about in an armchair where such realities as heat, biting insects, grime, improvised food, and disappointment—the constant disappointment of missed opportunities and simple misjudgment—do not intrude on the coolly worded summaries. Nor do wildlife reports provide many clues to the years of grueling effort that sometimes go into a single insight.

The two researchers for whom we will band birds this sultry July dawn are John Weske and John Buckalew, both former employees of the U.S. Fish and Wildlife Service. Buckalew started

129

banding birds in 1927, long before there was a Chincoteague National Wildlife Refuge for him to manage and near which he presently lives retired. By contrast, John Weske quit the service in mid-career when it sought to reassign him away from his beloved crested tern project—an effort he first began in the late 1960s. Now he continues the project, using his savings and odd-job money to finance the research, driving back and forth between the coast and his parents' home in suburban Washington, D.C., in an ancient automobile and towing a battered skiff and trailer.

Buckalew has banded almost 200,000 birds of about 180 species during the past half century. Although he is content to clamp an aluminum USFWS band around most any bird's leg, he is especially interested in the wanderings of the laughing gull. Weske, on the other hand, only began banding in 1959, and while he is willing to band other species, including helping Buckalew with his laughing-gull research, his priority—indeed, his obsession—is the second largest of all North American terns, the royal.

John Weske finds it difficult to explain how and why a boy born in Cleveland, Ohio, mostly reared in upstate New York, and who did graduate research at the inland University of Oklahoma should have developed such an abiding passion for a strictly saltwater species that nests on coastal islands from Mexico to southern Maryland. One reason, of course, may be that the royal is the most majestic of all the "sea swallows" or "strikers," as English-speaking watermen have called terns for centuries. Although the royal is not as large as the Caspian tern, the royal has a more deeply forked tail, less gull-like wings, and a less raucous cry than the Caspian. Furthermore, the royal eats only seafood (mostly small fishes of any available species and occasionally crustacea and squid) and does his own fishing, unlike the Caspian tern which commonly robs other terns of their fare as well as steals their eggs.

There are four North American species of terns with feathered crests on the backs of their heads: the Caspian, royal, sandwich, and the elegant, which looks very much like the royal tern and would cause considerable confusion among birders except that it is mostly found along the Pacific coast where the royal rarely strays. The sandwich tern has a distinctive "kirrik, kirrik" cry and normally fishes farther offshore than its larger royal and Caspian cousins. I have seen them twenty-five miles off the Virginia coast coursing over fifty-pound bluefin tuna, waiting for these pelagic predators to drive baitfish to the surface so the terns could dive for their share. The

Royal Terns

largest nesting colony of sandwich terns along the Atlantic coast is found on Ocracoke Island, North Carolina, which is, perhaps not coincidentally, closer to the Gulf Stream than any barrier stretch north of Florida's highly developed beaches—useless, of course, to nesting sandwich terns. This species is unique in having a bright yellow tip on the end of its slender black bill.

However tempting other members of the tern tribe may be, John Weske knows there are already people studying or who have studied the little tern—with a wingspan of only twenty inches, smallest of all North American terns; the Arctic, common, and roseate terns—which look generally alike except for bill color and which I'll leave the more detailed field guides to distinguish; the Forster's tern, which can only be easily distinguished from other similar-sized terns during the winter when it wears a narrow black eyepatch; the gull-billed tern, which, as its name suggests, looks like a small gull with a notched tail and is often seen hawking for insects over land; and such dark coastal visitors as the black tern—a tiny insect eater which breeds on freshwater marshes; the sooty tern, and the noddy tern—both of which snatch their prey from the surface rather than dive for it like other terns, and both of which breed along the U.S. Atlantic coast only on Dry Tortugas at the extreme end of the Florida Keys. Weske feels he would not be making as much of a contribution by reevaluating the work of other researchers as by getting afield himself and studying such a relatively unknown species as the royal tern. Surprisingly, before Weske began his work little more than a decade ago, no one had showed much scientific interest in the royal.

Ten years of more than a hundred juvenile roundups like the one we are on, of tracking down information stemming from the scant return of bands, of travel to remote islands to study the birds' wintering as well as breeding habits, and what has John learned about the royal tern?

He has discovered that royal terns are opportunistic colonizers, ready to move into new areas for breeding rather than clinging stubbornly—and, therefore, disastrously—to former breeding islands overrun by the children of man and his dogs and cats. This explains why Cobb Island, Virginia—uninhabited today and where we will band nearly a thousand young royals—had no record of breeding royal terns at the turn of the century when it was a popular resort for wealthy Northerners.

The flexibility of royal terns in responding to changing barrier island conditions makes them analogous to the shad family of fishes which select breeding rivers sometimes far removed from their natal streams if those new rivers are more suitable for propagation than the old. Many other Atlantic seabirds are less flexible than the royal tern, and the alcids, which include puffins and dovekies, are analogous to Atlantic salmon in that once a puffin or a salmon loses its natal ground, the total population of puffins or salmon shrinks by that number of nonreproducing birds and fish unless their eggs or young are artificially introduced elsewhere.

Another important fact about royal terns is that they rarely nest before they are three years of age. In all the years of Weske's research, he has found only one two-year-old bird in a breeding colony and that one may only have been a voyeur to the nuptial proceedings. Furthermore, he suspects that the majority of royals may not begin breeding until they are four years of age. This obviously raises special problems for the management of such a species. Most birds, like the popularly hunted puddle ducks, breed the spring after they hatch. Barring such natural calamities as drought or severe winters, mallards are a cinch to manage if the objective of management is to ensure sufficient survival to maintain the same approximate number of breeding pairs year after year.

However, management difficulties increase with each additional spring it takes for a species to reach sexual maturity. That may be why certain diving ducks, which are two and three years old before they begin breeding, have such unstable populations in comparison with the mallard or pintail. Hunting regulations can only be established by the U.S. Fish and Wildlife Service in consultation with the Canadian Wildlife Service based on this year's crop of goldeneye, not what may happen to those species' breeding sites during the next two years.

That is also why the Atlantic sturgeon and most sharks—species which take well over a decade to mature—are well nigh impossible to manage for sustained yields, and why commercial fisheries for such species always have collapsed. Finally, that is why it is irresponsible to exploit any resource before we understand its life cycle and ecological requirements, and why—although there is no longer a market for common tern wings and royal tern eggs as there once was along the Atlantic coast—the royal tern's population tends to fluctuate wildly, while the rapidly maturing common tern's numbers rise and fall more gradually. Of course, there is a kind of resilience built into the population dynamics of any species capable of reproducing many times before the individuals die. John Weske has recovered royal terns that were at least seventeen years of age, and older birds almost certainly exist, but bands sometimes fall off or their numbers become obliterated after longtime exposure to the marine environment.

Still, royal tern parents tend only one egg at a time. When they lose that one, they may make another nesting effort that season, but more often they do not. One year there may be more than five thousand successful breeding pairs of royal terns on Cobb Island; the next year, a summer storm overwashes the island and sweeps away every egg or chick. A significant portion of that entire species' year group has been lost, and four years down the road there will be a slump in reproduction even though breeding conditions seem ideal. Such slumps were once regarded as mysterious, but now are less so, thanks to John Weske's ongoing monitoring of the species.

For those who feel that security and "getting on" is what life is all about, John Weske has "wasted" his life. For those of us who feel that curiosity is a rare gift that should not be squandered doing what less gifted people can do, Weske's work takes on the quality of an odyssey, and each discovery becomes another small milestone in our longing to understand life.

After the terns were safely corralled, Weske gave me a carpenter's apron and a necklace of bands. I strapped on the apron and unclasped the necklace, sliding the bands into one of the apron's pockets. The other pocket contained a pliers for clasping the bands around the birds' legs.

"Any particular way you want this done?" I asked. "Right leg? Left leg? The band right side up?"

"I band all my birds' right legs. Other banders band the left. That's so we can tell our birds apart at a distance. Also, try to keep the band numbers up so we can read them later with a spotting scope."

"Can you really make out these tiny numbers on a free-flying bird?" I asked.

"Not flying, but free," interjected John Buckalew. "I get some of my best 'returns' on laughing gulls just sitting in my car in the Assateague parking lots with a pair of powerful glasses."

"Make sure you don't band any sandwich terns with the bands I gave you," said Weske. "They're strictly for royals. All baby terns

Laughing Gulls

look somewhat alike, so if you have any doubts, give John or me a shout."

Buckalew was already on his knees passing birds over the wire screen to three other volunteer assistants for banding. He managed to keep the volunteers supplied with terns and still band more birds than the rest of us combined.

"You seem to be experienced at this sort of thing," I said to Buckalew as I reached in for my first bird.

"You might say." Then with hardly a glance at the bird I was holding, he commented, "You better let me have that one. It's a sandwich tern."

As if in confirmation of the fact, as I passed the young bird to John, an adult sandwich tern swooped down between us. How had the parent picked its youngster out of the many hundreds of birds crowded in the corral?

Vocalization seems to be the key. Just as human parents can recognize the sound of their youngsters amid the din of a kindergarten, royal and sandwich terns can distinguish their young in the crèches into which the baby birds are herded and fed. Of course, there are subtle differences in coloring, and as John Buckalew could distinguish the pinkish baby sandwich tern bill and smaller bill and leg proportions from those of a baby royal tern with yellower bill, the parent terns probably identify equally subtle differences in plumage. However, such marks only confirm what their hearing has already told them: this chick is mine.

Buckalew quickly squeezed a smaller-sized band (3b) around the sandwich tern's leg and released it. The bird quickly trotted off across the sand with its parent hovering overhead and seeming to chide the youngster, as if it had somehow been responsible for the predicament of the past hour.

Cobb Island has a unique history that is at the same time typical of all Virginia's coastal islands which were settled early and abandoned in comparatively recent times as storm tides and the continually rising sea took their toll of human life and treasure. The next island north of Cobb Island, Hog Island, had a post office and daily mail service until Friday, February 15, 1941. Now only waterfowl hunters seasonally occupy a decommissioned Coast Guard station on the north end of the island, and sand blows through the broken windshields of vintage automobiles that once took summer visitors for Sunday-afternoon drives along the strand.

In 1833, Nathan Cobb, his wife, and their three sons sailed from Cape Cod to Virginia's Eastern Shore where Cobb bartered several hundred bags of salt boiled from a local seep for the barrier island that now bears his name. In those days, Cobb Island was nearly twice as large and considerably higher than it is today, and its southern end was more than half a mile east of its present location. Although our banding party had a half hour's boat run across Broadwater Bay to reach the island, back when the Cobb boys were courting local girls on the mainland, they had to sail more than half a day to reach Willis Wharf.

Eventually the boys returned to their father's island with their brides, and the extended family set up a successful market-gunning enterprise before the Civil War and then a luxury resort for triumphant Yankees after the war. Ducks, geese, swans, and shorebirds were shot for Northern food markets, and when the millinery trade took to using mounted whole terns and wings, the Cobbs cleverly charged their sporting guests a guide fee and a stiff price for shot and powder, and then the Cobbs sold the birds to schooner captains working up the coast. The most valuable tern was the tiny least, for which traders paid the Cobbs between 10 and 25 cents each, depending on condition and increasing scarcity. However, even common terns' wings were worth a few pennies since they could be styled into hats for ladies who could not afford to buy a chapeau with the whole mounted bird.

Cobb Island's relative distance from major fashion markets may have been the reason the Cobbs were not paid more for birds that sold for as much as $50 by the time they were converted into hats. Gunners on Long Island and in New Jersey received up to $1 a bird. Yet more modest prices for Southern birds did little to protect terns nesting along the Delmarva Peninsula. Upward of 40,000 terns were shipped from Cobb Island one summer, while farther north, according to ornithologist Frank Michler Chapman, Gull Island, Long Island, and Muskeget Island, Massachusetts, "are the only localities, from New Jersey to Maine, where the once abundant Common Tern, or Sea Swallow, can be found in any numbers." Every other colony had been blitzkrieged. "Now it is the Egret's turn," predicted Chapman.

Today, the Cobbs are long gone from the Virginia island named for them. Of all the grand buildings that once graced this strand, only a dilapidated Coast Guard station, an older life saving station, and a modern peregrine falcon hacking tower brave the periodic hurricanes. The last cemetery marker was sucked into the sea twenty-five years ago, and brown sharks now cruise over the site of the former resort's ballroom. The island has reverted to the wild, and the summer silences of the 1890s have been replaced by the cries of thousands of breeding birds.

Frank Chapman visited Cobb Island at least twice about the turn of the century and made museum history with specimens he collected there. Before 1900, mounted institutional wildlife was mostly displayed in dusty glass cases. While possibly useful to the specialist, bird collections were a bore to the general public. At last, the British Museum began experimenting with new display techniques, and an American sportsman and philanthropist, John L. Cadwalader, saw what the British were doing on one of his annual shooting trips to Scotland. He returned to America and offered Frank Chapman a generous sum of money if he could improve upon British efforts. In Chapman's own words:

"The result was the Cobb's Island, Virginia, group. It shows a section of beach six by 18 feet with its birds on their nests and in the air, and its vegetation so arranged to merge with a painted background of the ocean that, at a short distance, one cannot tell where the group itself ends and the painting begins. The desired illusion is, therefore, secured; the group conveys a feeling of the seashore and its life, and the birds, placed in their natural surroundings, can be studied in relation to their actual environment."

Chapman's more conservative and jealous colleagues hated the idea of mixing art and illusion with science and reality. They conspired to have the exhibit thrown out. However, Chapman's tenacity and the wisdom of a few senior board members of the American Museum of Natural History (including President Theodore Roosevelt) eventually swept the criticism aside, and this first wildlife group in diorama established a standard for museum displays imitated by institutions around the world to the present day.

Chapman was also an innovator in at least two other respects. In the 1900 edition of *Bird-Lore* (predecessor to today's *Audubon* and *American Birds*, published by the National Audubon Society), he proposed a "Christmas side hunt in the form of a Christmas bird census," to stand in contrast to the sporting side hunts that had gone out of fashion in which "everything in fur or feathers that crossed their path" were killed by local shooters. The concept caught on, and today about 125 million birds of several hundred different species are counted in more than 1140 count circles, 15 miles in diameter, from the Arctic to South America.

Chapman's other innovation was a bird identification guide for laymen. Ornithologist Elliott Coues (1842–1899) had created the first "keys" and "checklists" for North American birds beginning in 1872. However, these publications were for the already expert. Chapman's contribution was in recognizing the need for a manual to get the fledgling birder going.

In 1895, D. Appleton and Company published Chapman's *Handbook of Birds of Eastern North America*, and within a decade the book had gone through six "editions," in those days meaning printings. In 1920, Chapman published *What Bird Is That?* subtitled "A Pocket Museum of the Land Birds of The Eastern United States Arranged According to Season." This book had a less successful publishing history, and some editors may have thought that the field guide phenomenon was over. However, a decade later, a young illustrator and amateur ornithologist by the name of Roger Tory Peterson thought he could refine Chapman's concept by focusing on distinguishing field marks in a genuinely portable book that would at the same time eliminate much of the background information on birds which Chapman had stressed, but which was more suitable to armchair reading than quick reference for identification in the field.

Peterson published his first *Field Guide to the Birds* in 1934. The book has subsequently gone through four major revisions with dozens of printings in between.

As a guide to general rules of observation, Chapman's *Handbook* still contains much to recommend it. For example, on page 80 of the seventh edition (1907), Chapman tells us that the quickest way to distinguish a distant tern on the wing from a gull is that "a Tern points its bill directly downward, and looks, as Coues says, like a big mosquito, while a Gull's bill points forward in the plane of its body." Unfortunately, neither Chapman nor any modern guide tells us exactly where the black skimmer fits in. This bird looks like a hybrid ternxgull, and indeed, it even flies like one, with its head pointing neither directly down nor "in the plane of its body." The skimmer is a colonial nester on the same barrier islands where royal terns and laughing gulls breed. Its nest or scrape, no more than a slight depression in the sand, is often found in overwash areas behind the dunes close to tern colonies, and the aggressive defensiveness of terns near their own scrapes and crèches probably helps protect the eggs and chicks of the more passive skimmer from marauding herring and great black-backed gulls, both of which are

One immature and four adult Black Skimmers

extending their breeding range south along the Atlantic coast at the expense of other gulls and terns.

Skimmers and certain terns, along with such disparate species as flamingos, common eiders, and emperor penguins, share the habit of herding newly hatched young into nurseries where only a few adults guard them while the rest of the adults are out getting food. This nursery or, more properly, crèche phase lasts the four to five weeks (in the case of terns and skimmers) it takes the young birds to fledge and fly. By the way, contrary to popular misuse of the word, fledgings can fly; it is nestlings—or in this case, crèchlings (!) —that cannot.

The black skimmer, scissor-bill, or flood gull, as local watermen call the bird, is one of three species worldwide in the separate scientific family Rynchopidae. Its large red and black-tipped bill is distinctive, and not in color alone. The skimmer is the only North American bird whose lower mandible is longer than its upper. As Chapman wrote, "opening the mouth, the bladelike lower mandible is dropped just beneath the surface of the water; then, flying rapidly, they may be said to literally 'plow the main' in search of their food of small aquatic animals."

Since the skimmer is a tactile rather than a visual feeder, this species is the most nocturnal of all coastal birds except the night herons. In the evening, the wind dies, and skimmers sail across the calm surface of darkened coves or beneath the blinking lights of channel markers and snap up young menhaden and silversides swept by on the incoming moon tides. When in small flocks working a particularly productive turning in the marsh or possibly one illuminated by marine lights which serve to draw baitfish close to the surface, the birds clack and quack incessantly while executing spectacular turns and glissades to avoid collisions. Their constant chatter doubtless keeps each skimmer informed as to the whereabouts of his feeding kin.

The banding was nearly over. Fewer than a hundred terns remained in the holding pen. It was nine o'clock. We'd be finished and back in the shade on the mainland long before the sun gave us the full effect of its furnace glare and heat. And we had not lost a single bird.

I stood to stretch my legs and saw John Weske coming across the overwash with a bird and a fisherman's landing net. John had left us ten minutes earlier to make sure that the fledglings being

John Weske and the crippled tern

tended by adults south of our roundup area had already been banded. I met him halfway back to the corral.

"It's an adult royal tern with a broken wing," he explained. "I found it on the other side of the dunes. I know you have a federal salvage permit, and you know someone who rehabilitates injured wildlife. So I brought it back to you to make the choice."

The tern's left wing was broken in two places, and at one of the breaks, I felt splintered bone beneath the skin. Even if the wing was repaired with a splint, it would not mend so the bird could fly again. The bird would always be a cripple, and nature has no use for flightless or sightless terns. I held the bird's breast and began applying pressure on its lungs and heart with my thumb and forefinger.

The tern began to pant and tried to twist from my hand, but it quieted when I stroked its head with my free hand. Whether or not the bird was a breeder it had already shed the adult's black breeding cap, revealing the white feathered forehead which helps distinguish this tern through most of the year from the dark-foreheaded Caspian species.

"There is a man named Balram Pertab in Guyana," said John Weske, "who regularly reports band numbers from royal, roseate, and especially common terns. He apparently catches the birds for food. We'd like to discourage this practice, of course, but he says he has failed at everything else he has ever tried in life, except bird catching, and since there is no point in catching birds unless you eat them, we really shouldn't ask him to give up his livelihood. Since we naturally value the fact he is one of the few people in that part of the world to make the effort to report banded birds, we try to ignore what his numerous reports imply—especially when it comes to roseate terns which, because of their increasing scarcity, may become the first federally protected *Sterna* under the Endangered Species Act."

The royal tern's eyes had closed and its head lolled to one side. Alive, the bird had seemed larger and more substantial than its statistical eighteen-inch length. In death, the tern appeared smaller and strangely fragile.

I slipped off my shirt and carefully bound the tern's body to protect its plumage. I would mount the bird and give it to The Nature Conservancy which owns this island and most other islands in the Virginia barrier chain. Perhaps, one day a diorama of island life can be constructed at the mainland headquarters of the Virginia Coast Reserve, and people unable to visit the islands but curious to know about them will have a chance to see—and possibly to learn—something about coastal life-forms which no longer exist on islands that man can easily reach.

8

CETACEANS

It's better to be on the inside of a twelve-ton truck, looking out, than blown off the road by the gale force winds it generates. As Charlie Potter barreled along Route 13 in the flatbed monster donated by the Ford Motor Company to the Smithsonian Institution's marine mammal salvage program, we passed a pair of bicyclers wearing backpacks and helmets. When I looked in the rearview mirror on my side of the truck, the bikers were frantically weaving through hub-deep grass on the road's shoulder, trying to maintain their balance. One of them suddenly disappeared.

"Sorry about that," said Charlie, who had been watching them in his rearview mirror. "I would have pulled into the left lane except for that passing car. But then four-lane highways make lousy bike trails."

Charlie Potter and Jim Mead are the Smithsonian's marine mammal research team in which Charlie plays Archie Goodwin to Jim Mead's thinner version of Nero Wolfe. While Mead sits in his combination library and laboratory at the Smithsonian contemplating the life histories of whales, dolphins, and porpoises, Potter is at one or another strand along the Atlantic coast taking measurements and photographs, and pulling teeth, stomach contents, and gonads—often an entire skull—all of which may help solve one or another of the many mysteries about warm-blooded creatures that live in the sea.

However, while Nero Wolfe's sedentary detective style is self-imposed, Dr. Mead's is not. In fact, until he suffered an aneurysm in one of the arteries of his brain, Mead and Potter divided the salvage territory, especially when simultaneous strandings were reported from different sections of the coast. Jim had acquired a pilot's license to move more swiftly from one scene of action to the other. However, even though his flying days are over, Mead acquired so much material during his airborne years that he feels he now makes better use of his time by staying at the Smithsonian and fitting some of the already recovered pieces of the marine mammal puzzle together rather than personally trying to collect every new piece that washes ashore.

Jim's and Charlie's contrasting personalities suit them well for the scientific equivalent of Rex Stout's detecting duo. Potter is a restless, action-oriented bachelor with a degree in wildlife management. He likes roadwork, as he calls his long hauls down the highway. One rainy night after locating a pair of pilot whales in New Jersey—he decided it was easier to winch the animals aboard the movable flatbed and bring them back to Washington where he could count on some necropsial assistance in the morning rather than try to do the whole job by himself in the dark—Charlie stopped at

Pilot Whale or Blackfish

a bar and grill for coffee and a hamburger before pushing on. Two men at the bar were arguing about who had caught the bigger fish.

"Pikers!" announced Charlie finally, "You guys don't know what a big fish is. I've got something on the truck outside that will outweigh all the big fish you two guys ever caught combined!"

There were a few tense moments until the bartender suggested converting the challenge into money. He covered the bets, and it's a good thing he did. At least the barman had a sense of humor. The two customers did not, and Charlie is no Paul Bunyan. Fortunately, the bartender outweighed everybody but the pilot whales, and he made the braggarts pay up.

Jim Mead is a quieter, more contemplative personality. Or maybe his undergraduate years at Yale and his graduate work at the University of Texas (M.S.) and the University of Chicago (Ph.D.) tamed the boy who once liked to strip down automobiles to see what made them roar and who is still as fascinated by the technology of fishing—he and I once spent an afternoon driving some coastal roads in Virginia in order to check out the accuracy of a new loran unit— as he is by the fish and mammals taken in the fishery.

He has also indelibly stamped with his candor and enthusiasm the entire research atmosphere involving marine mammals. Where too many other well-educated men and women are inclined to dismiss the observations of lay enthusiasts, Jim Mead understands that most of what we know about marine mammals was the work of observant whalers, sealers, and other nonscientific people in years long gone by; that there is no way Charlie and he can encompass in the 1980s what all those hundreds of people covered in decades past; and that his limited budget could never reimburse a fraction of the hundreds of thoughtful amateurs who already contribute to marine-mammal spotting and salvage programs.

Since the name of the oceanic game is to make up for centuries of ignorance and decades of neglect in as short a time as possible, Mead welcomes other institutions' interest in marine mammals, and he is happy to share with less experienced university staffs his knowledge and the Smithsonian's specimens. Besides, he knows, as does shark researcher Jack Casey, with whom Jim shares an ability to coordinate the efforts of a navy of volunteers, that the sea offers dozens of marvelous contradictions for every immutable law we try to devise. Thus, while many of Jim's colleagues pursue fixed theories, he devises flexible rules of thumb.

Prior to the 1970s, a scientist who wanted to learn about whales went to a whaling station or booked passage on a factory whaler and promised to do his fair share of the labor or stay out of the way entirely. Unfortunately, from the moment a whale is harpooned until the last chunk of fat slips into the bubbling vats belowdecks, there is little time to take pictures and get measurements, much less extract organs or examine placentas. Some frustrated and/or intrepid researchers went off to harpoon whales on their own. Mostly their efforts were relegated to the smaller species, but businessman John Borden of Chicago set off on the yacht *Adventuress* to harpoon Arctic bowhead whales for the American Museum of Natural History. The trouble with that expedition was, as future American Museum director Roy Chapman Andrews, observed, "Yachting parties and serious natural history work do not mix."

Andrews began his own fieldwork in 1907 near the fishing village of Amagansett, Long Island, by salvaging the skeleton of a right whale, for which the American Museum of Natural History had paid $3,200 to keep the renderers at bay. Even though Andrews gave the local fishermen the valuable baleen, which are the whale's gums modified into furry fronds to strain small animal prey from the sea and once used by the corset industry to strain overweight women into sylphlike forms, the fishermen did little to help the young technician until a winter storm threatened to take the whale back out to sea. For their assistance, the fishermen got the blubber as well.

The good boys of Amagansett must have had many a laugh over how they ripped off the rube from the city. ("That museum fellow paid thirty-two hundred dollars for a whale and didn't even take the best parts!") By contrast, no part of a whale today is legal to salvage except by special permit, and no research institution has to pay anyone to remove any or all of a stranded marine mammal. Furthermore, whereas Andrews had few volunteers to help him, today there are often too many, and local town administrators are eager to do anything to help so long as the scientists promise to get the smelly hulk off the beach!

Before becoming famous as the man who led the expedition that discovered the first dinosaur eggs, Roy Chapman Andrews was known to a smaller number of people as the man who rediscovered the allegedly extinct Pacific gray whale off the coast of Korea where he examined more than forty harpooned specimens in six weeks. Despite ongoing whaling by the Koreans, the gray whale has reestablished itself on both sides of the North Pacific, but its Atlantic counterpart became extinct toward the end of the sixteenth or early seventeenth century.

Like his modern colleague, Jim Mead, Roy Chapman Andrews suffered horribly from seasickness, but he insisted on going aboard working whalers to get the kinds of data and photographs unobtainable at shore stations. Once after watching a pair of humpback whales make love, he begged the captain to spare them—to no avail.

Yet Andrews was not averse to the killing of whales under less romantic circumstances, and he even determined "to add the biggest of all animals to my game list." He managed to pull this stunt by guaranteeing his Japanese host a thousand dollars (the value of the whale) if he missed. He fired too soon and only knocked the animal out. Fortunately for his thousand-dollar security, the Japanese crew got the gun reloaded "just as the huge beast was beginning to notice things again," and he killed the finback with his second shot.

Since Roy Chapman Andrews, or "RCA" as the crowd down at the Explorers Club called him, didn't want to tell the gang about how he bounced a hundred-pound bar of iron propelled by three

Humpback Whale

hundred drams of black powder off the skull of a whale without then being able to assure them that he coldcocked the next animal, he again risked a thousand dollars and this time "did a very creditable job sending the harpoon smack into the heart" of a sei whale.

Years later when the British government became worried about the rate at which whales were being killed in the South Atlantic, RCA advised the government not to worry, because the ocean was big, there were many whales in it, and "with the whole ocean to roam in, I should judge that free love was the order of their lives"—thereby providing a moralistic as well as biological justification for killing every whale possible.

By contrast, although Jim Mead is an avid deer hunter, he has never felt an overwhelming compulsion to squeeze the trigger on any of the largest animals that have ever lived on earth. Rather the opposite seems true, for his knowledge today makes him feel an even greater awe for the great cetaceans than he felt as a callow and often seasick graduate student twenty-five years ago.

Furthermore, rather than underwrite the continuing exploitation of whales, Mead and his many scientific colleagues have generated data that have more effectively put the brakes on whaling overkill than all the sentimental Save the Whale campaigns combined. After all, an economic evil is best eliminated by demonstrating its cost-ineffectiveness, not by shouting "Murderers!" By providing well-supported numbers illustrating the forthcoming extinction of the whaling *industry*, Mead et al. got the attention and ultimately the cooperation of such unlikely bedfellows as Japan, South Africa, and the USSR, whereas similar information pointing only to the biological extinction of several whale species might not have elicited a second glance from Japanese, South African, and Russian accountants and money managers.

With the exception of the Arctic bowhead whale, still hunted by Alaskan natives, no marine mammal of commercial importance during this century is on the verge of biological extinction. That fact notwithstanding, all of the larger whale species are on the U.S. endangered species list, and most of these are also on the more scientific "red list" of the International Union for the Conservation of Nature (IUCN) headquartered in Morges, Switzerland.

Being listed does not necessarily mean that an animal is about to become extinct. The lists are merely official recognition that a threatened creature is entitled to protection so it can rebuild depleted stocks, an almost inevitable occurrence if the creature's habitat is still ample and wholesome. Often such endangered species are already commercially extinct—which means only that there are too few of them to support an industry on a sustained-yield basis despite, or because of, an increase in the value of their scarce, hence valuable products.

The whaling issue in particular has caused many Americans to be seized by a moralistic frenzy. It was not enough to say that we had killed too many, and that we would have to provide complete protection for several decades to allow stocks to recover. As we did with the bison campaign sixty years earlier, Americans converted the preservation of the whales into a religious or antiwar movement intense with talk about guilt and atonement. We converted the whale from a fascinating fellow creature into a passionate symbol for the saving blood of Christ.

All whale species were turned into one long-suffering martyrdom to crass materialism, and overnight, our society spawned a legion of whale gurus. Some alleged that because whales have large brains (actually, in proportion to their body size, whale brains are smaller than those of mice), they are more intelligent than humans, and we must dedicate ourselves to learning their language so they can tell us where and how we have gone wrong. Others, even more mystical, suggested that whales were Beings of Special Creation, and if you aspire to hear the word of God, lock arms, close your eyes, and sway to the song of the whale.

Poor Jim and Charlie! All they wanted to do was to salvage a little information about the life histories of marine mammals by examining dead and dying animals on the beach. However, the Marine Mammal Protection Act of 1972 prohibits even them from removing all or any part of a marine mammal without completing all the appropriate forms. The catch-22 is that the forms have to be completed before you touch the animal, and some species cannot be identified without moving the creature to check identifying marks and openings!

Another requirement of the Marine Mammal Protection Act is that you must do everything possible to save a stranded animal. Although Jim and Charlie know that whatever caused the animal to strand in the first place is likely to cause it to strand all over again somewhere else along the coast, they do what they can to alleviate its suffering while sometimes entire communities of people sweat and strain to push the derelict beast offshore.

"It's weird," says Charlie. "Here you are trying to stay out of the way of a flailing tail, which bears the same relationship to me as a flyswatter to a gnat, and here these crazies are swarming all over the animal, hugging it, kissing it, and telling it everything is going to be all right now that the doc—that's me—is here. Then when the animal makes any noise, everyone rushes up to ask, 'What did it say?' 'What did it say?' for God's sake! I hate to get flippant about any animal's suffering, but sometimes I relish telling the truth: 'That was no cosmic sigh you heard; it was just a fart!'"

There are many good new books about marine mammals, but seemingly none of them can be used as a field guide. This is because only the most fortunate observer sees sufficient numbers of marine mammals at sea often enough to develop some feeling for the subtle—and therefore, not guidebookable—differences between species within the same genus. The best guides to marine mammals may always be scientific keys to identifying stranded animals.

Yet there is one marine mammal most everybody thinks they know. This is *Tursiops truncatus*, the bottlenosed dolphin, the leaping, bell-ringing, rubberized creature that every kid wants to hug and take home with him. But even most of what we know about this species, besides its physiology, is what we have taught it.

Creatures in captivity are mirrors of our own egos and ambition. No one has ever been able to learn much about the population dynamics and behavior of wild *Tursiops*. Jim Mead thinks there may be two Atlantic populations: a large pelagic edition, and a smaller littoral variety. There may even be two distinct populations of the inshore variety: one that winters in Florida, and another that winters in North Carolina where from the 1750s to 1928, there was a midwinter fishery on the Outer Banks which annually reduced as many as three thousand animals to gallon canisters of oil and fertilizer.

When a scientist uses the word *whale*, he could be referring to almost any cetacean. But when a layman uses the word, he is almost certainly referring to one of several species of great whales. The most impressive of this lot belongs to the rorqual tribe which is distinguished by a series of grooves on their throats and bellies and by torpedo-shaped heads. In addition, unlike the right and gray whales, the furry baleen combs hanging from the upper jaws of rorquals are shorter and more numerous than in other baleen-equipped animals.

The largest rorqual is the blue whale, which reaches lengths of more than a hundred feet. In fact, it is the largest species of any animal that has ever lived on earth. A brief glimpse of a sounding blue whale gives you little sense of its immense size. However, a stranded blue does. Amazingly, the only possible stranding record of a blue whale from anywhere along the entire U.S. Atlantic coast occurred at Crisfield, Maryland, in the summer of 1876. Crisfield is situated more than sixty-five miles from the ocean, inside Chesapeake Bay!

The only distinguishing feature of surfacing blue whales is the species' unusually broad head compared to the heads of other great whales. However, you must have some elevation to perceive this characteristic, and you must have some experience to realize how much broader the blue's head is than other rorquals. Yet because blue whales are relative strangers to the northwestern Atlantic, the odds are frankly against your seeing one. There may be only about 15,000 of these animals remaining worldwide out of a prewhaling population of, perhaps, 300,000, and the survivors are more likely to congregate in areas where great quantities are found of *Euphausiids* —alias krill, a cold-water shrimp of which there are at least four species. It is sobering to consider that in the winter of 1930 alone, more than twice as many blue whales were killed as now exist in the world.

By contrast, the second largest of all whales is possibly the most abundant whale species off our Atlantic coast. The fin or finback grows up to seventy-five feet. I once helped salvage (appropriately enough, with a "Boston Whaler" boat) a *newborn* finback seventeen feet long. You stand in awe of such monumental feats of procreation!

When starting its dive, a finback usually shows a considerable length of back aft of the dorsal fin, as its common name implies. However, this is an unreliable way to distinguish finbacks from the closely related sei, Bryde's (pronounced Bru-da's), and minke whales because fin sizes and profiles, and the amount of back they may show in a dive, differ according to the individual, not the species.

Ashore, fin whales are quickly recognized by their unevenly colored lips and baleen plates. On the left side of the animal, both the lips and baleen are the same dark color as the back. However, on the right side, the lower lip, sometimes the upper lip, and always

Blue Whale and Great White Shark

the first third of the baleen are white or at least a paler gray than the back. By contrast, a stranded minke is characterized by a prominent white flipper patch.

The sei whale is a mysterious quantity in the North Atlantic. Although as many as a hundred of them were taken every year by ships working out of the old whaling station at Blandford, Nova Scotia, modern sightings of live animals by whale watchers in the western Atlantic are rare, and strandings are even rarer. In all the twentieth century, one animal came ashore at Cape Cod in August 1910, and another was found on North Carolina's Outer Banks in April 1975.

An even scarcer rorqual in this part of the Atlantic is the Bryde's whale, which is puzzling because of all the rorquals, the Bryde's is most avidly a consumer of gregarious fishes like mackerels and herring which, despite overfishing, would seem to be plentiful enough for a whale's purposes off these shores. A stranded Bryde's was found at the mouth of the Potomac River in March 1923, and it might have grounded itself while pursuing a school of spawning-run herring or hickory shad. The Bryde's offers no other records for this coast, but just in case, the way you distinguish a stranded Bryde's whale from a sei is to note that while both species have relatively short ventral grooves, the sei whale's terminate in front of the navel, while the Bryde's grooves extend as far back as the navel. If the animal is lying on its stomach, some authorities insist that the sei whale has many more oblong white spots caused by the parasitic copepods which plague all rorquals. However, Jim Mead doubts this, and his advice is to notify him or Charlie Potter at the Smithsonian.

The last of the rorquals to inhabit western Atlantic waters is, perhaps, the best known—certainly for its "song." The humpback has the most complex communication system discernible to human ears of any marine mammal. Furthermore, the pattern of this marvelous "music" apparently changes every year. Cetologist Roger Payne suggests that humpbacks off the British coast have the capability to communicate with other humpbacks as far away as Brazil. Possibly because of this eerie musical talent, of all the great whales, humpbacks are making the fastest population recovery now that they are protected by international law.

This species is easily distinguished from other rorquals by a variety of protuberances and knobs marking the head and flippers, and the flippers themselves often measure one-third the length of the animal. Humpbacks make frequent dramatic leaps, and when the

Right Whale

animal sounds, the rear edge of its flukes is scalloped, and the white and black color patterns on the flukes are so varied that individual humpbacks can be recognized and kept track of by photographing and comparing the tails' distinctive markings.

The adult right whale is a rotund, cumbersome, and barnacle-encrusted beast about forty feet long. Since the right whale is a slow swimmer, unimaginative under stress, and floats when dead, it was the "right whale" for Indians in their canoes, and later Europeans in their barks and dories, to harpoon from shore whaling stations all along the North Atlantic coast. Although each year, right whales migrate the length of the coast and have a predilection for entering bays and coves where they sometimes wreak havoc with channel markers and moorings by throwing their full, sixty-ton weights upon them in apparent play, marine mammologists do not often have the opportunity to work on a stranded right whale. Perhaps, because right whales spend more time closer to the shore than rorquals, the right is more adept at navigating through shallows, which may be the reason insufficient numbers of right whale study skulls from stranded specimens exist in museum collections. But that was not the only reason the head of a young male right whale salvaged on Long Island in March 1979 was kept in my backyard for close to a year while vultures, possums, and mostly insects cleaned the bones to Smithsonian specifications. The reason for that was that Jim and Charlie couldn't find anyone elsewhere along the coast to accept the grisly trophy! Although my neighbors must have been tempted to ask what I had back there, they never complained, and the local insect-eating bird population flourished on the halo of flies hovering around the whale's head.

Although unfamiliar to the general public, the Ziphiidae, or beaked whales, are currently the glamour issues among marine mammals—possibly *because* they are unfamiliar to the general public. They are medium-sized whales up to thirty feet long and once believed rare because strandings are relatively few and the whales are almost never recognized at sea. Little of their body is revealed when they take air, and their brief blow at the surface is more likely to be mistaken for a whitecap than an animal. When stranded, the elongated face is unusual in having only one or two pairs of teeth in the lower jaw, and none in the upper jaw. Male *Mesoplodon* (the most common genus in the family) regularly butt and rake each other with their teeth, leaving odd sets of parallel scars all over their bodies. A stranded Cuvier's beaked whale that Charlie, waterfowl hunting guide Grayson Chesser, Jr., and I worked on in January 1981 could be recognized even at a distance as a member of the family by model-railway-track-like marks on its flanks and belly. The Cuvier's beaked whale is unusual in that females, which this specimen was, are sometimes as scarified as the males. Cuvier's may be a more passionate species, and once rival males are driven off, the champion lustfully attacks his prize. Or maybe males must attack females to determine their sex by how they react to the masculine ramming. Incidentally, our female specimen was the victim of some thoughtless fisherman who had thrown overboard a load of fish scraps in a plastic bag. The whale had swallowed the bag, it had impacted the stomach, and the animal had apparently starved to death.

No one knows yet how many species of beaked whales there are.

Cuvier's Beaked Whale

There are at least seven species found in the North Atlantic: Sowerby's beaked whale, Gervais' beaked whale, True's beaked whale, Blainville's beaked whale, Gray's beaked whale, Cuvier's beaked whale, and the northern bottlenose whale. The only one of this lot to have a worldwide distribution is Blainville's, and Gray's is known in the North Atlantic from a single whale stranded in the Netherlands. The only three to strand with anything approaching regularity on the shores of the western mid-Atlantic, especially along the Outer Banks close to the very deep waters these animals inhabit, are Blainville's, True's, and Gervais'.

These animals are fortunate to live solitary existences in offshore waters. They are delicious to eat! Unlike other forms of whale meat, beaked whale holds up well in the freezer, and a two-year-old filet mignon is as choice as a fresh cut. A culinary credo has it that all creatures reflect their diets, and in some instances that is probably true. However, minke meat tastes like veal, not fish, and beaked whale meat tastes like Kobe beef—only better!

There is something pathetic about a stranded sperm whale that goes beyond tragedy for the particular animal. This was the species that made America's reputation in whaling. This is the sole producer of that mysterious unguent, ambergris, and the only whale from which we obtain that unparalleled lubricant, spermaceti oil. This is the creature from whose heavy ivory teeth exquisite scrimshaw ornaments were made, and whose battles with giant squid thousands of feet below the ocean's surface have fascinated storytellers and illustrators. Yet this is also the only species that the national museum does not need to salvage, because the Smithsonian already has crates of material, some of it dating from the heyday of American whaling.

Whereas coastal wreckers and fishermen once fought for the right to salvage a valuable sperm whale carcass, coastal city officials today wring their hands in despair lest they not find anyone willing to remove the smelly and unsightly sperm whale cadaver. Because the life history of the sperm whale is so well known, it is the least interesting of the great whales to science. And because the sperm whale is covered by both the Marine Mammal Protection Act and the U.S. Endangered Species Act, a stranded animal cannot be taken away for rendering. Its teeth can no longer be extracted by carvers or the merely curious, and its oil can no longer be recovered by local entrepreneurs. Swift federal retribution descends on anyone trying to recover a single dollar from the expense of removing the animal.

When the Smithsonian marine mammal program hot line rings, Jim or Charlie tries to identify the species of a stranded animal before they run for the truck. If it is a sperm whale, they tactfully decline, but notify other cetologists and institutions of the availability of the specimen. The Smithsonian researchers' time and their program's funds are too restricted to serve as a waste-disposal service for seaside resorts. Yet what an ironic conclusion to America's long involvement in the history of whaling: that the most sought-after species of the nineteenth century should become *cetacean non grata* in the twentieth century!

The sperm whale family, or Physeteridae, has two other members which most people would never associate with the sixty-ton leviathans of *Moby Dick*. The pigmy sperm whale and the dwarf sperm whale are nonetheless closely related to the great sperm whale, except they do not often exceed 1200 pounds in weight. *Kogia*, as they are known to science, are weird-looking whales with sharklike heads and false gill marks. Their steel-gray backs and white bellies contribute to their sharklike appearance. They probably inhabit most all the oceans of the world, but they normally stay in very deep waters feeding on squid and fish. Still, the pigmy sperm whale is the third most common species to strand after *Tursiops* and the harbor porpoise along the mid-Atlantic coast. Probably more *Kogia* strandings were not reported in earlier decades because people thought these creatures were baby whales of other species or deformed dolphins.

The largest family of whales includes many species that most people don't even consider whales. Delphinidae does include some whale-sized creatures like the pilot whale and killer whale. However, it also includes all the dolphins, while a closely related family, Phocoenidae, includes all the porpoises. And what is the difference between the two?

Actually, the words *porpoise* and *dolphin* are derived from different roots for the same animal. The ancient Minoans and Naboteans

believed these beasts were sacred. The Greeks called them *delphinus,* and Homer said Apollo disguised himself as a dolphin and led a Minoan ship to found the temple at Delphi, birthplace of man and first home of oracles. Aristotle compared dolphins to man and observed that they are born from a womb, take milk from nipples, breathe with lungs, utter a variety of sounds, copulate rather than spawn, and care for their young. Greek sailors venerated the dolphin and felt it criminal to kill one unless a ship's crew faced starvation as the alternative.

The Romans were different. They gave the same creatures the name *porpoise* from *porcus* ("pig") and *piscis* ("fish"). To these inheritors of the Mediterranean, the "sea pig" was simply a more succulent form of seafood. Nowhere is the contrast between ancient Greek and Roman values more striking than in this conflicting view

Bottlenosed Dolphins

of marine mammals. The sensitive Greeks revered them; the sensible Romans ate them.

Sacred and profane. Cetaceans are revered or adopted as pets; they are slaughtered for food and oil or because they compete with man for food fishes. Today, as millennia ago, there seems to be no middle ground. Marine mammals are a moral issue for some, a management issue for others. If history-in-the-making offers only variations on the past, it may be instructive to note that in the ancient world, the people who conceived of porpoises as food prevailed over those who believed dolphins were gods.

When scientists attempted to clarify the porpoise-dolphin dilemma, they unwittingly adhered to ancient distinctions, for as it turns out, those animals scientifically classified as porpoises—namely, beakless members of the *Phocoena* genus, usually small in size with a triangular dorsal fin and spade-shaped teeth—*are* good to eat, whereas dolphins generally are not. *Phocoena phocoena* is the most abundant porpoise on both sides of the North Atlantic. In preindustrial days, this animal, known as the harbor or common porpoise, would ascend tidal rivers for a hundred or more miles. The Indians hunted them, and the Passamaquoddy tribe in Maine still does—but most often the delicious meat is used to feed mink on the Indians' fur farms. In Europe, the diminutive (150 pounds average) harbor porpoise was such popular fare for the nobility that as early as 1098, the Normans restricted the size and number of harbor porpoises to be taken annually. During World War II, meat was so scarce in countries around the Baltic that the once plentiful stocks of common porpoise were extirpated in that brackish sea.

To describe the ten dolphins found in the northwestern Atlantic, including four members of the Family Stenidae, named for the Danish anatomist Nicolaus Steno, would require another chapter without, perhaps, succeeding in evoking the subtle differences between such closely related mammals. Yet one species—the prototypical dolphin—stands out as representative of all the rest.

In the great palace on Crete, a panel of dolphins leaps across the wall in one of the royal rooms. Although the painting is more than 3300 years old, there is no mistaking *Delphinus delphis*. Also called crisscross or saddleback, it is the most common dolphin of all the temperate and tropical deep waters of the world. In the Mediterranean, this was the species that swam before the bows of Minoan and Phoenician freighters, that rescued the musician Arion from

drowning at the hands of pirates, and sailed with King Agamemnon
to war:

> And dolphins, drunken with the lyre,
> Across the dark blue prows, like fire,
> Did bound and quiver,
> To cleave the way for Thetis' son,
> Fleet-in-the-wind Achilles, on
> To war, to war, till Troy be won
> Beside the reedy river.

When Americans think of dolphins, it's Flipper, the coastal
species, *Tursiops truncatus*, that most readily comes to mind. But
Delphinus is the dolphin described by Homer, Herodotus, Euripides
(in the excerpt from *Electra* above), Plato, Aristophanes, and
Lucian. Aesop composed four fables involving this dolphin, and
there are similar legends from Japan and India with *Delphinus* as
the hero.

The common dolphin's beak is narrower than that of the bottlenosed, and its coloration is more beautiful. *Delphinus* is black or
dark brown on the back and white on the belly. On each side there
are bands of gray, yellow, and white. A black ring circles the eye,
and a dark streak runs from it to the snout. Possibly the pelagic
dolphinfish (*Coryphaena* sp.)—even more spectacular with hues of
blue, pink, and green—took its common English name from the
mammal, because each creature bearing this name fades so suddenly and pathetically in death.

Yet, because *Delphinus* is an offshore species, marine mammal
salvagers rarely see its life colors. And because it lives, and therefore,
usually dies far from land, relatively few *Delphinus* ever wash ashore
for salvagers to work on. No more than an average of one *Delphinus*
a year comes ashore between Maine and Florida, and that's, perhaps,
just as well. Watching a great whale expire on a beach is sorrow
enough. Watching an animal electric with life and color yield its
energy to the sucking sands can devastate the human spirit.

9

COASTAL CAROLINA

The Outer Banks of North Carolina are a chain of sand shoals and dunes bulging into the Atlantic and forcing the Gulf Stream away from America toward its next landfall, Ireland. If you are sailing north before benign summer breezes with the Stream swelling beneath your hull, you view the sweeping Cape Hatteras light at night as a grand sight and suspect that disaster tales told about the Banks must be exaggerated. But if you sail too early in the spring or too late in the fall, you may dread that stabbing eye as howling winds and chaotic waves push you inexorably toward the beach.

Travelers ashore do not often experience such violent weather, but enough old-timers on the Outer Banks have been marooned by moving dunes, undermined bridges, and flooded roads to have developed a wary and occasionally fearful regard for these treacherous sands called barrier islands. For every two, three, or four people from elsewhere dreaming of retirement in coastal Carolina, there is at least one native son looking for a way out.

The Banks begin just below the Back Bay National Wildlife Refuge in Virginia and drift into the Atlantic east of Currituck, Roanoke, and Pamlico sounds. Many people don't like to think of *their* Banks as having much to do with the developed areas north of Oregon Inlet, but the sprawl of seaside chalets and instant eateries at Kill Devil Hill and Nags Head is only an elaborate variation on the folly of such towns as Avon and Buxton. The most substantial difference to be found along the Banks is in people's attitudes. Most old-timers accept the fact that periodically the sea gods try to destroy their homes and lives; many come-heres cannot imagine such a thing.

Starting above Oregon Inlet and sweeping south around the Pea Island National Wildlife Refuge and protecting all the coastline dunes and marshes outside a scattering of small towns is the Cape Hatteras National Seashore. It includes Ocracoke Island, and on Portsmouth Island blends into the Cape Lookout National Seashore all the way to Cape Lookout and the Shackleford Banks, terminating south of Beaufort on the mainland. These combined parks protect nearly 150 miles of ocean frontage from the poor judgment of people, for there is nothing any human agency can do in the long run to protect these islands from the sea. National seashores are great concepts partly because they are rooted in humility; they acknowledge we have no other choice but to try to preserve the unpreservable. At least that is more sensible than developing the shifting dunes and eventually losing our investments of asphalt, timber, and even flesh to the sea.

The Outer Banks have tragic connotations of another kind for me. In the fall of 1963, I had made plans to join my younger brother in North Carolina where we would spend his Thanksgiving holiday from Duke hunting waterfowl along the coast. Shortly before I was to catch my flight south from New York, President Kennedy was shot in Texas. This was still a time when many Americans took for granted that history and evolution provided evidence that law and reason would one day prevail over chaos. That was, of course, before we learned that evolution represents only change and accommodation, and sometimes accident, but rarely man-made im-

Flounder Fisherman

provement. And that was before we learned to dream in Vietnamese and wipe the blood of other men from our hands. I wept when I heard the President was dead—not for him, for I never knew him; but for a generation's loss of innocence.

I called my brother and asked if he wanted to cancel the hunt. No; too many wheels had been set in motion. So I flew to North Carolina, and on our way to the coast, a gas station attendant said, "I hope they get the man who did it"—we agreed—"and pin a medal on him." More lost innocence.

The Outer Banks felt far removed from such sleeve-worn hatreds. The people in the little towns knew what had occurred, of course, but an assassination was something foreign to their own daily concern with survival. I learned that islands are good places to restore perspective. And I also learned that November is too early to hunt ducks in North Carolina.

On our last day but one, with barely a buffllehead to our credit, we took the ferry to Ocracoke because we heard the barber there made exquisite miniature decoys. I bought a pair of flying mallards for twenty-five cents and a flying Canada goose for a dime, and we started north just as a squall brought down premature darkness. By the time we passed through Avon, the car was being buffeted by gale-force winds and rain fell through the headlights' glare in nearly horizontal sheets. Then we hit our first washout.

I got out of the car with a flashlight and followed the pavement center line below a foot of white-capped water while Johnny crawled the car behind. At one point, we saw a nutria swim across the highway. In the distance, we could see light diffused and reflected by a low wall of cloud. Finally, I was able to get back into the car, and we drove slowly into the town of Salvo.

A sign at a gas station swung wildly in the wind, but we parked out of range of its potential fall and prepared to stay the night. We supposed—correctly, as it turned out—that the ocean had reclaimed the road through the Pea Island National Wildlife Refuge while we were more or less safe on a slight rise of land two or three feet above the raging sea. Although Salvo looked deserted, we assumed somebody lived there, and just as we were snuggling down under all our hunting clothes—for the night had turned suddenly cold—a man rapped on the driver's-side window.

"You boys look cramped in there!" he yelled above the wind. "Come inside and have some coffee!"

He was E. Burgess Hooper, the owner of the gas station and

now the proprietor of the Salvo Inn Motel. Before the evening was over, he had fed us and moved his son out of his room onto the living-room couch and put us in his son's bed. The next morning he gave us breakfast, offered to have his son take us goose hunting— "It's always good after a blow"—and dismissed any suggestion that we could pay him for any part of the rescue. My brother and I became so immersed in Hooper's life at the edge of the sea that had the Kennedy murder been mentioned by a visiting neighbor, it would have been as remote for us as the Outer Banks were for the rest of the world.

Many other storms have swept across the Banks since November 1963, but the permanent population has recklessly doubled and the seasonal population increased manyfold. Problems of use and abuse of this unstable land have cropped up in the past two decades that were not even conceivable in the early 1960s. One is the advent of thousands of ORVs, or off-road vehicles. Of course, there is nothing new under the sun: the first car that ever appeared south of Oregon Inlet automatically became an ORV, because no paved roads were built there until after World War II. From the beginning, such vehicles helped accelerate the islands' normal pace of erosion.

In 1941, there were fewer than a hundred beach buggies along the Outer Banks, whereas today more than a hundred thousand such vehicles annually use the thirty-nine miles of shoreline specifically set aside for ORVs on Cape Hatteras National Seashore. Rather than drive from point A to point B for fishing or birding, too many ORV operators want to "bust dunes." Four-wheel-drive systems and special tires rarely make it necessary for such drivers to leave their air-conditioned and often stereo-equipped interiors, and although only 1 percent of all national seashore visitors are ORV visitors, they mar the landscape for others and even threaten the foundations of the islands themselves.

Concerned about increasing offroad vehicle use, the National Park Service began a five-year research program in 1974 under the direction of marine scientists Stephen P. Leatherman and Paul J. Godfrey to measure the effect of ORV use on coastal ecosystems. The studies confirmed conservationists' worst fears. Of all the coastal zones, only the intertidal ocean beach was not severely degraded by the passage of ORVs. Some crustacea and shellfish are destroyed, and feeding and/or resting birds may be harried. But since this is the least stable portion of a barrier island, physical damage is repaired daily by the tides.

However, on the high beach and through the dunes, the presence of ORVs can be disastrous. Their tires churn the "drift line" of flotsam and jetsam left on the beach by high water. This detritus contains seeds and roots of beach grass which, on unimpacted beaches, colonizes the upper tidal areas and helps stabilize the seaward foundation of dunes with new plants generated even from rhizome fragments. On ORV-visited beaches, only fifty passes by vehicles are needed to obliterate all seaward growth of the beach grass, and dunes in such areas tend to be lower and migrate westerly more readily, crossing roads and suffocating maritime woodlands behind the dunes.

Drs. Leatherman and Godfrey concluded that "there is no 'carrying capacity' for vehicular impact on coastal systems. Even low-level impacts can result in severe environmental degradation."

Possibly the most important parts of their research were recommendations on how to minimize the impact of ORVs when they

Off-Road Vehicles

do cross dunes. Paul Godfrey is himself an active ORV user, and he feels a complete ban of such vehicles is neither sensible nor enforceable. However, he stresses that trails should be designed to minimize steep grades and sharp turns, and wooden ramps must be placed over dune crests. Furthermore, the crossing sites should be periodically relocated to minimize the possibility of dune "blowouts" and to permit old tracks to be revegetated. Only a few passes by an ORV will obliterate such stabilizing vegetation as hairgrass and beach heather, and revegetation takes a minimum of four years and sometimes as long as ten.

Yet how many new dune crossings must be designed annually, and at what cost, to preserve Cape Hatteras National Seashore from the ever-waiting wind and sea? And what of Cape Lookout National Seashore? It represents 87 percent of the roadless public land in North Carolina's 308 miles of barrier island coast with only a handful of park personnel to ride herd on countless dune busters. More

than 2500 vehicles have been abandoned there, and more derelicts are due so long as the permit system enables people to buy one-way tickets to the islands for their clunkers. Although federal taxpayers have been saddled with the cost of hauling out the old cars, the Cape Lookout General Management Plan (May 1980) concedes that "it is difficult to collect all the rusty and salt-corroded parts and other debris that is [sic] buried in the dunes and scattered along the beach berm."

Female loggerhead turtles and even rarer leatherback turtles haul themselves ashore to lay eggs. Some become disoriented amid the deeply rutted trails and derelict vehicles on Shackleford and Core banks. A few cannot find the sea again and die. Of the 162 female sea turtles that crawled ashore in the summer of 1979, only 72 succeeded in nesting, and several of these nests were later compacted by passing vehicles so the hatchling turtles were unable to dig their way to the surface. Rather than be allowed to create such hazards to turtle survival, ORV owners should be briefed, and some even deputized, by Park Service personnel to protect the turtles from thoughtless or outlaw visitors who would confuse the nesting animals at night with too many strobe-lit photographs or even steal their eggs. Most everyone finds the threatened Family Chelonidae fascinating and would like to help save sea turtles. However, present Park Service policy treats the public like children and does nothing to convert their curiosity into an ongoing campaign to protect and restore turtle nesting habitat.

After ORVs, the greatest controversy on Cape Hatteras National Seashore is the proposed $114 million jetties for Oregon Inlet. In a classic case of wishful thinking cutting against the grain of environmental reality, the North Carolina legislature spent more than $8 million developing a seafood "industrial park"* at Wanchese not far inside Oregon Inlet. If this passage to the sea were in a rock-ribbed setting, the Wanchese fleet of more than fifty commercial fishing boats would be ideally situated by latitude for the most productive winter trawling off the entire Atlantic coast. Unfortunately, however, Oregon Inlet is composed of as much shifting sand as water, and the Army Corps of Engineers spends over $600,000 annually, but principally during the fall and winter, just to keep the inlet open.

Corps spokesmen argue that spending $114 million for a pair

* This phrase, "industrial park," is perhaps the best example of a contradiction of terms in the English language.

of jetties will save money in the long run, because the inlet will be stabilized, and there will be no need for further dredging. However, conservationists point to Murrells Inlet, South Carolina, where millions of dollars were spent on a similar but smaller pair of jetties, and where annual dredging is still necessary to move the ever-migrating sands from one side of the channel to the other. Furthermore, although army accountants justify the proposed $114 million expenditure as "an investment that will pay dividends to the year 2100," conservationists point out that land subsidence and a rising sea mean that much of the Outer Banks may be moved, if not drowned, within a century's time, leaving the jetties behind as curious mementos to twentieth-century man's ignorance about the workings of nature.

Not everyone who sides with nature in this dispute is opposed to the jetties. Some people accept the plan even though they know it is exorbitant and doomed to long-run failure. Although the jetties will aggravate shoaling in Pamlico Sound and accelerate erosion along the beach, especially south of the inlet on the Pea Island National Wildlife Refuge, a good many birders and recreational fishermen are looking forward to seeing new species of fish and wildlife drawn to the matched pair of artificial peninsulas. Purple sandpipers, eiders, and even harlequin ducks may appear, just as tautog, sea bass, and increasing numbers of drum, sea trout, and other

Purple Sandpiper

Peregrine Falcon

Sciaenidae will almost certainly take advantage of the massive boulder habitat.

Even without jetties, the Outer Banks are a birder's paradise. In October 1979, I fished with several executives of the National Wildlife Federation for king mackerel off Oregon Inlet. Driving north in the afternoon, we counted sixteen peregrine falcons sweeping down the dunes or sitting on telephone poles, including four birds in sight at one time. We didn't know then that this was part of the greatest peregrine migration ever recorded, with more than fifty birds seen on Cape Hatteras National Seashore during the weekend.

The birder who will most benefit from the proposed Oregon Inlet breakwaters is that most recondite of the breed: the pelagic birder. His pride is in noting species that cannot usually be seen from shore. When Henry T. Armistead, the Middle Atlantic coast regional editor for *American Birds,* saw glaucous gulls and an Iceland gull on the Outer Banks one recent New Year's Eve, his sighting of such exotic fare was disappointing to some open ocean colleagues who feel that Harry and his fellow observers should have been suffering more than seated in heated cars across the street from the restaurant where they had just eaten breakfast. A pelagic birder doesn't feel he has earned a rare sighting unless it has caused him some pain.

However, the first birders to go down to the sea in ships were not suburbanites sliding over the slippery decks of rolling headboats, but commercial fishermen who reckoned that their knowledge of the birds' feeding habits would enhance their own ability to catch fish. Even in today's electronic world, when fishermen's boats are outfitted with loran, depth recorders, surface-water temperature gauges, and other aids to navigation and fish location, old-timers cling to their practical knowledge of sea signs. They may not know the scientific names of the birds they see—or even much about their breeding habits or migrations—but the fishermen know when they should expect to see certain species and with what fishes each bird associates.

Beginning in the nineteenth century, when naturalists such as John James Audubon, Charles Darwin, and Thomas Huxley began to take their thoughtful curiosity to sea, our knowledge of more than the feeding habits of pelagic birds began to grow. Audubon collected and studied birds on his trip along the Florida coast to Key West in 1831, and Huxley did the same during his cruise along Australia's Great Barrier Reef in 1848. Their work was carried into the present century by such men as Charles William Beebe and Robert Cushman Murphy. Writing sixty years ago while aboard a steamship bound for British Guiana from New York, Beebe refers to "the amusing terrestrial instincts" of his fellow passengers who encase themselves "in the angular cocoons furnished for the purpose at one dollar each by the deck steward" and then "hibernate" for the duration of the voyage without taking the least interest in the sea around them.

By contrast, Beebe swung grapple irons to snag clumps of sargasso weed so he could fill collecting jars with the many fish species and crustacea which live in its fronds; he rigged a lady's silk stocking over the nozzle of the saltwater bath faucet in his cabin to collect plankton; and he climbed down onto the anchor so he could get closer to marine mammals surfing on the bow wave.

Mostly Beebe spent his time aboard ship in the crow's nest studying birds. He not only identified them but tried to understand how different species were adapted to different niches within the unstable environment of the open ocean. He learned that each niche is based largely on what each species eats and how it is peculiarly adapted to take food from the sea. At one end of the scale, there are the tiny

Storm Petrels

storm petrels daintily "walking" across the surface and plucking plankton from the film. At the other end are the great, gliding albatrosses, feeding mostly at night when they snatch squid seemingly drawn to the starlight overhead.

Thanks to the efforts of such observers, modern pelagic birders see not just the shearwater sweeping over the waves, perhaps trailing an outermost primary as its name implies, we understand the function of the bulge at the base of the bird's bill which enables such "tube-nosed" avifauna to excrete sodium chloride so their blood systems do not become saturated with salt.

We know how to distinguish the yellow-billed Cory's shearwater from the black-billed and black-capped greater shearwater, and our imaginations carry us to Bermuda and the Bahamas where the small Audubon's shearwater—popularly named for the naturalist who first collected this bird in the Florida Straits—breeds in rocky crevices or under heavy vegetation.

Although Beebe, Roger Tory Peterson, and many thousands of thoughtful birdmen and -women have facilitated our ability to identify pelagic birds and to answer most questions about their morphology, we still need to learn much more about their behavior and interspecific relationships. The British and Scandinavians have always been better at this sort of thing than Americans, who seem to feel that we've said most of what needs to be said about any subject once it has been counted or measured. Numbers are certainly useful tools in telling us *what* is happening, but they are not always helpful when it comes to *why*.

In the early 1920s, Poul Jespersen, a biologist aboard the Danish *Dana* expeditions in search of the breeding grounds of the *Anguilla* eel,* studied the correlation of seabird species and numbers to planktonic densities in the North Atlantic. In 1933, British ornithologist V. C. Wynne-Edwards repeatedly crossed the Atlantic aboard a passenger liner to learn how seabird species and numbers vary over the course of a summer and between one oceanic region and another. By contrast, half a century ago, American biologists thought of marine life exclusively in terms of creatures that live *in* the sea, while American ornithologists thought of seabirds only in terms of their terrestrial breeding habitat.†

Ecologist Rod Hennessey, manager of The Nature Conservancy's Virginia Coast Reserve, recalls being in a boat one wintry day with a group of marine biologists when a peregrine falcon suddenly appeared over the grass chasing a bufflehead that barely made it to the water by flying, not diving, into it.

"Wow! Did you see that?" yelled Rod. "Sensational!"

"What's he so excited about?" an oyster specialist asked a sea-worm man.

"I dunno," replied the sea-wormer. "Just a couple of birds chasing one another."

I have had comparable experiences with marine ornithologists. One day I was with a friend and birder off an Atlantic inlet when we discovered what Canadian researcher G. B. Brown calls a "tidal pump," in which swift currents moving over an abrupt rise in the bottom tumble a variety of sea life to the surface. The air was full of diving, screaming terns and gulls. Large predatory fish were attacking the bait from below, but after trying two or three different lures from my tackle box, I still hadn't got a strike. I asked my friend who was watching the spectacle with binoculars to see if he could make out what kind of bait the birds were feeding on so I could improvise a facsimile.

---

* Although no one has yet seen eels breed or found their eggs, a Danish marine biologist with the help of nearly thirty Danish merchant skippers willing to tow plankton nets for half-hour intervals in midocean shipping lanes finally tracked down the eels' spawning grounds in the Sargasso Sea south of Bermuda.

† By nesting on pack ice, rather than land, the Emperor penguin becomes the only wholly marine bird species extant.

With genuine disgust, my birding friend said, "How can you think about fish at a time like this?"

Seabirds never stop thinking about fish. However, as human populations continue to swell beyond reasonable bounds, increasing numbers of entrepreneurs are turning to marine fishes as low-investment (no breeding, feeding, or housing requirements) sources of protein. Since most of these entrepreneurs know little enough about the marine species they seek to exploit, it is absurd to imagine they know or care much about the seabirds that are dependent on these very same aquatic species for their existence.

Yet there is at least one pelagic bird species that has done well in the context of man's increasing exploitation of the seas. In a world in which *millions* of seabirds die annually in the nets of fishermen or in the oil slicks of merchant mariners, many birders are thrilled to learn that the northern fulmar has a worldwide population growth of almost 7 percent, compounded annually. The fulmar's success seems to imply that we must be doing something right if such a wild ingredient—unlike the semidomestic gulls at our dumps or rats in our sewers—is flourishing on a planet we dominate.

Unfortunately, exaggerated growth of even apparently healthy cells must be categorized as cancer, whether they flourish in the microcosm of the human body or in the macrocosm of the planet. All species seek to inherit the earth, but nature's infinite wisdom lies in its diversity of predators, parasites, diseases, and even accidents that keep any one species from overpowering the others. The fulmar's mushrooming population is neither proof that some wild species can flourish despite people's omnipresence on earth, nor that the seas are still unimpacted by our activities. The case of the fulmar is one for concern, not celebration.

In the western Atlantic, fulmars are the first seabirds to begin the breeding cycle each year. Some pairs arrive in Newfoundland in December to set up housekeeping on cliffs and ledges overlooking the sea not far from where that cold ocean's version of the pelican, the gannet, finished fledging its young only a few short months earlier. The entire nesting effort of each pair of fulmars consists of a single egg. If a gull finds it, or if it is accidentally tumbled from the slight depression in which it sits and falls to the rocks or sea below, the female fulmar will not replace it. Considering this, the rigorous season they start nesting, and the fact that fulmars do not normally begin breeding until their seventh year, nothing natural helped make

Fulmars in two color phases: gray and white, and all gray

this species flourish so that literally millions of pairs occupy the wintry sea cliffs of Newfoundland, southern Greenland, and Baffin Island.

Like the herring gull, the mallard, and the starling, the northern fulmar has become one of the most abundant bird species on earth because of us, not despite us. As early as the seventeenth century when whaling activities spread into the North Atlantic, the scavenging fulmar began expanding its numbers and range. During the past four hundred years, whalers have noted, and several have described in their ships' logs, the characteristic gliding flight, occasional rapid wingbeats, and peculiar chuckle of these otherwise gull-like birds as they planed over the waves picking up scraps of blubber and offal.

Today, whaling activities have all but ceased in the North Atlantic, but huge factory-fishing fleets from a dozen nations are busy gleaning every fish, crab, and squid they can find on the continental shelves. The waste products from the gutting and packaging of these animals is flushed over the ships' sides in a constant stream of food for fulmars and other Procellariiformes (tube-nosed birds).

We have nearly overreached the North Atlantic's capacity to

sustain us. Inevitably, the oceanic food web will unravel, and fulmar populations will collapse. Yet when that time comes, we will be too concerned with our own predicament to give much thought to such human-dependent scavengers as the fulmar. In the long run we will probably treat this species the way we treated all large birds before the Golden Age of Northern Europe and North America: we will gather its eggs and kill its adults for food.

Most of the seabirds seen regularly off the Outer Banks breed on distant coasts. For example, the Manx shearwater breeds in burrows on the sea islands of Northern Europe with a very few western Atlantic records including Massachusetts. Once fledged, some of the juveniles join adult shearwaters off Hatteras where schools of yellowfin tuna and pods of white marlin push squid and baitfish to the surface where the birds can reach them. In winter, after most pelagic fishes have retreated from the Carolinas to the Caribbean, mature Manx shearwaters return to Scotland or Norway to continue the breeding cycle.

The Manx shearwater shares its nesting ground with puffins and petrels which arrive in April, usually to find the best burrows already taken by the shearwaters. In most cases, the puffins and petrels dig side tunnels off the shearwater burrows, but in a few cases, when the shearwater goes to sea for ten days or two weeks to build up fat reserves for the ordeal of egg incubation, a newly arrived puffin or petrel will expropriate the shearwater burrow, egg and all.

Puffins differ from shearwaters and petrels in that the "sea parrots" are diurnally active so that their peers and other birds will see their distinctive plumage complete with broadly red-tipped bills and orange feet. By contrast, even when the weather is foggy or stormy, the drab shearwaters and petrels will fish throughout the night and find their burrows again before dawn. If one of a pair of Manx shearwaters does not return before first light, it relies on its mate to incubate the egg or brood the chick until the following night. Shearwaters are so awkward on land, it is safer for them to spend the daylight hours soaring over the sea and occasionally swooping down for a young herring than to return ashore and run the risk not only of betraying the burrow's location but of being torn apart by a black-backed gull before the shearwater can shuffle out of sight.

Such avoidance of the coast during the daylight hours does not mean that Manx shearwaters are casual parents. When one was removed from its British burrow and flown to Boston, Massachusetts, and released, the bird was back on its nest twelve nights later. The shearwater's nocturnal nesting routine is predicated on the black-backed gull's diurnal dining schedule. During their overlapping breeding seasons, blackbacks prey on shearwaters to such an extent that in one British study, only 21 percent of the waste near the nests of black-backed gulls consisted of fish. The rest were a few rabbits' bones and hundreds of Manx shearwater skins. The gulls catch the shearwaters just before dawn when they try to sneak back to their burrows, or on moonlit nights, and so furiously shake the prey, the shearwaters' skins are turned inside out. In 1957 on Skokholm Island off the coast of Wales, 2536 Manx shearwater skins were found near just twenty-seven nests of great black-backed gulls. Five years later, after most of the gulls had been destroyed in an effort to keep the shearwater colony active, 646 skins still ended up in the vicinity of the five surviving pairs of blackbacks. Although the lesser black-backed gull is not as large as his great cousin, he is as rapacious, and it is disconcerting to thoughtful American ornithologists that just as the great black-backed gull is extending his breeding range south along the western Atlantic coast, the European-nesting lesser black-backed gull is wintering with increasing regularity along our shores.

However, there is a pelagic predator even more fierce than the black-backed gulls. Although the wingspan of a great black-backed gull is twice that of a skua, this falconlike seabird will swarm down on a flying blackback and buffet it with its wings to force the gull to land so the skua can blind the blackback and then eat it. Sometimes the skua is itself injured in the ferocity of its onslaught, and other skuas will then attack and tear apart their handicapped brethren.

Unlike the closely related jaegers, which make their livings by harrying terns and black-legged kittiwakes until they disgorge or drop the fish they have caught, skuas will feed directly on other birds and particularly on puffins and young kittiwakes on their breeding grounds. Skuas have two methods for taking puffins: one requiring patience, the other requiring speed. The skua will wait to one side of the entrance of a puffin burrow and ambush the unsuspecting bird when it emerges for its daily feeding flight. Or the skua will stoop on a gathering of puffins and force the panicked birds into the air. The skua then selects one bird as its victim, pursues it like a falcon, but captures the puffin with its beak, rather than with its relatively weak feet.

Skua attacking Puffins

Two skua species can be seen off the Outer Banks. In the fall and winter, the great skua sweeps down from its nesting range in the subarctic regions of the North Atlantic. Over the open ocean on its way south, the great skua continues to hunt puffins and the closely related dovekie. These Alcidae escape by diving, and skuas may be one reason no alcid spends much time on the wing after it leaves the breeding cliffs.

Once skuas leave their nesting range, they are more inclined to exploit the fishing skills of other large seabirds than kill them. That way the gulls and shearwaters provide fish and squid on a sustained-yield basis. When the great skua moves north in the spring to breed, the south polar skua sometimes appears off the Outer Banks from its nesting grounds in the Antarctic. Since both skuas are about the same size and color,* a zealous bird counter might be able to claim a south polar skua for his life list if he sees a skua off North Carolina during the summer months when great skuas should be in the Arctic. However, not all individuals of any species follow rules of convenience promulgated by man, and the wise birder simply says "skua."

Although most pelagic birders are generalists, interested in any and all species that fly by, as with any human activity, there are

---

* They are built like a stocky herring gull but fly like a fighter plane. Both are dark with white wing patches, but the south polar skua sometimes has a blond color phase.

specialists. One of the most interesting of these is the individual obsessed with esoteric "firsts"—his first white-tailed tropic bird, for example, sighted off North Carolina. This sport is for professional birders only, those who have or are aspiring for a *reputation*. For instance, although sooty terns have been "confirmed" off the coasts of North Carolina and Maryland, none have yet been documented off Virginia. That is, none have been seen by people whose impeccable birding credentials make such sightings official.

Of course, sooty terns have been seen by a goodly number of amateur birders off Virginia. However, because the gospel according to Chandler S. Robbins, Bertel Bruun, and Herbert S. Zim (who collectively created one of the continent's best field guides) states unequivocally that sooty terns are "seen on Atlantic and Gulf coasts only during hurricanes," even some top-seeded birders who spot a sooty tern under different conditions will not trust their eyes. Unless a hurricane is blowing, has just blown, or is about to blow, the black-backed, fork-tailed tern without a white collar* thirty yards off the bow just *can't* be a sooty tern!

Offshore birding expeditions are available from Bar Harbor, Maine—where the ferry to Yarmouth, Nova Scotia, features sightings of Alcidae, especially puffins, murres, and black guillemots—to Key West, Florida, where you may spot a red-footed booby or sooty terns and brown noddies fishing east of their breeding colony at Dry Tortugas.

Oregon Inlet trips offer wonderful proximity to the Gulf Stream, and you are at the southern extreme of some Arctic birds' ranges and the northern extreme of some tropical species' wanderings. For example, the greater shearwater is usually a bird of cool temperate waters well north of the Gulf Stream, while the Cory's shearwater prefers the warmer waters on the edge or within the Stream. Off the Outer Banks, however, it is not unusual to see both species during the same day's trip at any time between May and October.

Unusual varieties like the band-rumped storm petrel, white-faced storm petrel, little shearwater, and South Trinidad petrel have all been seen off North Carolina, and there is always the chance that

---

* A white collar helps distinguish the bridled tern which, to confuse matters, Roger Tory Peterson in his most recent revision of A *Field Guide to the Birds* suggests is *the* tropical tern to be looked for after hurricanes. This bird appears regularly, with or without hurricanes, along the edge of the Gulf Stream as far north as Cape Hatteras.

your particular expedition will be blessed with that most magnificent of all seabird sightings, an albatross, coasting on flexed, seven-foot wings which are never flapped once during the twenty minutes or so of turns, sweeps, and circles the bird makes of your wallowing hull.

If there are no pelagic birding trips advertised in the port from which you'd like to sail, ask around. Most fishing guides are in the business because they love the sea. Most will respect your enthusiasm for seabirds, and all of them will appreciate the opportunity to earn some extra money, particularly if it is during a slow season for angling. The more people you can persuade to go, the cheaper will be everybody's portion.

Mid-October. Five ruddy turnstones zigzagged down from the sky over Myrtle Beach, South Carolina. Dodging an Air Force jet practicing takeoffs and landings on a runway southwest of the city, the birds darted toward the boulder jetty jaws of Murrells Inlet.

The turnstones had flown nonstop from the huge breakwaters at Lewes, Delaware, covering five hundred miles in less than thirteen hours. Four days earlier, they had run and probed on groins and jetties near Belmar, New Jersey, and the week before that, this same group of turnstones had found food hidden in the folds and fissures of the Chicago harbor breakwater.

The birds had been late leaving their summering habitat near Hudson Bay, and, weeks behind the main movement of shorebirds down the Atlantic Flyway, each new northwest wind with the faintest taste of snow had swept them from Canada to the mid-Atlantic coast and beyond. The first week of December would find them on the north jetty at Stuart Inlet, Florida, and the birds would spend Christmas Day near the old turtle pens on Grand Cayman Island.

In the meanwhile, Indian summer weather and an abundance of food would persuade the turnstones to linger at Murrells Inlet. Although the birds had already lost the crisscross blacks, russets, and white plumage of spring and summer, they were not quite in the drab brown uniform of winter. Thus, the birds looked like nothing ever illustrated in a field guide—except for the legs and feet. Their bright orange color signaled "turnstone," even if their restless behavior and undistinguished body color said only "shorebird."

As soon as the turnstones landed, they began picking at the barnacles and sea lettuce exposed by low tide. Three dozen fishermen were scattered along the inside of the south jetty waiting for the

Turnstones in their fall plumage

tide to start in and bring some sea trout, spottail bass, and southern
flounder to their cut baits. Most of the fishermen ignored the birds,
but one small boy threw a slice of bread to the turnstones, thinking
they would attack the oversize food as gulls do. The turnstones took
off in a burst of indignant "tuk-a-tuks" and flitted across the water
to the unpaved north-side jetty where there were no fishermen. The
birds landed in a group but immediately scattered to give each individual more foraging room.

Don Millus and I sat in his fourteen-foot aluminum boat within
comfortable casting range of the jetty and tossed soft plastic lures
into the shallow, surging sea around the rocks. The turnstones
trotted and pecked within the sloppy undulations of the water's edge.
Like children playing a game to see who could get closest without
also getting wet, the birds hopped from rock to rock and ran after
retreating panes of water to pluck unseen life from below the molten
surface before leaping sideways onto other rocks to avoid spray washing over the boulders they had just left. A person on the rocks might
have frightened the birds. However, shorebirds perceive that danger
comes only from the beach behind them or the sky above. Hence,
the turnstones only fluttered from one rock to another when one
of our lures plopped too close.

Ornithologists have known for over a century that many shorebirds, including the yellowlegs, woodcock, and that most impressive

of shorebird wanderers, the golden plover, will proceed along elliptic migration routes to take advantage of the ocean's moderating influence which keeps coastal areas warmer and ice-free longer in the autumn and cooler longer in the spring. Hence, even the woodcock, least shore-bound of shorebirds, will drift to the coast from interior nesting grounds north of the Great Lakes and New England and congregate at Cape May, New Jersey, or Cape Charles, Virginia, before the majority of adults angle over the mountains to prime wintering areas in Louisiana and Mississippi. Other woodcock, mostly juveniles, will stay along the coast where they are invariably inventoried by Christmas birders from Myrtle Beach to northern Florida before joining their elders for the main spring flight up the Mississippi and Ohio valleys.

Likewise, both species of yellowlegs will winter along the southeastern Atlantic coast, while some specimens of the greater yellowlegs will linger as far north as the edges of Long Island Sound. But when spring comes, these hardy birds will sometimes fly southwest to join yellowlegs moving up the Mississippi Flyway before the combined flocks fan out across northern Canada.

As for the golden plover, you may be lucky to see a few in the fall coursing over an Atlantic beach on their way to South America, but you have almost certainly seen its larger cousin, the black-bellied plover, if you see within easy flight of the coast in the spring a black-necked (the color change from drab winter plumage begins with

Woodcock and Christmas Fern

that portion of the anatomy) and black-breasted shorebird that runs in short starts and stops like a robin.

One recent May, wildlife artist Ned Smith and I saw several thousand black-bellied plover in fields on the Eastern Shore of Virginia. It never occurred to us to question whether there might be a golden plover in the flocks. The careful observations of thousands of birders before us assured us that by May most every golden plover was already over midwestern Canada on its way to the tundra and Arctic islands where black-bellied plovers would shortly join the goldens via the coastal route.

I had managed to catch three spottail bass before Don got his first strike. Up until that point, Don referred to me as the guest whom he wanted to show a good time. Then, "Whoopee! I've got him, Reiger! Oh, boy, this is no puny spottail! Look at him go! Look at him roll! Come on, Reiger, get with the program! This is a trout, a winter trout! Get the net! Don't bungle the job! Ah! One of these is worth four of your spottails!"

The most enthusiastic of outdoorsmen never grow up, at least not that part of them that loves the outdoors. Don served as an army officer in Vietnam before completing his doctoral thesis in Renaissance literature at Yale University. He has had his fill of sophistication and knows it has no place on a fishing trip. He has also had his fill of pretension from marine scientists who sound more knowledgeable than they are.

"Here along the Grand Strand," said this associate professor at Coastal Carolina College, exulting over his four-pound catch, "this is a winter trout, to be distinguished from the summer trout which Virginians call gray trout, New Jersey anglers call weakfish, Long Islanders call tiderunners, and New Englanders call squeteague. South of us, the summer trout has no common name because it doesn't exist.

"Ah, but our winter trout is found right around into the Gulf of Mexico where it is called speckled trout, which confuses New Englanders because that's their name for the brook trout, which sometimes runs to the sea and is called a salter. Meanwhile most everybody else calls our winter trout the spotted sea trout. And this is to distinguish it from a smaller and unspotted sea trout with the same range called the silver or white trout. Finally, British visitors would call none of these fishes 'sea trout' because that's their common name for sea-run brown trout.

"Biologists laugh at fishermen for having so many confusing

names for the same fish. Yet the biologists themselves are still trying to figure out what Latin names to apply to a good many species. Just a few years ago, they took the striped bass out of the genus *Roccus* and turned him into a *Morone* which, as far as I'm concerned, makes a fine fish sound dumb. But best of all, our local flounders give them fits!"

Dr. Richard Moore, Coastal Carolina's dean of the School of Sciences, an ichthyologist and an active birder, reluctantly agrees. "Taxonomic debate among fisheries experts is probably not as intense as it is among bird experts, because ichthyology attracts fewer amateurs with just enough knowledge to confuse issues. However, our taxonomic arguments are probably more complex, because there are so many more fish species than birds. For example, there are more flounder species in the world—five hundred or so—than there are birds in eastern North America. Remember that flounders represent only a very few fish families while American birds comprise everything from loons and eagles to warblers and hummingbirds. Furthermore, while it is a rare event to find a new bird species, the discovery of a new fish species, or an unexpected range extension for a known species, is almost a monthly event."

The difficulty of classifying the humble flounder begins with the question of how many New World families exist. Some experts say six. Others lump halibuts and flukes in with Pleuronectidae (the whiffs and sand dabs) to come up with four. The "splitters" (scientists favoring six flounder families) argue that the behavior and habitat of halibuts and flukes have little in common with those of whiffs and sand dabs, while the "lumpers" (scientists desiring to streamline marine taxonomy) insist that there is really only one

Spotted Sea Trout

significant difference between most flatfishes: some are "right-handed" (Pleuronectidae) and some are "left-handed" (Bothidae).

What this means is that while all flounder larvae start out looking and swimming like other fishes, the right eyes of Bothidae move around to join their left eyes as the fish take up their side-to-bottom juvenile and adult postures. As you look down on such fish, so their left side corresponds to your own, the mouth of these flounders is, or seems to be, on the left. Just the reverse is true of Pleuronectidae.

One would have more sympathy with the lumpers' perspective if their left-handed and right-handed generalizations were foolproof or even evolutionarily significant. Unfortunately, however, varying percentages of every species in both families include individuals with eyes on the side opposite to that on which they are supposed to be found. Now the lumpers are quick to reassure you that "internally, these reversed individuals can still properly be placed, for in the left-eyed Bothidae the nerve of the right eye is always dorsal and the reverse is always true in the right-eyed Pleuronectidae" (James S. Böhlke and Charles C. G. Chaplin). But such internal distinctions don't do the ordinary angler much good. As it is, he is inclined to separate flatfish into only two "families": those that can be caught on hook and line and, therefore, are large enough to eat; and those so small they can only be caught in nets but are occasionally used as live bait.

Into this live-bait category go tonguefish of the Family Cynoglossidae. This species is not uncommon between North Carolina and Florida, but scientists know very little about its life history. Bait fishermen know that it grows up to eight inches long and that they sometimes catch one while cast-netting mullet in coastal estuaries.

The equally small hogchoker flounder, which is found from Massachusetts Bay to Panama and was one of the species that did well in our Naval Academy aquariums, is frequently caught by bait fishermen seining for silversides. A little more is known about its life history because of its success in fresh, brackish, or saltwater laboratory tanks. However, scientists still argue about whether it should be in the general family of soles, Achiridae, or the more specialized broadsole family, Soleidae.

Of greater interest to coastal Carolina anglers is the fact that the northern fluke, southern fluke, Gulf flounder, and four-spotted fluke can all be taken off Carolina beaches and in Carolina inlets. Even the sundial or windowpane flounder occurs here, although it runs generally smaller than its occasional two-pound New England cousins. Well offshore in waters down to four hundred feet, the halibutlike *Paralichthys squamilentus* offers sport and fine flavor in weights up to twenty and thirty pounds. This fish is distinguished not only by its hefty size but its gray to black underside.

Just as some flounders have reversed eyes, a certain percentage are ambicolored, which means that their normally white ventral and dark dorsal sides, or portions thereof, are reversed. Significantly, many reversed-eyed flounders also have ambicoloration. Such specimens are sometimes thrown back by fishermen who think that such strangely pigmented creatures must be diseased. Likewise, the southern fluke that swim several dozen miles from the Carolina coast up the freshwater Waccamaw River to be entrained by the Grainger Steam Plant's cooling system and pumped into Lake Busbee bewilder fishermen who imagine they have hooked a deformed crappie!

Since the usual definition of commercial value includes only those fishes caught for sale by professional fishermen, many species which are of far greater aesthetic and even dollar value do not come in for their fair share of the research pie. For example, much more money is spent by rod-and-reel fishermen catching flounders than can possibly be earned by trawlermen netting and selling flatfish. In the economic scheme of things, because it takes fewer flatfish to make a recreational angler happy than it does to pay the bills of a commercial dragger, and because each flounder is, therefore, worth so much more as a recreational resource than as food alone, the recreational fisherman should be the entity for whom this resource is managed and research moneys dispersed.

But bureaucracies are only impressed by statistics, and we have few firm numbers concerning recreational angling anywhere along the Atlantic coast. In order to shake lose federal Sea Grant funds to study the parasite, *Trypanoplasma bullocki*, which attacks and ultimately kills young northern fluke, ichthyologists at Virginia's Institute of Marine Science had to stress that the flounder was "the most important food finfish" commercially caught in the commonwealth. Yet the ten million or less pounds of flounder annually taken in commercial nets in Virginia are only a fraction of the flounder caught in that state on rod and reel. And if sustained yield is the ultimate objective of all resource management, many marine fishes would find not only their highest economic value as game fishes, they would be managed more effectively at the recreational level, because recreational fishermen can release undersize fish while trawlermen necessarily kill most everything they scoop up in their enormous mesh sacks.

Unfortunately, marine recreational anglers in the Atlantic do not buy a license to fish. As a result, there is no revenue for research pertaining to the few exclusively marine recreational fishes—like Florida's snook or South Carolina's striped bass—unless the money comes out of the already overburdened freshwater fisherman's license fees. Because there is no such thing as a recreational fishing license in the Atlantic, we don't even know how many coastal fishermen there are. Some estimates say no more than eight million; others go as high as twenty-two million! To date the ocean has been a commons which everybody uses but for which no one is responsible. A recreational fishing license would not only help remedy this impossible situation, it might help stimulate a more thoughtful view of the sea's awesome but strangely fragile diversity so that a few more amateurs might join the thin ranks of those already involved in oceanic research. Ichthyological amateurs have already contributed much to our understanding of fish migrations. There is no reason why amateurs should not, also, be able to expand our knowledge of the life histories of fishes with funny names like sundial, sand dab, whiff, and fluke.

10

CHARLESTON'S BIRDS

Charleston, South Carolina, has just one association for those unfamiliar with Charleston history: It is the place where the Civil War —or as it is more often called in the South, the War Between the States—began.

Yet before that war, Charleston rivaled Boston and Philadelphia as cultural wellsprings in the New World. Distinguished visitors to America might miss money-mad New York or muddy, muddled Washington, but they passed up no opportunity to sail to salubrious Charleston.

When William Makepeace Thackeray began writing novels to pay for the support of his insane wife and his two daughters, he twice toured the United States to help promote his books by doing the nineteenth-century version of talk shows—giving lectures on such subjects as English humorists of the eighteenth century and the four royal Georges. Naturally he found a large and enthusiastic audience (meaning eager to buy his books) among the cosmopolitan stock of Anglo-Saxons, French Huguenots, Caribbean Celts, and European Jews who once dominated the intellectual and social life of Charleston.

Likewise, when that scientific genius and showman, Louis Agassiz, was thumping his revolutionary concepts in geology and ichthyology, he knew his campaign to convert the best minds in America would not be complete until he lectured in Charleston— which he did at the medical school during the winter of 1851–52.

Yet even modern Charlestonians sometimes have difficulty reconciling the image of their city as a theatrical pioneer—which it was when the Dock Street Theatre opened its doors in 1736—with the picture of its affluent, but intemperate political leaders demanding that their state secede from the Union.

My mother's family was not from South Carolina, but when Edmund Ruffin fired the shell that exploded over Fort Sumter on the morning of April 12, 1861, he sealed the fate of six of the seven male members of the Virginia Dances and Johnsons who died in the next four years of fighting.

When the war began, a war which many Virginians were reluctant to enter, my great-grandfather did not rush off to enlist. Wesley Mayes Dance had five children and a farm to look after. There was spring planting to be done. Let the hotbloods who started the war finish it.

By the summer of '63, that point of view was no longer tenable. About the same time that the survivors of Pickett's charge were drifting back across a field near Gettysburg and two Confederate officers were entering Grant's siege lines at Vicksburg to discuss surrender terms, Wesley Dance made up his mind to go to war. On August 15 he enlisted in the 3d Company C of the 59th Virginia Infantry Regiment and was immediately sent by rail to help reinforce the defenders of Charleston.

At this point in the war, Wilmington, North Carolina, and Charleston were the only major Atlantic ports left to the Confederacy, and although the quantity of supplies which slipped through the Union blockade was a trickle compared to prewar trade, it was an indispensable trickle for Southern morale if not material well-being.

In April 1863, Union monitors had steamed into Charleston harbor to pound Fort Sumter into submission. Instead, the monitors were pounded into submission. The *Montauk* was hit fourteen times and the *Weehawken* fifty-three times and nearly sunk. By the time Wesley Dance's company arrived, the Union forces had emplaced huge Parrott rifles on Morris Island within range of the city, and the 59th Virginia Infantry Regiment spent the rest of the year trying to dislodge these eight-inch guns, prevent Union forces from establishing any more artillery sites or seizing any part of the city, and helping to feed the civilian population as well as themselves with the fish and crabs the soldiers caught in the rivers and the shorebirds and herons they shot in the marshes.

Wesley Dance and other Halifax and Mecklenburg County farmers may have managed to get home the following spring for planting. At least their last skirmish with the Yankees near Charleston was on February 11, 1864, and the next time the men of Company C, now known as the South of Dan Rebels, appear in military chronicles is on May 4 while consolidating a defensive position near Petersburg, Virginia.

Unlike the South Carolina "Gamecocks" who began the war or the North Carolina "Tarheels" who stubbornly stayed with it, Virginians were known as "Sorebacks," because they often subscribed to the theory that discretion was the better part of valor. Still, when a fellow Virginian or a South Carolinian, for whom the men of the 59th Infantry Regiment had developed an affection during their long months of service at Charleston, was in trouble, the men of Company C fought like fury. So it was that when a huge Union mine exploded under a South Carolina battery on July 30, 1864, and breached a gap in the defenses of Petersburg, the South of Dan Rebels plugged the hole, and my great-grandfather was killed in the fierce fighting at the Crater.

A little more than a century later, as I lay on my belly in a Saigon hospital while two corpsmen probed for shrapnel in my back, a man with a clipboard came by asking for the names of family to notify. I asked him to play down the seriousness of my injuries, for I was concerned about the reaction of my mother who had not been happy when I volunteered for duty in Vietnam. I needn't have worried: A week later, I got a letter from my mother noting that, for a change, her "sorebacked son" was taking after her side of the family!

Southerners are renowned for long memories and family ties. However, memory becomes a flaw when it broods on past humiliations, and family ties become a curse when they emphasize the differences in "outsiders" rather than the many similarities shared by all Americans. Perhaps the greatest of all ingredients that frame the American experience is our common view of the importance of nature.

In the eighteenth and nineteenth centuries, irrespective of whether we were from the North or South, frontiersmen or city sophisticates, Americans looked on the wilderness as something to be domesticated or destroyed. In the present century, our singleness of purpose has been modified by a vast accumulation of proof that we are fundamentally dependent on the many ecosystems our forefathers sought to subdue.

In retrospect, the eighteenth-century advent of an urban environment as rich in cultural amenities as Charleston's is less remarkable than the advent of such naturalists and sportsmen as John James Audubon, who visited Charleston on his way to Florida to collect and paint birds, and South Carolina's own William Elliott, who commemorated nature in his writings rather than condemning it.

William Elliott (1788–1863) will never rank as an outdoor journalist on the order of Henry William Herbert or Henry David Thoreau—both of whom were his Northern contemporaries—but Elliott was a significant regional reporter for a landscape and a culture which have largely vanished over the past century and a half.

Elliott was born and brought up on a large estate founded by his grandfather near Beaufort. The young man was estranged from many of his neighbors by his Harvard education, his wanderlust, and his sympathy for the Union. Just as his experience convinced him there was no way the agrarian South could win in a war with the industrial North, his familiarity with northern coasts convinced him there was no more subtly beautiful strand of the Atlantic than that of his native Carolina.

Yet he also knew how fragile this beauty could be. Writing in 1845, Elliott describes a barrier island bar which disappeared in his time and whose geographical location is about a mile east of the present beach:

"[Egg Bank] lies, or more properly speaking did lie, south of the public lot at Bay Point—distant half a mile [near the mouth of Port Royal Sound]. Covering several acres in extent and lifting its head a few feet above [the] high water mark, it served as the secure roosting-place of the curlews, sea gulls, and other aquatic birds; and here, too, in the spring they deposited their eggs.

"But the hurricanes which periodically sweep along our coasts have so obliterated it, that its existence as an egg bank will become, in a few years, a matter of tradition. It is now covered at half flood —and its site is marked in stormy weather by the waves, that rushing together from opposite quarters, meet at its summit, and jutting upwards into the air, fall in a sheet of foam.

"When the bank stood above water, it formed a barrier against the sea; and while the surf beat on the outer side, the inner was protected so that a boat could land in security. I used to push over from Bay Point at early flood, land on the inner side of the bank, and, leaving a few oarsmen to take charge of the boat, walk over to the seaside of the bank with a servant or two to carry bait and lines

Long-billed Curlew

—and, wading out into the surf waist-deep, toss my line into the breakers in quest of [spottail] bass."

Because so much has changed along the Carolina coast, we can only speculate about the specific aquatic birds that kept Elliott company on his fishing expeditions. Probably there were laughing gulls and royal terns, but what kind of "curlews" did he see? As late as 1891, Thomas Nuttall in his *Popular Handbook of the Birds of the United States and Canada* observed that the largest of all curlews, the long-billed curlew, wintered in the marshes of South Carolina, "as I have observed specimens on the muddy shores of the Santee, near Charleston, in the month of January." Furthermore, there are nesting records for these nominal western breeders from at least as far south as the salt marshes near Cape May, New Jersey.

However, due to intensive market gunning and the alteration and settlement of most of the Atlantic margin, the long-billed curlew is rarely seen today east of the Mississippi. Whether or not it ever bred as far south as the Carolinas is as conjectural as whether or not the species could be reestablished as a breeder anywhere near the Atlantic. Although there is still suitable salt marsh habitat all along the coast—indeed, more and generally better habitat than exists along the U.S. Pacific coast—there are still more private places for this wary bird in Mexico and Canada than in the eastern United States. Today, of all the larger shorebirds that may once have shared

Elliott's Egg Bank, only the willet both nests and winters along this southern strand.

Occasionally a flight of Hudsonian curlew, alias whimbrel, is seen near or over Charleston harbor as this species migrates from its South American wintering grounds to its Arctic breeding areas. Sometimes flocks of whimbrels settle in local marshes to gorge on fiddler crabs and other mud-loving invertebrates before rising again with wild cries to begin the next long leg of their intercontinental journey. Sunday sailors in Charleston harbor sometimes note the flights of whimbrels; however, rarely do the boaters realize they may be witnessing the passage of most of this species' Atlantic Flyway population.

Comparatively few Charlestonians—even those educated to appreciate the city's cultural heritage—know about its equally wonderful natural heritage, including a relatively recent contribution known as Drum Island. Many local residents pass daily over the Cooper River Bridges without realizing that below them is the largest wading-bird rookery in eastern North America. Every year Drum Island hosts over 50,000 nesting birds of at least ten different species.

The island's importance as a rookery began with the damming of the Cooper River as part of the Santee-Cooper power project which generates electricity and upstream recreation on Lakes Marion and Moultrie. The U.S. Army Corps of Engineers reversed an older and possibly wiser water-flow pattern completed in 1800 that directed the Santee River through Lake Moultrie down the Cooper River and through Charleston to the sea. The nineteenth-century diversion meant that although Charleston's docks and White Point Gardens were subject to periodic flooding, the enlarged volume of water down the Cooper River scoured the harbor and its channels so that little dredging was required to maintain Charleston's preeminence as a Southern port.

All that changed in 1941 when both the Santee and Cooper rivers were dammed, and the silt that settled out of the slow-flowing Ashley and Wando rivers and the now tidal lower Cooper accumulated in great quantities on the harbor bottom. South Carolinians who boast of the "cheap power" generated by the Santee-Cooper project never calculate the additional cost—hence, energy loss—of the nearly annual dredging of Charleston harbor. Nor do they see any further deficit in the Corps's present plan to divert the Cooper so the mild overburden of silt still carried by the weakened river will be eliminated entirely.

Drum Island was originally a low-lying salt marsh with a small nesting colony of laughing gulls in addition to scattered nests of clapper rails, willets, and seaside sparrows. Eggers worked the laughing-gull colony into the 1940s, and they are sometimes blamed for the eventual decline of this colony. However, it was the conversion of Drum Island from salt marsh to lowland scrub by the concentrations of dredge spoils sucked out of the harbor by the Army Corps of Engineers that drove away the laughing gulls, not the egging activities of a few subsistence-living watermen.

Still, the laughing gulls' loss was the herons' gain, and the greatest of these success stories—indeed, one of the most dramatic restorations of a formerly endangered species anywhere on earth—involves the snowy egret. These birds were on the verge of extinction by 1900 due to relentless slaughter on their nesting grounds. Ornithological expeditions were mounted to penetrate Florida's unmapped southern coast to locate the last egret rookeries with the hope that protection could be given such sites.

The American Egret, also known as a Common or Great Egret (top) and Snowy Egret (bottom)

Boat-tailed Grackles: the female left, the male right

In order to save the species from the feather merchants, scientists allied themselves with wildlife preservationists. Many of these used sentimental appeals involving grieving "widows" and "orphaned" birds to influence legislators creating laws to protect the endangered birds. Ironically, these same laws later made it difficult for scientists to acquire trapping, collecting, or salvaging permits to study endangered wildlife.

In a similarly ironic vein, local Charlestonians who lost their fight to maintain Drum Island as a salt marsh are now resisting efforts by ornithologists to manage the island as an egret, ibis, and heron rookery. In order to do that, the climax coastal growth of mulberry, red cedar, and hackberry must be cut back and the Army Corps of Engineers encouraged to continue using the site as a dumping ground for dredge spoils.

There are two stages of plant succession before the climax phase for all Atlantic coastal islands. First, salt-tolerant (halophytic) plants appear characterized by the herbaceous grasses, *Spartina*. Then small woody shrubs, like marsh elder and sea myrtle, appear, followed by the larger saltwater cedar and wax myrtle.

This woody shrub phase is the one preferred by nesting waders. Although some waders will nest in trees, such climax vegetation is also the preferred habitat of boat-tailed grackles and fish crows, which prey on the waders' eggs and young. Yet, despite the fact the entire northern end of Drum Island has reached this less desirable phase of plant succession, with the rest of the island destined for the same fate, most Charleston bird lovers don't want to alter this already completely artificial environment.

Yet the successful restoration of any species is only partially possible through protection. In the case of the snowy egret, the digging of the Intracoastal Waterway—accompanied by the creation of thousands of spoil islands and potential rookery sites along the Atlantic coast—eventually enabled this uniquely "golden-slippered" species to recover its entire former range as much as did the prohibition of the plume trade in 1910.

Artist and ornithologist Alexander Wilson collected snowy egrets in 1812 near Cape May, New Jersey. Not until after World War II did the snowy return to that area, and not until 1953 was the first snowy egret nest discovered on Long Island. Now the species is common around New York City—thanks, in part, to spoil islands, created without any thought of birds, for boaters who now benefit aesthetically from the sight of the elegant egrets.

That protection alone is not enough to effect a rapid about-face for the population of any species can be seen in the example of the most distinguished of all white herons, the American egret. Like the snowy egret, the American egret was extirpated from most of its former Atlantic breeding range by plume hunters before the turn of the century. Unlike the snowy egret, the American egret has been slow to recover. This may be, in part, because the American egret is less tolerant of the presence of man than his snowy cousin. Or it may be that the American egret is like dozens of other bird species that find survival difficult once their populations fall below undefined, but critical levels. Unless bird lovers are willing to allow wildlife professionals to manage this species for maximum (hence, artificially maintained) production, there is the possibility that the American egret will decline in the face of continuing coastal development after making only a tentative recovery in the first half century following cessation of the plume trade.

The most common nesting species on Drum Island is the white ibis, which numbers at least 38,000 individuals between early March and the end of June. In addition to their long, decurved bills, ibises in the air can be distinguished from other waders by their outstretched necks, rapid wingbeats, and alternately flapping and gliding flight.

The white ibis is a curious piece in one of the puzzles of the avian world. Why is it that several completely unrelated species of large bird have all-white bodies and wings with only black wing tips? What evolutionary advantage is there in adult white ibises, whooping cranes, snow geese, white pelicans, gannets, and (although there is more black on the wings and head than in the other species named) wood storks sharing the same color pattern?

One answer has it that white is characteristic of birds which evolved along the fringes of the periodic ice sheets. However, how does this involve ibises, which apparently never associated with ice sheets? Another concept says that since all the birds which possess this pattern have more or less permanent pair bonds, and since complex plumage patterns are not important to such species, white with black wing tips is about as uncomplicated a pattern as nature can design. Yet would not an all-white plumage, as in swans, or an all-black plumage, as in vultures, be simpler still? The mystery remains.

Several hundred of the closely related and darkly maroon glossy ibis also nest on Drum Island. Not many years ago, the mere sighting of a glossy ibis would have made a South Carolina birder's reputation—if his colleagues believed him, that is. In fact, the first nesting pair in South Carolina were shot to confirm their occurrence. Unlike the formerly exploited egrets, which have used the past seventy years to recover lost ground, the unexploited glossy ibis has used the same time frame to expand its range. Frank M. Chapman noted at the turn of the century that "this is a rare species in the eastern United States." Today, nesting colonies can be found on spoil islands and behind barrier beaches all the way up the coast to New Jersey.

With their sepulchral mutterings and manner, glossy ibises have become one of the eerier harbingers of spring in the Carolinas as they wheel inland to feed in flooded fields on toads and drowned earthworms. Later, as the sun warms the estuaries, the ibises return to the brackish margins to feed on insects, fiddler crabs, baby turtles, and an occasional small snake.

Although the greatest of all Atlantic coastal waders, the great blue heron, feeds and winters in the vicinity of Drum Island, this species nests in tall trees, most often in quiet, inland river bottoms. The great blue heron is the supreme predator among waders, and besides its usual fare of fish and frogs, this bird will eat swamp rabbits, muskrats, surprisingly large snakes, and baby alligators as well as other birds. In Florida, they have killed brown pelicans and people's pets apparently just to be rid of the competition.

Black-crowned Night Heron, flying, and a Great Blue Heron

The principal predator of other species' nestlings on Drum Island is the black-crowned night heron. Although the closely related yellow-crowned night heron and the cattle egret will occasionally steal an unguarded chick from another nest, only the black-crowned night heron makes something of a specialty of cannibalism.

You have to feel a little sorry for this dapper little trapper (only twenty inches tall) which sports two or sometimes three elegant white nuptial plumes from the nape of his black neck. If he were allowed to go straight, he might do so, for in circumstances where the black-crowned night heron is not at the bottom of the herons' interspecific pecking order, the black-crown will feed by day on fish and frogs. On Drum Island, however, the adults cannot compete with the many more efficient fishers around them, and so they skulk in the dark at the edges of the white ibis and cattle egret concentrations, waiting for the parents to take off for their feeding grounds. Then quick as Mack the Knife, the night heron strikes and scurries off through the underbrush with a squalling nestling.

There are other forms of mortality among the young birds, of course. During the 1950s, local crabbers used the nestlings to bait their traps. This practice was stopped, however, and now a thriving colony of rats picks off the many young birds that are shoved out of nests by their more precocious siblings. Fish crows and boat-tailed grackles will sometimes kill or scavenge some of these dispossessed birds, but since neither crows nor grackles feel safe in the shadowy understory below the nesting herons and ibises, rats remain the principal ground-level predators.

Since adult herons, egrets, and ibises rarely concern themselves with any of their fallen progeny, a relatively quick death from the jaws of a rat is probably preferable to the only alternative, slow starvation. Yet even with what amounts to an occasional cornucopia in unattended nestlings at ground level, black-crowned night herons still seem to prefer to plunder unattended young in their nests. Perhaps they view the risk of a possibly crippling jab from an irate parent a more sporting proposition than competing with rats and grackles for a sure thing.

Beach walking is a wonderfully solitary exercise. Even when done in company, conversation cannot interfere with the ocean's hold on the imagination. And there is nothing that can occur on a beach—not even a whale stranding or a bluefish bonanza—greater than the planetary breathing of the sea itself.

In a similar, but more microcosmic manner, the daily acts of life and death among colonial nesters are submerged within the rhythm and cacophony of the colony. As you huddle inside a hotly suffocating and mosquito-dense blind, you look out portholes at the rookery as though you were in a submarine staring into a fantastic undersea garden. However, while you would hear only a faint buzzing, or the occasional snap of a shrimp or grunt of a fish, beneath the waves, you are saturated with sounds in a heronry.

Male black-crowned night herons attract their mates by swaying from one foot to the other and making a noise comparable to steam escaping from a boiler. Displaying male cattle egrets make peculiar "rick-rack" cries, while little blue herons and Louisiana herons stretch and pump their bodies, snap and rattle their mandibles, and perforate this performance with occasional ecstatic groans. Snowy egrets stretch, pump, bark, and cry "wah-wah-wah" like a human baby; American egrets maintain a more dignified murmur of cawing and churring. Yet all these sounds are mere punctuation marks amid the coliseum roars of jabbering ibises. If a Hollywood director needed to dub in the noises made by an unruly army for a film with a cast of thousands, he couldn't do better than use a recording of a wading bird colony in full breeding voice.

No wonder the first European settlers were overwhelmed by wild America! Coming from an overcrowded and thoroughly domesticated landscape, many of them felt threatened by the fecundity and exuberance of this continent's wildlife. In a sense, even John James Audubon and William Elliott were typical of their contemporaries in wanting to control and confine nature—except they used pens and brushes as well as guns and axes.

How fortunate we are to be the heirs of such observers! They were so busy stringing lights in the darkness, they had little time to let their own eyes become fully acclimated to the wonder and meaning of the American spectacle. Elliott and Audubon would have viewed Drum Island as an opportunity to collect a few study skins and jot a few notes in their diaries before rushing off to their next appointment in an impossible effort to accumulate all knowledge.

Today we live not only with the systematic perception of nature they bequeathed, but with the understanding that we are only recent pieces in the ancient mosaic of natural history. At the same time, we know that we have the power to exterminate—and to restore—most any species, including our own. Increasingly, we distinguish between acts of cruelty involving men and apparent acts of cruelty involving wild predators and prey. And we no longer seek to destroy all black-crowned night herons and crows because they earn their keep in ways repellent to our own finer sensibilities. In this, and, perhaps, in this way alone, we are making progress.

11

GEORGIA'S MARSHES

Georgia schoolchildren must still memorize some of the verses of Sidney Lanier, but most young Americans have never heard of him. And little wonder. Southerners once read Lanier less because of the sentiments he expressed than because he had been a soldier in the lost Confederate cause. And because he had been a Confederate, many Northerners dismissed him as a "regional poet." Yet there are few sweeter testaments to nature's paradoxical combinations of delicacy and power, of life and death, than in the verses of Sidney Lanier. And there is no more compelling psalm to the beauty of the merging sea and shore than "The Marshes of Glynn."

> *A league and a league of marsh grass, waist-high,*
>   *broad in the blade,*
> *Green, and all of a height, and unflecked with a light*
>   *or a shade,*
> *Stretch leisurely off, in a pleasant plain,*
> *To the terminal blue of the main.*

Glynn County, Georgia, still has leagues of marsh grass stretching off in a pleasant plain. However, Interstate 95, the city of Brunswick, and the development of Jekyll, St. Simons, and Sea islands have cast shadows across the formerly unsullied sea marshes. Furthermore, the settlement of upland Georgia, with the consequent conversion of blackwater rivers like the Big Satilla and the Altamaha from occasionally muddy streams into waters orange with clay, has ensured that "the terminal blue of the main" now lies many miles east of where it might still have been seen from shore in Lanier's day.

Still the peace and the healing quality of the salt marsh remain:

Somehow my soul seems suddenly free
From the weighing of fate and the sad discussion of sin,
By the length and the breadth and the sweep of the
marshes of Glynn.
Ye marshes, how candid and simple and nothing-
withholding and free
Ye publish yourselves to the sky and offer yourselves to
the sea!

The rocky coasts of the North Atlantic have a more flamboyant beauty than our coastal marshlands. High winds create sound and light spectacles where jagged cliffs stand opposed to the thundering sea. The contrasts and leitmotifs are Wagner or Richard Strauss, but the music of the Georgia salt marshes is Brahms or Lanier or even Johnny Mercer whose wistful whimsy was inspired in part by the marshy tidal creeks on which he grew up near Savannah, Georgia.

My wife was born in Savannah and her best friend's uncle was Johnny Mercer. Her generation, like his, still heard the daily cries of the Gulah women selling shrimp and crabcakes and other products of the coastal waters. Below Savannah are sea meadows through which freighters and tankers glide like ships in a prairie mirage. Despite pollution in the creeks and river so bad at times that not even barnacles can grow on the channel markers, striped bass—some up to fifty-five pounds—red and black drum, spotted sea trout and southern flounder move in with the flooding tide to pursue bait fish and shrimp. One lazy, hazy summer day, my wife, four friends, and I caught all these fishes anchored just downstream from Savannah while holding on for dear life every time a great ship passed and rolled enormous waves up at us out of the channel.

Savannah's ties to the sea are more substantial than many Northerners imagine. Ever since the heyday of the Yankee clipper and whaling ship, the nation has accepted the mostly-Massachusetts-made myth that our best sailors come principally from New England. Yet the history of the U.S. Navy, Merchant Marine, and Coast Guard is star-studded by senior officers from the south, and a boy who used to pedal over on his bike to teach my wife to play chess when they were youngsters growing up in Savannah successfully defended the America's Cup and the country's maritime honor as skipper of the *Courageous*. Ted Turner may be brash and arrogant, but those faults are intrinsic to a competitive spirit which sails circles around less intrepid yachtsmen.

Savannah is also headquarters for an organization which has helped educate the last three Washington administrations as to the recreational values of our sea resources and, in the process, helped write federal legislation affecting dozens of different coastal activities. The National Coalition for Marine Conservation was founded by Frank E. Carlton, a Savannah-based urologist, who converted his anger at the commercially biased way in which the National Marine Fisheries Service used to conduct its business into leadership of an action-oriented consortium of influential friends and fellow anglers who have succeeded in carrying a message to Congress that the nation's twenty million marine recreational fishermen have at least as great a stake in fisheries management as the few tens of thousands of commercial fish boat owners and operators.

While Dr. Carlton has tried to suppress his partiality for the Georgia coast through his efforts in other areas, particularly the preservation of bluefin tuna and the restoration of Atlantic salmon to New England and eastern Canada, he fortunately could not forbear to include Gray's Reef lying fifteen miles east of Sapelo Island, Georgia, in a proposal to expand the nation's marine sanctuary program—a proposal which in no way interferes with traditional uses of this area, such as recreational and commercial fishing, but which does raise storm signals if offshore drilling or mining industries show interest.

Gray's Reef is enriched by life and detritus flowing from the marshes of Glynn and McIntosh counties. Its biotic diversity encompasses species characteristic of both littoral and pelagic zones of northern waters as well as those of the tropics. Grouper and northern porgy may be found gliding through sea whips and around hard coral heads while above them, amberjack feed on butterfish. Over the surrounding sands, sometimes tens of thousands of wintering scoters dive for tiny *Crassinella* and *Cyclocardia* clams.

Gray's Reef and its vicinity are riddled with ecological anomalies and contradictions, and its wonders are not perceived by people with purely political outlooks. General James Edward Oglethorpe saw Georgia only as a front line between the British Carolinas and Spanish-held Florida. Disappointed that his colonists of 1733 were more interested in building homes and businesses in Savannah than in killing Spaniards, Oglethorpe was finally able to recruit some professional soldiers to annihilate a Spanish force on June 9, 1742, in the marshes of St. Simons Island. Although the general was ultimately frustrated in his efforts to drive the Spanish out of St. Augustine, he did enable Charleston to emerge as the foremost British colony in the South by using Brunswick and the marshes of Glynn as buffers between South Carolina and Florida less than a hundred miles apart as the Spanish warships sailed.

Today, while American history buffs make pilgrimages to the battlefields of Bloody Marsh near Fort Frederica National Monument on St. Simons, natural history buffs make comparable pilgrimages to Sapelo Island just up the coast where much of our knowledge of salt marsh ecology evolved.

Although salt marshes are found up the Atlantic coast as far as Nova Scotia, they do not reach their most luxuriant growth in individual plant size or area until the land merges more gradually with the sea from the mid-Atlantic coastal plain south. In addition, the rock-ribbed rivers of Canada and New England are parsimonious with mineral overburdens in contrast to the silty rivers of the Carolinas and Georgia. And ever since erosion-prone farming practices were introduced by European colonists in the seventeenth century, agriculture's losses of topsoil have been the littoral zone's gain in marshes.

Two plants of one genus dominate the salt marsh. As silts are washed from uplands and carried down to the estuaries, they begin to settle where the downstream currents are counteracted by incoming tides. As silt banks build, they become potential seedbeds for a variety of brackish-loving organisms including oysters and the pioneering form of *Spartina* known as *alterniflora*.

Spartina will germinate in seawater after being submerged for many weeks, but the sweeter the water, the less time it takes for the germination process to begin. This is why the most vigorous marshes lie in or close to brackish water estuaries like those in the Chesapeake or the marshes of Glynn. This is also why upstream damming and the diversion of sweet water can cause the decline of downstream marshes as has occurred along parts of the Texas coast.

Seeds dropped farthest up an estuary and, hence, in a preferred location for marsh expansion are quick to germinate before drifting off on some ebbing tide to more saline environments. Once a seed misses its chance to propagate in the estuary that spawned it, or when a seed is dropped by a plant growing on the backside of a barrier island already far removed from estuarine influences, it becomes an oceanic space probe in which all metabolic processes are delayed with the evolutionary hope that the seed may eventually lodge in the muds of some previously unvegetated sandbar or flat.

An established marsh's vigor depends less on its seeds than on its rootstocks. *Spartina alterniflora* dies back each winter, leaving only a coarse stubble. However, each spring—unless a dry winter intervenes—emerald grass grows up, sometimes four feet high, from the old rhizomes. The lushness of this growth is dependent on injections of rainwater or estuarine mixing, and a dry winter can lead to stunted growth, even from well-established rhizomes, the following summer.

Similarly, an oil spill can suffocate a salt marsh's potential to renew itself in the spring by coating the rhizomes with tars or saturating the peat with chemicals having the effect of herbicides. However, unless an impervious crust forms over the rootstock, most salt marshes appear to recover from most forms of oil contamination within a year or two, even though all the subtle relationships between other plants and animals living within the *Spartina* matrix may not be reestablished for many years or even decades afterward.

The development of salt marshes parallels the millennial rise of the sea. Old barrier islands are washed away and tidal lagoons are drowned, but new marshes continue to emerge as fresh deposits of minerals are made off river mouths. There is an eternal standoff between the sea and the grass. Some years, the sea makes greater headway than the marsh—perhaps helped by the excavations of man and muskrat as well as by coastal subsidence due to tectonic plate

Spartina patens

Cattle Egret standing in Needlerush

movement. Other years and more often during the past several centuries, the marsh creeps out into the sea.

The fact that the marsh can rise as fast or slightly faster than the sea is due to the sod substrate created by the latticework root system of *S. alterniflora*. As each year's growth dies back, new plants find life in the peat of former years, and millimeter by precious millimeter, the marsh builds upon itself until it is no longer flooded twice a day by tidal waters and *Spartina patens* takes over the task of marsh consolidation.

S. patens—known as salt hay grass in New England, salt meadow hay in the mid-Atlantic, and marsh hay cordgrass in the South—is programmed to prevent the marsh from rising more than one foot above mean high water. It does this through the biologically clever expedient of creating such a dense and permanent mat of itself that nothing but its own kind ever has a chance to germinate in those areas where *S. patens* is most lush. However, where unusually high tides deposit mats of old *Spartina* cane on top of a marsh hay meadow, *S. patens* runs the risk of having itself overshadowed by a host of plants ready and eager to invade the detritus-enriched and elevated sod.

First, there is black needlerush, with spiky leaf tips and coarse rhizomes which form dense mats resistant both to erosion and to challenge from *S. patens* once it has been supplanted by needlerush in the marsh. In drier or sandy areas of an upland marsh, saltwort or glasswort often assumes dominance. Many long-time coastal dwellers are happy about this, for they pickle and preserve the succulent terminal branches of saltwort and say the flavor is comparable to watermelon rind. And in the days before the sea goose called brant learned to feed in upland fields, the nutrient-rich *Salicornia* was an important late winter food for these birds after local supplies of eelgrass and sea lettuce were all consumed.

Sea oxeye is a yellow flowering plant found in dense colonies along the upper fringe of almost every salt marsh from Virginia to Florida and, wonderfully enough, in Bermuda. Although dark brown, burrlike seed heads appear in late autumn, the most common method of propagation is by way of underground rhizomes that result in dense colonies which compete, wherever an additional millimeter of elevation allows them, with *Spartina patens*.

Still, the most substantial threat to *S. patens'* accommodation with the sea is the saltbush community dominated by marsh elder and groundsel. Although most people assume these similar-looking plants are the same, they are readily distinguished by the fact that

Sea Oxeye

marsh elder's toothed and thicker leaves are oppositely arranged on their stems, while groundsel's thinner, more rounded (but still slightly toothed) leaves are alternately arranged. These salt-tolerant shrubs are found on the fringes of every salt marsh and intrude into S. *patens'* sphere of influence by trapping great mats of flotsam and jetsam on their branches during extreme high tides which then settle and shade out the lower-growing S. *patens.*

Of course, these typical steps in plant succession are disrupted wherever man goes with his draglines and backhoes. The concern is not that man alters the environment. After all, nature does that continually. But while nature always acts within the logic of its own imperatives, man simply doesn't know very much about what he is doing. He *thinks* he is dredging a marina or creating landfill for a housing development, but he invariably does the littoral equivalent of opening Pandora's box. Because man is a single-minded animal absorbed by immediate pleasures and profits, he rarely considers the dozens of chain-related consequences generated by even a single morning's work.

The question is not whether the U.S. Army Corps of Engineers should dredge, but only what to do with the endless tons of often highly contaminated spoils. The cost of dredging doubles for every half mile you must move the spoil from a dredge site, and most coastal cities long ago filled up every possibly cost-effective site within and without their corporate limits.

Savannah is plagued by silting that prevents ships beyond increasingly shallow drafts from moving upstream to off-load. Dredging is done periodically, but the former scouring effect of the Savannah River has been greatly diminished by upstream dams creating impoundments that straddle the Georgia–South Carolina border. Another dam that will eliminate a major portion of the free-flowing watershed that still exists between Augusta and the sea is on the engineering drawing board, and despite occasional political and fiscal setbacks, the Russell Dam seems fated to be built. It may provide some more largemouth bass habitat but it will do nothing but aggravate Savannah's increasingly tenuous commercial relationship with the sea.

Although man knows better, time and again he lets economic expediency overrule his common sense. In addition to the horrors that dumping toxic wastes and raw sewage wreaks on local water quality, such dumping inevitably contributes to shoaling when the many solids in each unfiltered discharge settle to the bottom. Yet for a long time Savannah dumped her municipal and industrial wastes directly into the river. The struggle between environmentalists and the business community culminated in 1972 when, being confronted by a December 31 court-ordered deadline, the American Cyanamid Corporation announced that it would no longer dump two thousand tons of surfuric acid and heavy metal traces every twenty-four hours into the Savannah River. Furthermore, it was abandoning plans to dump the wastes offshore in the Gulf Stream. Instead, American Cyanamid would create additional jobs and profits by using the wastes to manufacture dry wall for the housing market. After such a powerful adversary became their ally, environmentalists found that improvement of local water quality became a steady, although occasionally setback, activity. Today Savannah and the marshes of Chatham County are no more polluted than Brunswick and the marshes of Glynn. That statement may sound cynical, but in comparison with what the situation was only twenty-five years ago, genuine progress has been made.

Nature has an apt symbol for man's foolhardy finagling with marine marshes and their water quality. It is a gigantic nonnative grass found almost everywhere Americans have disturbed or contaminated coastal wetlands. From Jamaica Bay, New York—where mountains of garbage cover vast acreages of once fertile fields of *Spartina*—to Glynn County, Georgia—where causeways across the marsh disrupt ancient patterns of water flow—reed grass or *Phragmites* flourishes where few other plants can survive.

Phragmites grows up to twelve feet high. This coarse exotic is often mistaken by people unfamiliar with wholesome marshes as characteristic of any marsh because *Phragmites* is characteristic of areas where marshes used to be. In the late fall, *Phragmites* develops feathery seed heads which are collected by coastal visitors and carried home to fill vases to decorate holiday sideboards. Such aesthetic gestures guarantee the spread of this subtle intruder into still more disturbed ecosystems.

This highly adaptable plant mirrors man's own adaptability, and its aggressive rhizomes enable it to spread rapidly once its feathery seeds have given it a toehold. Eventually it excludes all vegetative competition. *Phragmites* has adapted to both freshwater and tidal environments and, thanks to well-intentioned tourists, it is now found throughout the world. It provides no food for wildlife, but in some areas it provides impenetrable shelter for colonies of rats which forage out onto the nearby garbage mounds or littered roadways.

Redwinged Blackbird among *Phragmites*

Man has used *Phragmites* to stabilize spoil banks, to provide windbreaks (difficult to eradicate once you decide to plant the area with something else), and in Eastern Europe, some people still make paper from its fibers. Finally, since it is such a super assimilator of all available nutrients in poor or salty soils, sanitation engineers are trying to learn whether filtering waste water through *Phragmites* stands will offer cheaper, but as thorough, secondary treatment as sewage plants.

Fortunately, once you leave roads, dikes, and spoil sites behind as you wander out over the marsh, you leave behind this emblem of man's degradation. It is then that you encounter the salt marsh's own symbol, the clapper rail.

> As the marsh-hen secretly builds on the watery sod,
> Behold I will build me a nest on the greatness of God;
> I will fly in the greatness of God as the marsh-hen flies
> In the freedom that fills all the space 'twixt the marsh
> and the skies.

Several members of the Family Rallidae are found as transients in the marshes of Glynn. The Virginia rail, sora rail, and the American coot are frequent migrant visitors. And the black and yellow rails may be far more common in Georgia marshes than their secretive ways permit local birders to know. These marshes are, also, well within the breeding and wintering range of both the common gallinule and the purple gallinule. However, none of these birds is as common to all the coastal marshes running from New England to Mexico as the marsh hen, alias clapper rail, alias *Rallus longirostris*.

My favorite moment in the marsh is just before the peak of high tide. During the spring and fall equinoxes, particularly if there is a steady northeast wind, water completely inundates the marsh and sometimes covers coastal roads so that cars appear to be running over the surface of an enlarged bay. When the tide finally turns in furious retreat to the sea, the marsh hens skulking in the roadside reeds herald the change with raucous laughter as though they themselves had turned the tide.

The marsh hen is a clown. Waiting in my duck punt for the sudden sight of waterfowl hovering overhead, I've become so engrossed with the fussy antics of an ablutionary clapper that ducks have come and gone without my notice. Once, in a flooded blind, a marsh hen and I played peekaboo, with the bird peering at me from the roof in a curious upside-down fashion and me trying to sneak my hand up to grab the bird's downcurved bill before it could pull away. The game went on for half an hour, and I never did catch the rail—or shoot a duck.

The call of the red-winged blackbird may define spring along the fringes of the upland marsh as the muttering of waterfowl defines autumn in the tidal guts and creeks. However, in most every season, the changing tides, the dawns and dusks, are signaled by the clamor of the clapper rail.

Marsh hens eat a variety of insects, fish, and crustacea, but the most important food in its diet is one of three species of fiddler crabs, *Uca minax*, *U. pugilator*, and *U. pugnax*. Two of its three specific names suggest a pugnacious temperament for this crab, and certainly the oversized cheliped or claw of the male gives them a formidable appearance. Furthermore, because the fiddler is predominately diurnal, casual human observers see what appears to be a good deal of fighting in the crab colonies. However, this apparent combat has more to do with love than war.

Uca minax, known as the mud fiddler, is the largest fiddler and found farthest up estuaries where its tolerance for low salinities enables it to survive where other crabs cannot. *U. pugilator*, the chinaback fiddler, displays a cream-colored shell interrupted by purple patterns. It inhabits sandy areas and is found running over the dunes some distance from the sea. *U. pugnax* is the marsh fiddler, and the smallest and most abundant of the trio. It is normally a dark brown color, which makes these sun-loving creatures inconspicuous against the marsh mud they inhabit.

Fiddlers hibernate during cold weather, which means more than

Clapper Rail and Fiddler Crabs

five months in northern latitudes and, perhaps, three months in Georgia. However, a spell of warm weather in February is likely to bring them forth trotting in droves across a bar or the males hypnotically waving their major chelipeds by their burrows.

Light intensity and tides dictate the rhythms of fiddler existence. As soon as lengthening days assure the male fiddler that spring will not renege on its promise of lasting warmth, the crab repairs his burrow which consists of two chambers at either end of an underground passageway. Spoil is packed into pellets and carried to the surface by using two or three legs on one side of his body as a cradle. The pellets are deposited to one side of the burrow's entrance and sometimes used to fashion a cone or hood as added protection from both the sun's desiccating radiation at low tide or as an extra millimeter of flood control at high tide. The china-back fiddler can create no such sophisticated constructions in sand, so it solves its home-maintenance problem by building burrows well above the high-tide line and often where it can receive some shade from the western sun by a convenient ridge or dune.

Of the two behaviors commonly seen in fiddler crabs—droving and cheliped waving—only the latter has an obvious explanation. As to why the crabs periodically move about in sizable hordes, the theory that these are migratory or dispersal marches, or that they represent feeding binges, is not supported by details within the activity itself. Here is an instance in which a thoughtful observer could make a significant contribution to our understanding of a major component of the marsh ecosystem.

By contrast, there is no mystery about waving displays. They are used by male crabs to advertise their presence to other fiddlers. The waving is a warning to other males to keep away. At the same time, it allures reproductively active females. From dawn to dusk during all low tides, male fiddlers spend almost every moment waving their oversized chelipeds. Only after the tide reaches the halfway mark will the male crabs take time out to eat or repair their burrows. Otherwise, like conductors of silent symphonies, fiddlers scattered all along the muddy berm wave their massive batons.

When a female crab strolls into one of these amphitheaters, the tempo of claw waving becomes frantic. From a Brahms third symphonic movement, the orchestra suddenly switches to a Beethoven symphonic fourth. The nearest male dashes out to meet the female with his major cheliped held high. He attempts to herd her toward his burrow, and as she flirtatiously darts away, both crabs suddenly find they are in the territory of another male who may rush out to lock claws with the interloping male. As the two males scuffle in a ritualized struggle designed to get the invader back onto his territory with a minimum of damage to the adversaries, the female may wander onto the territory of still another male who finally succeeds in forcing the female into his burrow. Quickly he follows, plugs the entrance, and blocks any of her attempts to leave until she lays eggs in the far chamber. At that point, the male may emerge to feed, for he intuitively knows that once the female has laid eggs, she will stay in his burrow to incubate them.

When the eggs are ready to hatch, the female carries them in her apron, a chitinous integument beneath the belly carapace, out of the burrow and to the water's edge where the brood is released as planktonic larvae. This is no random dispersal of young. The larvae are always released on a neap tide during the first or third quarters of the moon when the tidal range and, consequently, water movement are at a minimum. This timing ensures that during the first few days of their development, when the larvae are most vulnerable, they will not be subjected to the additional hazard of being swept far from their natal shore.

Yet, the larvae are not entirely passive passengers of the tidal flux. They swim to the surface on incoming tides to take advantage of the greater flow of water in the upper layers so they can remain close to future potential landing sites. Contrariwise, when the tide begins to ebb, the larvae sink toward the bottom to be out of the mainstream of outflowing water. After twenty-one days, the fiddler larvae have metamorphosed into adults and are ready to come ashore on a higher-than-usual spring tide which occurs on the new or full moon.

Within the simple cycles of existence in the marsh, procreation is nature's most compelling synonym for life itself. When the sun sets on the waving chelipeds of male *Uca* so that females can no longer see their come-hither movements, the males tap their feet, drum their chelipeds, or stridulate their body parts the way crickets "sing" in the dark to attract females throughout the night.

Each female crab must breed once a month during the warmer months of her brief life for her species to perpetuate itself. Thus, although such fundamental activities as feeding and burrowing are triggered by the sun, procreation is triggered by the moon's effect on the sea. The tide, not sunlight, is what gives life to the fiddler crab.

How still the plains of the waters be!
The tide is in his ecstasy.
The tide is at his highest height:
And it is night.

The marshes at night murmur with sound. The ticking of yellow rail and the snapping of shrimp are heard against the subtle background rustle of water rising through the reeds. Periodically a plop says "muskrat," or a frantic splash describes an otter closing on fish, or a clapper rail so intent on extracting a fiddler crab from his burrow that the rail fails to notice the sibilant wings of a short-eared owl coursing over the flooding grass.

But who will reveal to our waking ken
The forms that swim and the shapes that creep
Under the waters of sleep?

Thanks to enterprising fisheries biologists, we know a great deal more than Sidney Lanier could have imagined about the forms that swim and the shapes that creep within the marvelous marshes of Glynn. Although the littoral diversity seems typical of all the coast from Cape Hatteras to central Florida, an amazing variety of summer juveniles including grouper and angelfishes reminds the seiner of tropical waters farther south, much as winter visitors like tautog and weakfish recall the chilly waters of New England.

However, there are larger visitors to the marshes of Glynn that would have awed Lanier had he known of their existence "below when the tide comes in." Each May and June, tarpon, some of which weigh more than 150 pounds, and blacktip sharks, some more than seven feet long, move north along the beaches and into the bays behind the barrier islands to feed on the croaker and sea trout they find there in abundance. These fish are gypsies, and because you see a leaping, spiraling blacktip or a rolling, armor-scaled tarpon reflecting the late afternoon sun in a tidal channel one day does not mean they will be there the next.

Equally nomadic and far more awesome are the huge lemon sharks that pursue their ancient prey, stingrays, well into the marshes of Glynn. Some of the great predators are eleven feet long and weigh many hundreds of pounds, yet they can be found on the flooding tides at night in drains where men cull oysters in ankle-deep water by day.

Lemon sharks are Cacharhiniformes, which comprise the largest order of sharks, totaling 8 families, 47 genera, and approximately 199 species. The lemon is a member of the requiem shark family, which includes numerous "man-eaters" such as the bull, bronze whaler, oceanic whitetip, and tiger; the lemon shark itself has been credited with several attacks.

The horror of being eaten by a shark is compounded in most people's minds by the alleged primitiveness of sharks in general. While it is no less fatal to be eaten by a bear or tiger, such a prospect is not so terrible in our imaginations, perhaps, because we share the land and warm blood with bears and tigers. We may feel sufficient courage to try talking one of these terrestrial predators out of attacking us or even, in extremis, we may counterattack the mammal. However, a shark has no cerebrum, and it is not intimidated by the mystery of the human voice nor by defensive-aggressive displays that, indeed, may only trigger the shark's feeding urge when it sees what it interprets to be an awkwardly swimming—hence, injured—marine animal.

The lemon shark is supremely well adapted to survive and flourish within the littoral zone, that area of the sea where man is most frequently found. It is no more primitive for its lack of a cerebrum than we are for not being able to outswim such creatures. In fact, sharks and man share a significant but rare predatory attribute: we are both able to feed on creatures larger than ourselves.

However, man maintains an ideal of instantaneous death which we call "humane," and much of our horror of sharks is based on our knowledge that not only do some species regularly attack large and warm-blooded prey, but that they cannot kill this larger prey humanely. In fact, the ideal of the tiny cookie-cutter shark is never to kill its prey at all! The cookie-cutter merely bites chunks out of a whale or dolphin until the frantic animal escapes—and by escaping, ensures that there will be future meals for cookie-cutter sharks elsewhere in the ocean.

Thus, while the sea trout and bluefish found in the marshes of Glynn are limited to prey they can swallow at one fell swoop or, at most, chomp up in two or three quick bites, a lemon shark can prey on sea trout, bluefish, or especially stingrays many times larger than its mouth. Such prey is seized, shaken, and a piece torn out and swallowed. If the prey is still available, it is seized again and again until all has been eaten or the shark's appetite has been satisfied. When such habits are applied to a human swimmer, it soothes our imaginations not one whit to know that the shark is not acting out of malicious intent.

The lemon shark is not only the largest predator found in the marshes of Glynn, its tolerance for a broad range of salinities and temperatures makes it a hardy research species from which scientists hope to learn more about the physiology and behavior of sharks in general. Already researchers have discovered how lemon sharks can exist in warm tidal backwaters and other environments with a low oxygen content. Like human fetuses and burrowing animals, the lemon shark's blood has a high affinity for oxygen. When a lemon shark senses that the stingray it is trailing is on the verge of entering water too shallow for the shark to follow, an abundance of red blood cells suddenly inundates the shark's bloodstream and 20 percent more of the shark's gill surface is exposed to water flowing through the creature's mouth to extract all the oxygen possible from the surrounding environment. The shark accelerates to striking speed, and by the time the first chunk of the ray's wing has been ripped from its body, the shark's blood is saturated with oxygen at a partial pressure 200 percent lower than in most fishes at any activity level.

Cruising lemon sharks patrol more than a mile of new territory every hour. They are strongly affected by sunlight, and at dawn and dusk they generally move toward it. Thus, as the sun sets, lemon sharks off Georgia beaches move inshore, through inlets, and, if under the spell of a flooding tide, well up into the marshes to feed. As the tide turns, the sharks move back to the deeper channels within the marsh and bays until the rising sun draws them offshore again.

Even more curious, a lemon shark's hunger seems to wax and wane within four-day cycles. Lemon sharks consume the equivalent of 3 percent of their body weight daily, but this is average consumption over the four-day periods. Every fourth night lemon sharks appear to be more aggressively hungry and will attack more prey than during other nights of the cycle. Thus, a 400-pound lemon shark is more likely to eat one 48-pound meal to hold him 96 hours than 12 pounds of flesh every night for 4 consecutive nights.

Every Georgia summer, a small and secretive number of recreational fishermen angle for the huge lemon sharks that move into the marshes at night. The fishing is considered most sporting if it is done from a stationary platform like a dock or launch ramp. Balloons are used to suspend the bait just off bottom so crabs and other scavengers can't chew up the fresh ray's wing before a cruising lemon shark discovers it.

Water-skiers also use the marsh channels for their recreation, and one afternoon several years ago, three boys and a girl were taking turns behind their speedboat when one of them spotted a balloon moving slowly in the current. They ran over to it, caught up the end of the broken line, and were excited to feel a live weight at the other end. However, when a shark's head broke the surface whose eyes were "an ax handle apart," they dropped the line and switched their water skiing to Lake Sinclair 120 miles away and inland!

Unlike Sidney Lanier, they had never wondered "what swimmeth below when the tide comes in on the length and the breadth of the marvellous marshes of Glynn." Also unlike Lanier, they wanted to know nothing more about it!

12

MAN AND MANGROVES

When we think of railroads in this country, we think of the West. We are stirred by old images of Indian attacks on railway crews, the ceremonial meeting of engines and the driving of golden spikes, the slaughter of the buffalo from cowcatchers and train windows, and later the piles of bison bones waiting at prairie depots to be shipped east and ground into fertilizer.

Yet the building of the railroads was the most important developmental step for every region of the nation, and although historians and publishers find few prints or pictures to illustrate the cutting of rail lines through the mangrove forests of Florida and the crossing of the Florida Keys, the railroad was more essential to the settlement of our southernmost Atlantic state than it was to the West where land-hungry immigrants would have gone on horseback or foot if the rail lines and later highways had not made the journey less arduous.

Florida is a 447-mile-long thumb of coquina limestone, much of it less than a dozen feet above sea level, that turns the Gulf Stream southward in its clockwise orbit within the Gulf of Mexico. At the bottom of Florida—through the Keys, the Marquesas, and the Dry Tortugas—the Gulf Stream is entrained by and merges with the Antilles Current surging up from the islands for which it is named. This combined current sweeps north along the Florida coast, sometimes undulating only half a dozen miles off the beach at Stuart, and its proximity and tropical warmth are what once provided southern Florida with some of the most vigorous onshore mangrove and offshore coral reef communities in the world.

When naturalists began poking along the Florida coast in the early nineteenth century, they were amazed by the diversity and abundance of fish and wildlife found here and nowhere else in coastal North America. Creatures like the manatee and the alligator may stray along the coast as far north as the Carolinas or even the Chesapeake, but the warm, fresh, and brackish waters of Florida are clearly their wellsprings. The flamingo, the snail kite, and the crocodile are more characteristic of the West Indies than any area north of the Tropic of Cancer. However, they all established toeholds in South Florida and are still found there today—the flamingo, artificially, and wild ones, occasionally; the snail or Everglades kite and the crocodile, barely—because the lower end of this peninsula is ecologically part of the West Indies.

Prior to the 1830s, the entire peninsula was a refuge for runaway slaves and Indians of the Creek culture who had fled the usurpation of their native lands in Alabama and Georgia. The pre-Columbian Indians had been mostly killed off or packed away as slaves by the Spanish, and the newcomers, regardless of whether they spoke Hitchiti or Muskogee, were called "Seminolies" by the British who briefly ruled Florida.

In 1823, a treaty was ratified between the U.S. government and thirty-two chiefs representing all the Seminoles in northern Florida. The Treaty of Moultrie Creek called for moving the Indians south of their adopted area to a fertile but soggy four-million-acre reservation in central Florida between Ocala and Lake Okeechobee. The treaty promised that this area was being set aside for the Seminoles "in perpetuity"; today, Disney World is located not far from one of the principal Indian campgrounds.

The problem was that the Seminoles were hospitable to runaway slaves, and the slaveowners wanted them back. Furthermore, a group of slaveowning businessmen saw the sugar-growing potential of the Okeechobee region. They contributed to the electoral campaign of their old Seminole-fighting friend, Andrew Jackson, and helped make him a U.S. senator and, later, a president, from which office he personally directed operations for moving every last redskin west of the Mississippi—or killing those who refused to go.

From the mid-1820s to the eve of the Civil War, our armed forces were trained by hunting Seminoles through the jungles and savannahs of central and southern Florida. We have no record of how many Indians were killed, but we do know that in six and a half years of some of the most severe fighting, the U.S. Army lost 1466 men, including 215 officers, while the U.S. Navy lost 69 sailors on riverine patrols.

The Indians had their heroes—Osceola, for example, who was treacherously seized under a flag of truce and died in captivity in a South Carolina fort ironically with the same name as the treaty for which he fought. And the whites had theirs—Lieutenant Colonel William S. Hainey, for instance, who guided ninety men in sixteen canoes up the Miami River, across the Everglades, and down the river now named for him to the Gulf of Mexico. Along the way he killed the Seminole chief, Chekika, and many of his followers and family.

This Seminole "relocation program" slowed down as the tension between the Northern and Southern states warmed up. When the War Department began withdrawing troops from Florida for duty elsewhere, it shrewdly offered civilians bounties for live Indians ($500 for a male, $250 and up for a female, and $100 for a child) and, thereby, recruited an unpaid army of bounty hunters who criss-crossed the Big Cypress and Everglades helping to harry and de-moralize those Seminoles they couldn't actually capture. In 1858, the last significant chief, Billy Bowlegs, surrendered with 123 of his followers, most of them women and children. They were promptly exiled to Oklahoma.

A few Indians remained in Florida, and their silent and often sullen descendants now run airboats in the Everglades or sell the tourists handicrafts along the Tamiami Trail. Like red men any-where in the Americas, they have learned that their survival depends on never developing an attachment for anything a white man might ever want.

The South Florida refuge denied to the Seminoles was then sought by several generations of white renegades and nonconformists. Whether people came to subsistence-live along the coast or to roll for high stakes in farming, logging, fishing, or even trading in this enervating realm, they did so with the knowledge that when you went to Florida, you were more completely turning your back on the mainstream of human society than if you went to almost any other corner of North America. You had better want to be alone, for surely you would be.

In one sense, that is still true today. While towns like Palm Beach and Hobe Sound throb with wealth and reputation, Florida is still not a place where you can readily make your name in the larger world. You must bring your money and position with you. Florida is a museum of the rich; some might say a mausoleum.

My brothers and I have all lived in Florida at various times in our lives, and I once asked Tony, my older brother, what difference he saw between his years there and the past twenty-five years when he has lived in Alaska.

"That's easy," he replied. "Alaska is still the frontier that Florida used to be. Alaskans are people who have given up something to come here to live. Floridians are people who have given up nothing to go there to die."

Some readers will resent my brother's remark. Yet as someone who first went to Florida when the unsettled conditions of some portions of the land and the diversity and abundance of its resources were part of an optimistic dream—when living coral reefs thrived as far north as Stuart, and Marathon in the Keys was nothing more than a bus stop and a bait shop—he is entitled to his opinion of the Florida that is, for he weeps for the Florida that was.

My younger brother, John, until recently lived there, teaching at the University of Miami. It is an emblem of our fraternal sorrow for the peninsula's littoral Paradise Lost that he turned his back on the Atlantic coast and sought his recreation as an archaeologist in the Everglades, looking for artifacts used by Floridians who flourished long ago without stone tools, much less iron.

There is a legend that when Juan Ponce de León sailed in search of Bimini and found Florida, he was looking for a spring which gave eternal life to anyone who tasted its waters. In the more than four and a half centuries since Ponce de León's death, a good many other people preoccupied with longevity, if not eternal life, have come to Florida. Whether or not their lives were extended by being there, their ever-increasing numbers have overwhelmed a good many nonhuman Florida natives. Although the manipulation of complex and fragile water systems by cattlemen, farmers, and engineers has caused the most pervasive harm to Florida's ecosystems, the most visible damage has been done by visionaries with too much money and absolutely no understanding of nature. Foremost among these was a railway builder and a bevy of satellite real-estate promoters.

Savannah and Tampa were connected by rail as early as 1884, but the east coast of Florida took longer to develop, principally because of the red and black mangroves that once formed impenetrable jungles of curving prop roots and stalagmitelike pneumatophores, or breathing roots, along every tidal stream and bay in southern Florida.

The Indians had maintained trails from the slightly higher ground or hammocks where they lived to the channels where mangroves could not grow and which formed rivers that curled through the perennially green forest. The Spanish used these rivers and trails to find the Indians and the hammocks where giant mahogany and lignum vitae were cut after the Indians were enslaved to do the work. American loggers later used these same trails to reach stands of bald cypress, black ironwood—so dense it sinks in water and for that reason makes termite-resistant fence posts—and buttonwood, which grows just behind the mangroves in dry, but salty soil and which in prekerosene days was the primary source of charcoal for cooking in Florida homes.

Except for these pathways, all travel in southeastern Florida was by boat until the advent of Henry Morrison Flagler, who, like many of the incredibly rich men of his generation, had made his money in lucrative association with the Standard Oil Company. Flagler came from Connecticut and knew nothing about Florida until he first visited Jacksonville in 1878 on a trip for his wife's health. When he was told that while he could sail to Key West, there was no proper resort elsewhere along the coast, forty-eight-year-old Flagler was transfigured by the vision of a railroad connecting several exclusive resorts where the right people, meaning very rich people like himself, could live, and possibly prolong their golden years.

The first Mrs. Flagler died in 1881, and he was encouraged in his vision of an earthly paradise by the younger, second Mrs. Flagler whom he married in 1883. The plan was that he would move down the coast, laying tracks to coincide with the building of new hotels which would open with the arrival of the first train. A first step was the Ponce de León (locally pronounced "Ponsi-dee-leone") Hotel which opened in 1888 for 450 guests aboard Flagler's Florida East Coast Railway. The hotel was a Moorish confection of domes, spires, minarets, marble fountains, mosaic arches, and Oriental rugs that sprawled over six acres of downtown St. Augustine. After Flagler opened up more southerly portions of the coast, the Ponce de León began to lose its chic. However, it lingered well into the 1950s as a retreat for a steadily shrinking clientele of wealthy people who associated the hotel with their own lost youth until it was converted into a girls' school in 1967.

Next Flagler built an impressive caravansary (now a nursing

home) at Ormond Beach where his former patron, John D. Rockefeller, was to spend the last twenty winters of his life. Yet by 1892 Flagler was soon up and moving his railway crews again through the coastal forests to Daytona Beach.

He lingered there. For one thing, Daytona has an especially beautiful beach whose broad intertidal sands once attracted multitudes of nesting sea turtles and whose hard-packed sands now attract auto racers and multitudes of their fans. For another thing, Flagler was busy consolidating a deal with the state's political bosses who agreed to give him 8000 acres for every mile of railway track he laid south of Daytona.

Flagler sent his labor crews back into the jungle. It would have been easier for them to hack their way through the slash pine and saw palmetto of Florida's interior. But Flagler expected most of his future rail business to be in tourism and tourists want to be near the sea. So from Daytona, Flagler directed his crews south to Titusville, where boats were provided for hunting and fishing around Merritt Island between the Indian and Banana rivers. Some of the more intrepid visitors camped on Cape Canaveral, where excellent shorebird shooting was to be had after the scaup left in the spring.

Vero Beach, Fort Pierce, and Stuart became important railway towns, but Flagler did not stop until he reached and incorporated into his own railroad system a narrow-gauge track that ran between the coastal villages of Jupiter, Mars, Venus, and Juno. The so-called Celestial Railway was already popular with tourists when Flagler obtained it. Women in flounces and crinolines decorated the train in the evenings, while men sat with shotguns and rifles on the early-morning runs and shot at every flying, sitting, or swimming target they spied.

Not far south of Juno was a barrier island where, about the same time Flagler first visited Florida, a Spanish ship bound for Barcelona with a load of coconuts from the Caribbean had gone aground and lost her cargo. Many of the coconuts had taken root in the sands, and Flagler was charmed by the sight of these exotic plants amid the native seagrape and bay cedar, joewood and sea lavender. He decided to end his railroad on the mainland opposite this island and build the most sumptuous hotel in the world on what was known as Palm Beach.

The Royal Poinciana cost one million 1893 dollars but took only nine months to complete from the cutting of the first mangrove to installing the last flagpole in the last cup of the hotel's second eighteen-hole golf course. In our modern world of unionized specialization, it is difficult to imagine such an architectural feat. The hotel had rooms for 1200 guests, and the dining room could seat 1600. Many varieties of exotic flora were planted in elegant gardens through which black men pedaled the wheelchair-carriages that Flagler invented and called "Afromobiles." The guests were pedaled to the tennis courts, the marina, or to afternoon teas on the beach where the setting sun warmed their backs while they gazed at the darkening sea. From a balloonist's view, the hotel grounds were laid out in the shape of a gigantic letter F, which the more naive visitors thought stood for Florida.

Of the many trees which Flagler's plantings helped disperse throughout the region, none were more significant that that future symbol of Palm Beach, the royal palm—which is a Florida native, although all of Flagler's plantings came from Cuba—and various members of the citrus family which came from Asia and the Near East by way of Spain. The orange was already important to Florida commerce, and Flagler enjoyed Palm Beach, in part, because he believed he had come far enough south to avoid the orange-killing frosts of northern Florida. Meanwhile, down in Dade County, Mrs. Julia D. Tuttle and William B. Brickell had offered Flagler half of their many thousands of acres if he would extend his railroad to Miami. When an unusual cold snap killed his Palm Beach citrus buds in the winter of 1894, Julia Tuttle sent Flagler a bouquet of orange blossoms which persuaded him to push on.

The mangroves grew more dense and stubborn the farther south Flagler moved. It took his crews more than two years to reach the banks of the Miami River where, within a year, a newspaper was founded, 343 voters incorporated the city, and Flagler opened another hotel, the Royal Palm, at the river's mouth. This was a tidy, functional inn rather than a luxury hotel, and one suspects that at sixty-seven, Flagler was beginning to shed some of his fierce determination to control all the development of Florida's Atlantic coast. His railroad went to Homestead in 1903 and began its worker-killing push for Key West when Flagler's plan for a solid causeway connecting the Keys brought him unwanted international recognition. The British especially were worried that Flagler's causeway would block Gulf Stream currents through the Keys, with possibly dire consequences for the climate of Northern Europe which depends on the Gulf Stream to bring moisture and moderate winter's extremes. In Flagler's stubborn youth, he might have told the British Foreign Office and the U.S. State Department to go to hell and insist on building the cheaper causeway. However, at seventy-five, he wanted only to reach Key West before he died. So he spent $50 million putting his tracks across concrete pilings and, in 1912, finally rode all the way to the isle of the setting sun and pronounced his dream "fulfilled" and himself able to "die happy." Shortly thereafter, he did.

Meanwhile, down around Miami, two entrepreneurs vied with one another for fortune and eternal glory. Carl Graham Fisher was busy "inventing" Miami Beach while George Edgar Merrick was "creating" Coral Gables. It is difficult to say who was the more obsessive-compulsive of the two. Alfred Browning Parker, whose father was Merrick's sales manager, says that "Merrick had the kind of charisma and magnetism that the mad often have. He could sell anything."

Merrick started with 160 acres he had inherited from his father and borrowed money from bankers as taken with his charisma and magnetism as Alfred Parker had been. First Merrick built the Miami Biltmore Hotel for $10 million. Then he laid out a championship golf course and a country club with an Olympic-sized pool and began selling houses in a South Pacific–Mediterranean style. Merrick had never visited either the Pacific or the Mediterranean, but he knew that each of these oceans inspired a different dream of Sybaritic living in his countrymen. If he combined the dreams, he figured he would strike it rich.

Merrick was right. Within the first few months of the Coral Gables boom, he sold $150 million worth of unimproved lots on the fringe of his model township. When sales tapered off to $100 million a year later, he revived them by digging forty miles of canals and importing Venetian gondolas and gondoliers to pole Tahitian dancers up and down the waterways. Sales went back up.

Whenever business slackened, Merrick rushed in with a new idea. William Jennings Bryan was hired at $100,000 a year to preach a curious sermon about gold, godliness, and the glory of living in Coral Gables. Writer Rex Beach was paid $25,000 to write a novel called *The Miracle of Coral Gables*. Olympian Johnny Weissmuller was hired to swim at regular hours through the underwater limestone caves of the Venetian Pool. And Paul Whiteman and his entire orchestra stood waist-deep one night in a "fountain of youth," playing Merrick's written-to-order theme song, "When the Moon Shines on Coral Gables."

Meanwhile Carl Fisher was letting no mangroves take root under his feet. He told his young wife, Jane, as they slapped mosquitoes and pushed their way through the seagrapes on the barrier island protecting Biscayne Bay and Miami, "I'm going to build a city here! A city like magic, like romantic places you read and dream about, but never see!"

In her biography of Fisher called the *Fabulous Hoosier*, Jane recalls that "Carl was like a man seeing visions. He had pulled a stick and peeled it on the way through the swamp, and when we reached the clean sand he drew upon it a plan of streets and square designs that represented buildings. That damp sand on which he drew is now Lincoln Road."

That was in 1912. Three years later, Fisher led a cavalcade of fifteen cars (one for each year of the new century) down his self-styled "Dixie Highway" from the Indianapolis Speedway, which he had built, to the newly completed Collins Bridge which he helped build across the bay to Miami Beach. Although the bridge was conceived and named by John S. Collins, a horticulturist from New Jersey, Fisher had put $50,000 into completing it. Collins needed the bridge to take fertilizer to his avocado, mango, guava, and other exotic fruit orchards on the beach. He had experimented with coconut palms from Trinidad, but equally exotic Norway rats kept eating the seedlings. In exchange for his $50,000, Fisher got bonds on the bridge and a one-third-mile-wide strip running from the bridge across the island to the ocean. He bought 260 acres alongside this right of way and offered the oceanside end of the road free to anyone who would build a $200,000 hotel there.

That was in 1914, and World War I was brewing. There were no takers until after the war when N. B. T. ("No Back Talk") Roney built his $2.8 million Roney Plaza Hotel on the site. Then development took off. Fisher belonged to an unofficial club of self-made Indiana men, including Barney Oldfield, the racing driver; Gar Wood, the future speedboat king; James A. Allison, inventor of the Allison aircraft engine and Fisher's partner in a company they eventually sold to Union Carbide for $9 million; and pilot Eddie Rickenbacker. All were invited by Fisher to Miami Beach to do their thing, and the press was always on hand to cover their visits.

Fisher tried to provide Miami Beach with attractions found at no other Florida resort. Polo, for example, brought yeast-king Julius L. Fleischmann and rubber-king Harvey S. Firestone to Miami Beach. Fisher staged a powerboat race among ten famous auto racers. Fisher made sure none of the men had ever driven a boat before, and when six of the boats collided and sank, the newspapers gave the accident their headlines, not the fact that Louis Chevrolet had won the race. Fisher even persuaded genial Warren G. Harding to come to Miami Beach after his inauguration. When the president played golf, Fisher had an Indian elephant named Rosie serve as his caddy. The publicity was worth hundreds of thousands of dollars in additional lot sales.

One of the few personalities of the era to find the situation ludicrous was Will Rogers, who dubbed the dredge "the national emblem of Florida." Of Fisher, Rogers said, "Carl rowed the customers out in the ocean and let them pick out some nice smooth water where they would like to build, and then he replaced the water with an island." Of course, many other land hucksters did not even do that much. When Will Rogers was asked what he really thought of dredges, he called them "all-day suckers"—and clearly had more than machinery in mind.

In 1925, there was a national economic recession which was felt most severely in Florida where land prices had long since outstripped common sense. A few Miami banks quietly closed their doors, and a few others began calling in loans. The following spring, however, the real-estate promoters themselves triggered the most serious decline by initiating an advertising campaign with the negative theme "Don't sell Florida short!" The 1926 hurricane finished the boom by destroying more than $105 million worth of property and taking hundreds of lives. The general stock market collapse three years later came as an anticlimax.

George Merrick wandered the streets of Miami well into the 1930s, a threadbare figure who would come alive whenever he could buttonhole somebody new about his dream of Coral Gables. Carl Fisher lived until 1939, and although he had taken his profits from Miami Beach before the going got grim, he lost most of this money in an effort to make Montauk, not Manhattan, the principal transatlantic passenger port of the New World. When he died in a small house off a Miami Beach side street, the City Council offered to allow his heirs to use the $40,000 he had left them to build a mausoleum for Fisher in a park bearing his name. The council explained that this was the greatest honor the city could bestow. Miami Beach was dedicated to the principle of eternal youth; no one had ever been buried there, and no one but Fisher ever would. Carl might have enjoyed the council's con game, but his heirs had his body shipped back to Indianapolis.

Except for a portrait of Merrick that hangs in the Coral Gables Country Club, there is no memory in South Florida of the men who helped shape its social history and redesign its natural history. Ironically, the name Flagler and his fortune has a better chance of being honored in the next century thanks to the preservation of barrier islands, not their development. Starting in 1970, The Nature Conservancy has tapped the Mary Flagler Cary Charitable Trust for more than $8 million to acquire eight barrier islands along the Eastern Shore of Virginia. The United Nations has declared these islands stretching for forty-five miles along the Atlantic coast and providing habitat for tens of thousands of nesting or wintering waders, waterfowl, and seabirds to be one of its select Man and the Biosphere Reserves. However, the loggerhead turtles that labor ashore there in early summer and the peregrines that sweep down the beaches in late winter are testimonials to Mrs. Cary's vision, not to her grandfather's. Indeed, these remnant turtles and falcons are melancholy reminders of their many kin that once used the beaches of southern Florida, but do so no more.

The dense seagrape thickets along the beaches and the mangrove forests along the bays once kept many exotic life-forms from entering Florida's ecosystems. Today the disrupted landscape seems to conspire against certain natives. For example, the Australian pine was introduced to Miami Beach by John Collins to protect his fruit trees from salty breezes. The pines spread across Biscayne Bay and were soon being used as windbreaks by homeowners, farmers, and the Army Corps of Engineers throughout the southern mainland. Today they are symbolic of the Tamiami Trail and grow so densely along many of Florida Bay's beaches, they prevent nesting sea turtles from reaching the higher sands where their eggs must be laid if they are to hatch.

South Florida is a horticultural paradise—or a nightmare—depending on how much of the forest a naturalist can see for the trees. Sea mahoe is a salt-tolerant ornamental that has escaped from hotel gardens where it was first planted and is now found even in remote hammocks of the Everglades National Park where tides or birds

have carried its rough seedpods. Brazilian pepper is another ornamental whose red fruits are attractive to birds which have dispersed
the seeds in droppings throughout southern Florida. Tamarind is still
another ornamental—we used to have several forty-foot specimens
growing in the yard of our home on upper Biscayne Bay—which is
fiercely competitive with native flora and can be found in the most
unlikely corners of southern Florida supplanting vegetation that is
more compatible or essential to the region's unique ecosystems.

The avian mélange is possibly more confusing. On a recent walk
through Coral Gables, I saw canary-winged parakeets and red-crested
cardinals from South America, budgerigars from Australia, house
sparrows from England, and Java sparrows and hill mynahs from
Asia. I saw only one native, a mockingbird.

Although most of the tropical introductions will be prevented
from spreading beyond southern Florida by the unsuitability of temperate habitats to the north, there have been some worrisome excep-
tions. The monk parakeet is notorious for despoiling fruit orchards
in its native Argentina, and consequently its presence in a number
of Atlantic coastal states from Florida to Massachusetts has caused
alarm wherever the birds have been found constructing their bulky
nests. Fortunately, the large nests are readily discovered and all have
been destroyed before the monk parakeet could become established.
At least, we hope so.

While most introduced species offer some benefits—even starlings eat pest beetle grubs and looper caterpillars—by definition, an
exotic enters a realm where there are few or no biological controls
affecting its species. This leads to a population explosion in which
the exotic invariably overwhelms some native species usually of far
greater benefit to man and the local habitat. For example, the
eastern bluebird once nested throughout the Miami area, helping to
control some of the biting flies that breed there in abundance.
Starlings, which cannot catch flying insects and prefer feeding on
seeds, berries, and the bits of meat and French fried potatoes found
in the garbage near instant-food eateries, usurped the bluebird's nesting holes, and the best place in South Florida today to look for the
pretty blue thrushes with the rusty-red breasts is in the scrublands
to the west. Like the Seminoles, the bluebird is making his last stand
in the Big Cypress and Everglades.

Floridian fauna has also seen some cold-blooded introductions.
Giant marine toads from South America eat small native birds and
mammals, and their skin-gland secretions are highly toxic to raccoons

Bluebirds: the female left, the male right

and other potential predators. Cobras from Africa and Asia eat bene-
ficial native snakes as well as harmful exotic rats and threaten the
lives of workers in the cane fields around Lake Okeechobee. Walking
catfish move overland at night to new waters where they crowd out
native sunfishes and catfishes, and the occasional piranha caught in
a Florida canal raises the specter of schools of these aggressive predators attacking everything in their environment from native fishes to
swimming dogs.

The marine toad and the walking catfish are now definitely
part of Florida's fauna. We can only cross our fingers that the cobras
and the piranhas are not. Tragically, not a year passes that such dangerous creatures receive reinforcements from the homes of careless
fish and reptile fanciers, or from psychopathic people who find it
funny to terrorize other people and contaminate delicate ecosystems
in the process.

Exotic introductions have affected indigenous life patterns
within the littoral zone less than the destruction of the mangroves
and consequent development have done. Mangroves serve many of
the same functions as *Spartina* marshes. They filter and purify coastal
waters, yet their fallen and decaying leaves provide nutrients for a
myriad of larval and juvenile creatures that use the maze of the
mangrove root system for a nursery. Mangrove roots also stabilize
insecure shorelines better than iron or concrete bulkheads which have

Walking Catfish

replaced them throughout most of tidal Florida. Tens of thousands of waterfront homeowners in Florida annually spend tens of millions of dollars repairing seawalls where nature did not intend seawalls to be.

Like *Spartina alterniflora*, the red mangrove is a terrestrially conceived plant that has adapted to life at the edge of the sea. Red mangrove seeds are unable to germinate in seawater, so they send out their first roots while still hanging within the fruits of the parent tree. The seedlings grow nearly thirty centimeters and develop spikelike tips. If they fall while the tide is out, they spear themselves into the mud and immediately begin the process of producing another tree alongside their parent. However, if the tide is in when the seedlings fall, they plunge toward the bottom, bob back horizontally to the surface, and drift away.

For several weeks red mangrove seedlings float on their sides and travel wherever the tides and winds carry them. Gradually, however, as the roots continue to grow and become heavier in the tips, each seedling assumes both a vertical posture and a neutral buoyancy. They are preparing themselves, like gliders putting down landing gear, to complete their wandering when next they drift into suitably shallow and docile waters where the surge of the sea cannot wrench them from the nourishing silts and sands.

Red mangroves are further like *Spartina* in that the cell sap on the surface of their roots has the density of fresh water. Instead of losing moisture through the tendency of solutions of unequal densities to move through a semipermeable membrane until both solutions are the same, the less dense cell sap of mangrove and *Spartina* roots reverse the osmotic process to draw in nutrients and oxygen.

The red mangrove is more successful at excluding salt than its brackish-living cousin, the black mangrove, so this latter plant, along with both species of *Spartina*, use special glands on the surfaces of their leaves to excrete salt. The moisture in the excreted solution evaporates, and a faint residue of sparkling salt crystals remains for the next rain to wash back into the sea.

Another survival challenge for black mangroves which neither the red mangrove nor *Spartina* has to contend with is how to extract oxygen from the undisturbed anaerobic muds in which the black mangrove takes root. Red mangroves and *S. alterniflora* live on the fringes of such septic mires, while *S. patens* forms turflike mats over them. The low profile and interlocking rhizome mass of *S. patens* prevent storms from uprooting individual plants, but the black mangrove's elevated center of gravity would make it vulnerable to high winds without a compensatingly deep root system. Thus, in order to extract oxygen despite the anaerobic muds in which they are anchored, black mangrove roots send up pneumatophores, or aerial roots, that rise through the oxygenless layers to the water, atmosphere, and light above.

In the early 1950s, the Reigers lived on the residential Bay Harbor (now spelled Harbour) Island at the north end of Biscayne Bay. The island and its commercial Bay Harbour twin had been created out of dredge spoils dumped on top of marginal terrain where mangroves had flourished and German prisoners were kept during World War II. Seawalls ringed both islands, and Australian and slash pine, seagrape and sand spurs quickly took root in the artificial environment. Anole lizards and bobwhite quail had colonized the islands before the war, and the anoles, once sold in pet shops and circuses as "chameleons," remained and flourished ever after the last lots were developed.

At dawn, my younger brother and I would patrol the seawalls, cursing the sand spurs when we stepped on them with bare feet and observing and occasionally hurling gigs at a remarkable spectrum of marine creatures. Some, like the rays and the shortnose batfish, were

there because of an atavistic memory of the shallow flats where the seawalls now stood. The rays of several species were in continual motion along the seawall, except when they stopped to suck a crab or shellfish from the substrate. But the batfish rarely moved except to feed. Batfishes are among the most highly evolved fishes in the world, and like any highly evolved group of animals, they are so specialized in their feeding and breeding behavior, they are unable to adapt when their environment is altered, as happened to upper Biscayne Bay.

Batfishes are broad, flattened creatures that walk about on large, armlike pectoral fins and smaller ventral fins. However, "walk" is not quite an accurate description for how they move. Batfishes more

Great White Heron in a
Red Mangrove swamp
(the seed-pods are
in the foreground)

often hop like toads or bound along like rabbits. Or they can run along the bottom like an awkward aquatic puppy. Their principal defense, however, is not to move at all. They pretend they are inanimate objects, like discarded shells. Even when turned upside down, batfishes, reversing the ploy used by hognose snakes, will give the game away by righting themselves.

Since upper Biscayne Bay's waters were still crystal clear on incoming tides in the early fifties, we often saw various species of grunts —especially the colorful blue-striped grunt and porkfish—and angelfishes, such as immature rock beauties and French angelfish, beginning to colonize the reeflike substrate of concrete bulkheads and pilings. For two or three years a wonderful combination of reef and flats fishes existed near and under our dock, but then pollution and siltation overwhelmed the cleansing effect of tidal currents, and even the mud-grubbing mullets became less frequent sights in the progressively more murky water.

The most breathtaking moments in our morning walkabouts came when jack crevalle suddenly rushed out of the channels to drive schools of mullet up against the seawall where they could not escape. Time and again the mullet leaped desperately against the wall until its rough surface and barnacles had completely scaled the most energetic among them. When the feeding frenzy ceased, usually as suddenly as it had begun, these survivors continued swimming weakly at the surface alongside the wall as though still trying to find a way round the obstacle that had caused their living deaths.

Across the bay from us was a large tract of mangroves that had as yet been overlooked by developers. Through it wound a mahogany-colored tidal stream in which we caught snook, ladyfish, and mangrove snappers. Closely related to the mangrove snapper, and often found in our mangrove backwater was the schoolmaster snapper. This yellowish-barred fish with orange fins has just a dash of blue

Snook among Mangrove roots

beneath its eye to give it a rakish, rather than an academic, look. However, the "schoolmaster" in the fish's popular name refers to its cleverness in distinguishing between food with and without hooks. As specimens get older, they move into deeper water and idle away their days in the company of mangrove snappers and lane snappers, whose reddish hues and upper lateral black spot makes this species seem like a smaller edition of the commercially important mutton snapper. As the sun sets, however, the mangrove and lane snappers fan out over the reefs to feed, while the schoolmaster often returns to the mangroves of its youth to search for shrimp, crabs, and small fishes.

On the flats and in the channels and holes that lay between this mangrove forest and the inlet known as Baker's Haulover, the Reiger boys dived on incoming tides for spiny lobsters and octopus we found in the fifty-five-gallon drums we had taken from construction sites where they were used to burn scrap lumber and which we converted into artificial reefs. We also caught gag grouper and sand perch, both members of the flavorful sea-bass family. On outgoing tides, we fished for tarpon concentrated in the inlet to feed on the shrimp and baitfish funneled to them from everywhere in the upper bay, but particularly from the mahogany-stained waters of the mangrove forest.

My father had bought his three sons a sixteen-foot plywood boat with a "one-lunger" Onan engine. We were strictly admonished to stay inside the bay, but we were soon tempted by the king mackerel runs offshore. Thirty years ago, we used the old Kenilworth Hotel— the only high-rise on the upper beach—as a navigational reference point. Farther south and offshore we used the daily cloud of gulls over "the Rose Bowl"—the city's massive sewage outfall—as another reference point.

When fishing was slow elsewhere, we trolled or drifted through the Rose Bowl and made some outstanding catches. I once brought in a twenty-pound mutton snapper streaming toilet paper from its pectoral fins the way biplane pilots once streamed silk scarfs from their necks in sui generis gestures of gallantry.

Many king mackerel were caught at the Rose Bowl, and because this far-wandering species is seasonally abundant there, the many fishermen who used this facility rationalized that what was good for the fishes was also good for them. We all concurred with the Chamber of Commerce in not making a fuss about the fecal matter that frequently drifted up on Miami Beach. On the contrary, we make jokes about how gullible tourists thought such filth was "sea slugs" or the spawn of "sewer sharks."

Because of a technicality in the Clean Water Act, municipalities which *dump* their raw sewage at sea can be prosecuted by the federal government, but municipalities like Boston and Miami Beach, which *pump* their sewage into the sea, cannot be prosecuted. Hence, thirty years after the Reiger boys last trolled through the swelling effluent of the Rose Bowl, it is still swelling—and occasionally smelling—strong.

In the early fifties, we had not yet heard of eutrophication, but we were intrigued by the fact that the formerly fertile reefs off Miami Beach seemed to be dying. We further noted that the best side for fishing Baker's Haulover was on the north where the mahogany-stained and detritus-enriched waters from the mangrove swamp predominated and could be distinguished on outgoing tides from the chalky-colored and sewage-contaminated waters along the south shore of the inlet—even though the southern pier was more varied and interesting from a structural standpoint.

From the old Haulover Bridge looking down, you could see the rich brown and chalky green waters begin to curl into one another as they swept to sea. Our best tarpon fishing was along this interface, and our mother finally discovered us one afternoon in our breach of contract regarding the boat's use when she happened to drive over the Haulover Bridge at the precise moment we were battling a sixty-pound tarpon and some pretty fierce waves.

By the time our family moved from Bay Harbour in 1952, it was evident that both upper Biscayne Bay and the near-shore waters off Miami Beach were dying. At the time, however, the only alarm expressed by the City Council was for the fact that the beach itself was washing away. Although most of the city's larger hotels built one or more freshwater swimming pools for the increasing numbers of guests reluctant to swim in the sea, the hotel owners were eager to have the beach refurbished because it would be embarrassing for Miami Beach not to have a beach and, even more important, because the foundations of their hotels needed protection from the scouring action of high winds and tides.

I had not been back in Miami Beach for nearly thirty years when in 1980 I was invited there to give a speech and receive a conservation award from the National Wildlife Federation. The city had recently persuaded Congress to spend 50 cents for every man, woman, and child in the nation to restore the beach once more by pumping sand from deep water onto the intertidal berm. Barring a major storm, such engineering fixes are good for up to ten years, when Congress will have to approve funds to do it all over again.

One consolation of this Sisyphean enterprise is that Miami Beach's beach now belongs to all of us and not merely to the hotel owners. Thirty years ago, each hotel had constructed groins, jetties, and barricades in a futile effort to keep the sands from leaving their premises and in a more successful effort to keep guests at one hotel from trespassing on the beach of another. Since every taxpayer has helped support the Army Corps of Engineers' contractors in their beach-building program, this new beach belongs to anyone who may want to walk or jog its many miles. However, most hotels have signs at their beachfront doors warning guests to beware of the tars and other industrial residues prevalent in the dredged sands and to clean their shoes or feet carefully before reentering the hotel.

As I strolled along the edge of what had been a coastal jungle a century ago, what reporters had called Fisher's Dream sixty years ago, and what conservationists now refer to as an ecological disaster, I was perversely optimistic. True, there are no longer any mangroves anywhere on Miami Beach. Yet whereas in the fifties only a handful of environmental specialists regretted that fact, today tens of thousands of thoughtful people do. Thirty years ago beaches were only something to exploit for tourism; today Congress is gradually eliminating the subsidies and other public guarantees that have made the exploitation of barrier beaches possible. The taxpayers will be saddled with "nourishing" Miami Beach for decades to come. But where it once stood as a shining example of what all seaside "wastelands" could become, it now stands as a reminder of our folly and hubris in imagining, like the Danish King Canute who commanded the sea to be still, that we are superior to the winds and tides.

13

LAND'S END

Key West may be the end of the road, but it is not the end of the U.S. littoral zone. In fact, it is not even the end of man's habitation of those tiny coral islands stringing south from the Florida mainland which the Spanish called "cays" and the English-speaking fishermen and wreckers known as Conchs anglicized to "keys." Sixty-eight miles west of Key West is a curious monument to nineteenth-century imperialism known as Fort Jefferson. Since it is part of the national park chain of custodianship, two or more park rangers and their families live there the year around.

Seen from the air, Fort Jefferson has all the quality of a floating toy fort dropped into the middle of an azure sea. Almost everything in the way of fast land lies within the fort's hexagonal walls, and only when your seaplane tilts for the landing turn, do you perceive that the fort rests precariously on top of a small cay surrounded by shallow green water through which you're lucky to spot a sea turtle and then a pair of sharks languorously making their way over the sand.

Of the eleven islands discovered here by Juan Ponce de León in 1513, only seven remain, and it won't be many decades more before this cay, too, will subside under the massive weight of Fort Jefferson. A century or so from now, Spanish hogfish will swim through drowned battlements constructed by American slaves to keep everything Spanish out of Florida.

Begun in 1846, the fort was originally designed to be fifty feet high with eight-foot-thick walls. It was supposed to guard the western approach to the Straits of Florida and handicap Spain's hegemony in the Caribbean. The fort was planned to house 1500 men and 450 cannons.

After the fort was started, however, a youthful strategist in the War Department pointed out that by sailing closer to Cuba, Spanish fleets could simply bypass the fort's mighty guns, and without a sizable harbor, no significant tonnage of American warships could extend the range of the fort's stationary weapons.

Finally, how would the fort be supplied with water? Early navigators had called this cluster of islands the *Dry* Tortugas, implying that while it was a good area to find spawning sea turtles for food, you had to look elsewhere for water.

The young officer's observations fell on deaf ears. Bureaucracies are slow to make decisions, but once made, they require acts of God or Congress, not mere common sense, to alter. The fort would be built, and as if to underline the government's commitment to faith over facts, the island on which it would sit was renamed Garden Key with, perhaps, the childish hope that wishing would make it so.

Sixteen million bricks were eventually mortared into walls around the perimeter of Garden Key, but the War Department's original design was never finished. Only 141 guns were mounted, and fewer than 500 men were ever garrisoned at the fort. The island's wells were soon salty, and today visitors who want to camp overnight must bring their own fresh water.

Although the War Department eventually realized it had a white elephant on its hands, it was not able to unload Fort Jefferson onto a sister agency until 1935 when President Franklin D. Roosevelt declared it to be a national monument. The Interior Department has even less money to maintain the fort than the War Department had. However, the Park Service does not try to explain this to visitors who complain of the increasing number of areas of the fort closed to them because stairs and walls are decaying and have become dangerous. Instead, the rangers tell visitors that the Park Service is using the fort as a living laboratory of the ocean's effect on man-made structures—as though we ever had any other choice.

Most visitors come out of curiosity. A few want to see the cell where Dr. Samuel A. Mudd was wrongfully incarcerated for having rightfully given medical aid to a disguised John Wilkes Booth after he had murdered Abraham Lincoln. Dr. Mudd was eventually pardoned after valiantly working during a yellow fever epidemic to save many of the garrison and his fellow prisoners when fifty-eight men, including the fort's surgeon, died. However, rather than maintain his memory as a martyr to the too common practice of assigning guilt based solely on association, his name—except in the pejorative expression "his name is Mudd"—has been largely forgotten. Most biographical dictionaries no longer carry him.

However, they do carry Ernest Hemingway whose life and art have a vital connection with Fort Jefferson. In 1928 Hemingway met Carlos Gutiérrez, the owner of a Cuban fishing smack, in Fort Jefferson's tiny harbor. Hemingway was there to catch marlin in the blue water beyond the reefs; Gutiérrez was there to catch bait so he could return to Cuba where he fished for marlin off Coijimar, a coastal village about ten miles east of Havana. Gutiérrez had been following this routine since 1884 when he went to sea with his father at the age of six.

Naturally Hemingway, the tyro, was fascinated by Carlos' marlin fishing stories. Two in particular stuck in Hemingway's mind. One was about a huge white marlin which Carlos hooked but which was seized in turn by another unknown marlin over which Carlos had no control. After a long while, the greater fish let go, and Carlos brought his 150-pound catch, crushed and dead, to the surface.

The other story concerned an old man who went out fishing alone and hooked a big fish which dragged him far out to sea. Two days later, the old man was picked up with the head and tail of an enormous blue marlin lashed to his skiff. He had fought the fish for two days and two nights with a handline, finally bringing it close enough to harpoon. Then, finding the marlin too large to pull into his small boat, the old man tied it alongside. Sharks arrived, and despite stubborn resistance with clubs and gaffs, the old man lost half his catch. When he was picked up, sharks still circled the boat, and the old man was sobbing in frustration and exhaustion. The marlin's scant remains weighed eight hundred pounds.

Thus, on a still tropic night anchored off Fort Jefferson's derelict coaling dock, while fish splashed and rolled in the shallows, Ernest Hemingway first heard the tale that he would one day refine into a Pulitzer Prize called *The Old Man and the Sea*. Hemingway eventually fished in Cuba, looked up Carlos, and made him his guide, and from him and his own observations learned enough about billfish to write a twenty-six-page scientific treatise, *Marlin Off Cuba*, which was published the year Fort Jefferson became a national monument.

However, the story of the old man and a victory that transcended inevitable defeat was something that Hemingway had to wrestle with and nurture for twenty-four years before it was finished in his mind.

Then *The Old Man and the Sea* took just eight weeks to complete with practically no rewriting.

Yet earlier than Hemingway's fateful meeting with Gutiérrez, and even earlier than the injustice done Dr. Mudd, Fort Jefferson served as the site for a major contribution to marine biology. In 1843, Charles Darwin published his first monograph, *The Structure and Distribution of Coral-Reefs*, which theorized that all reefs begin by growing next to an island or continental platform (fringing reefs), that they continue growing upon themselves while the land mass begins to subside (barrier reefs), and that they still continue growing after the land mass, usually an island, has long since sunk beneath the waves (atolls). The core of Darwin's thesis assumed an adaptability and relatively fast growth rate for coral reefs that most scientists of his day were unwilling to credit.

To test Darwin's theory, Louis Agassiz and Spencer Fullerton Baird asked their mutual friend, Joseph Bassett Holder, in 1859 to collect specimens and to study the growth of corals near Key West

Wrasse swimming among Brain Coral

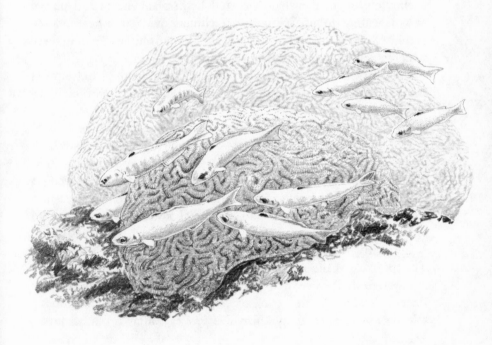

where Dr. Holder was surgeon-in-charge of the government's engineering facilities. When the Civil War broke out and Dr. Holder became the health officer for the military prison at Fort Jefferson, he delegated his marine scientific work to his precocious son, Charles Frederick, who took measurements of the coral growing in the seawater moat which nearly surrounds the fort.

Young Holder learned that while massive brain corals do grow slowly, branched corals grow much faster than had previously been realized—as much as 12.5 centimeters per year in the warm, shallow, and protected waters of the moat. He further found that some, particularly younger, corals can double their diameters within six months to a year. Although Joseph Bassett Holder continued to supervise the scientific correspondence that sailed between Garden Key and Agassiz' Museum of Comparative Zoology at Harvard and Baird's Smithsonian Institution, both scientists in the North knew that the fieldwork was being done by a ten-year-old boy. Nonetheless, Agassiz and Baird revised their estimates on the development of barrier reefs and coral atolls which they had formerly assumed grew from the bottom up rather than merely being relics of fringing reefs.

Well over a century later, some of the same corals that young Holder studied still grow at Fort Jefferson. Periodic hurricanes have done less damage to these intricate animal colonies than to the fort itself. Left to their own devices and barring an unexpected plague of coral-eating fishes, sponges, or echinoderms (starfishes and sea urchins), or a catastrophe of cold water, there is no reason why these same corals might not outlive the fort.

I return to my campsite, put on my mask, snorkel, and flippers and enter the water between Fort Jefferson's new dock and the pilings of the old.

I have largely given up spear fishing—which is anyway prohibited in the waters around the fort—and shell collecting—also, prohibited—because such physical contact with my surroundings ruins the dreamlike quality of being underwater. My hands, gloved to protect them from inadvertent contact with red fire sponges and stinging corals, seem to belong to somebody else or, perhaps, to nobody at all.

Twenty years ago, I dived the way film addicts go to the movies. The spectacle of the sea became more important to me than anything in my terrestrial existence. Then a would-be assassin swam off the screen and shocked me out of my reverie. In June 1964, I was diving solo over a ledge in about thirty-five feet of water. In those days I had undamaged ears and a lung capacity that allowed me to free-dive to such depths. I was pursuing a snapper with my spear gun when the shadow of a large fish passed over me. I looked up and saw that the nine-foot requiem-type shark above me lacked the penislike appendages known as claspers which trail from the male shark's pelvic fins and which are used to hold the female and insert semen. By observing such details, I tried to avoid thinking about the fact that the shark was interested in me.

I surfaced and began a slow retreat toward the beach several hundred yards away. The shark turned and came within ten feet before veering off and disappearing into the blue haze of deep water. A moment or so elapsed and she was suddenly there again, this time coming from the beach directly behind me. Again and again, she disappeared in one direction and reappeared from another. She was a cat and I was her mouse. Each time she reappeared, she seemed to swim a little faster and turn away a little closer.

As I got into shallower water, the shark could only approach from the offshore side, but she also came toward me after increasingly shorter intervals which took her only to the limit of my underwater vision before she turned and with a flick of the tail sped toward me. Finally, she came so close I used the butt of my spear gun and my gloved right hand to shear her away. At that point, my carefully calculated retreat turned into a rout. I churned and stumbled the remaining yards from the water to the sand, expecting at any instant to feel the shark bite into one of my legs!

But she was gone—possibly as startled by the contact as I was. Up until the moment I actually put my hands on the shark, she had been only a forbidding character in an underwater scenario in which the hero (me) could always wake up (come ashore) when the suspense became unbearable. At the moment of contact, however, I felt an intimation of my own mortality.

René Tillich, my partner on that camping trip who had taken a siesta while I had recklessly dived by myself, was unable to find enough clothes and blankets in our combined duffels to stop my violent trembling. He suggested we move up the coast a few miles, and we did, but it was a day before I could swim much beyond where I could stand.

The first structure-dependent fish to greet me is a sergeant major, a yellowish-and-black-striped member of the damselfish family. Distributed throughout the warmer waters of the world, damselfishes, one of whose species is famous for being able to live within the stinging tentacles of sea anemones, are distinguished from the equally colorful and tropically abundant butterflyfishes and angelfishes by the damselfishes' single nostril on each side of the snout, rather than two.

The names of damselfishes are almost as colorful as the family itself. Besides the sergeant major, they include such descriptive identities as the night sergeant, beau gregory, blue chromis, and honey damselfish. The family's present representative darts between me and its piling territory. Male sergeant majors guard the female's eggs which are attached individually by an adhesive filament to a solid substrate. I circle the piling to look for the eggs but find none. Another diver might interpret the sergeant major's boldness as playfulness, but I detect a desperate urgency in its apparent game of hide-and-seek, so I move on.

I have set myself the goal of circumnavigating the fort underwater, and if I'm to make the circuit before dark, I must keep swimming.

I take a breath when I reach the first underwater section of the fort's outer wall and dive to investigate a pair of antennae jutting from a cavity in the wall's foundation. The antennae belong to an enormous crawfish or spiny lobster, and for a moment I regret that the fort is a national monument and that I can't, therefore, have the lobster for dinner.

While holding on to the wall and trying to keep my position near bottom, I stir up little storms of sand investigated by three slippery dicks. They dart here and there, and one seems to capture prey that is invisible to me. Then the black-striped, cigar-shaped fish scull away, swimming mostly with their pectoral fins and giving the impression they are dragging their tails behind them.

Slippery dicks are wrasses, the Labridae, one of the largest (possibly six hundred species) and most successful of all fish families. Around Fort Jefferson they range in size from the six-inch slippery dick to three-foot hogfish, one of the most desirable food and game reef-fishes in the Caribbean. However, Labridae in the Indo-Pacific grow even larger. My friend and fellow outdoor writer, Boyd Pfeiffer, once caught a hump-headed Maori wrasse off Lizard Island in Australia's Great Barrier Reef. The fish weighed 35 pounds, but Boyd's hosts assured him it was a "baby." This wrasse commonly exceeds 100 pounds, and one caught off Australia's Hayman Island weighed 420 pounds.

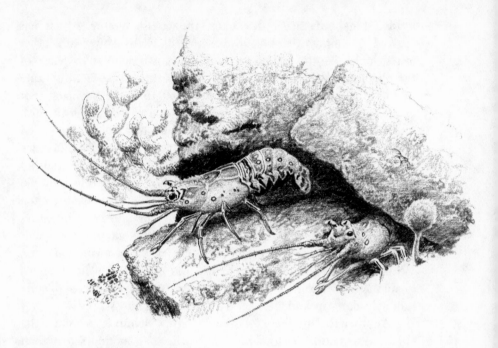

Spiny Lobster: Finger Coral at left,
Merman's Shavingbrush at far right

Another common wrasse of the Dry Tortugas is the bluehead. This fish is sexually dimorphic, which means most males and females have different coloration and sometimes slightly different forms. For example, many male blueheads are not only colored differently from the females, but they develop streamer rays at the tops and bottoms of their tails. Sexual dimorphism is found in some other wrasses as well as in some parrotfishes, the Scaridae. However, whereas in most of these other species, all individuals start out as males or females (usually the latter) and a change in color indicates a change in sex, a bluehead adult male may be either blue-headed or yellow, which is the only color females can be. Even more curious, whereas spawning between a bluehead male and a yellow female is always a private affair, spawning between yellow males and yellow females is always a group enterprise.

To cap this puzzling phenomenon with sheer bewilderment, yellow bluehead wrasse pick parasites off other fishes, but the blue-headed blueheads never do. Thus, the wrasse blenny, which has evolved to mimic the bluehead's trusted relationship with other fishes, looks like the yellow and not the blue-headed color phase of the bluehead. Although the wrasse blenny is a near perfect duplicate of the bluehead's yellow color phase—even to the little black spot on the anterior portion of the dorsal fin—we can easily distinguish the true bluehead from the phony by the former's obviously scaled body. Yet for some reason, other fishes cannot detect this difference which seems so apparent to a human. The wrasse blenny waits in its burrow, often utilizing one originally dug by a boring mollusk, for a yellow-phase bluehead to swim by. The wrasse blenny then slips out and innocently tags along. Sooner or later, the bluehead will visit a cleaning station where a grouper or moray eel waits with open mouth and gills for the cleaner to pick off annoying parasites. While the larger fish sits contentedly and the true bluehead begins to snip away the sources of the host's aggravation, the wrasse blenny suddenly darts in and nips off a piece of the host's lip!

Another feeding technique used by this blenny is to mimic the bluehead's smooth, pectoral-propelled swimming motion rather than reveal its blenny heritage with erratic jerky movements. The wrasse blenny glides deceitfully in among a school of tiny fish, which assume that the blenny, like a bluehead or they themselves, are intent on a meal of small copepods. With a sudden rush, the four-inch wrasse blenny will swallow one or two of the smaller fish. These juveniles and, more especially older and presumably wiser groupers and morays, never seem to learn that blueheads with distinctly scaled bodies can be trusted while bluehead look-alikes with apparently scaleless bodies are to be avoided—or to be eaten.

As I round a corner of the fort's moat wall, a midnight parrotfish spies me and sculls furiously away from the cluster of coral spikes it had been grazing. The midnight is a dark violet parrotfish with bright blue markings and green buck teeth. The midnight and other parrotfishes play a significant role—if not *the* significant role—in creating many of the beautiful white beaches of the Florida Keys and the Caribbean. Most Scaridae feed on the algae and animal polyps that form or live within corals. However, in order to reach the polyps and algae, parrotfishes must consume the limestone exoskeletons. Like herds of cattle feeding across a pasture, schools of parrotfish will grind down all the prominent features of a reef, and much like cattle chewing cud, parrotfish will mumble the limestone material back and forth between horny plates on the roofs of their mouths and tongues and expectorate the stony residues as sand. Storms carry the calcareous material ashore where Northern tourists remark on how "crunchy" tropical beaches feel in comparison to their denser quartzite strands at home.

Corals, sea anemones, hydrozoans, and jellyfishes all belong to a group of animals called coelenterates. One of their characteristics is that coelenterates have the capacity to reproduce themselves sexually by combing sperm and eggs or asexually by subdividing themselves. A new coral colony usually begins when a fertilized egg is ejected into the sea and becomes part of the zooplanktonic community drifting over the reef. About the size of a pinhead, the coral larva moves with the aid of cilia, or tiny hairs, lining the periphery of its body. While jellyfish larvae continue developing as drifting forms, coral larvae eventually sink, and if they are fortunate enough to find a hard surface—a discarded shell or a brick at the base of Fort Jefferson's wall—they immediately begin to secrete a limestone shelter made of calcium carbonate filtered from the sea. Once a larva is anchored within its calcareous cup, it metamorphoses further into a fragile polyp capped by a mouth surrounded by petallike tentacles. Even as the polyp begins to sweep food into its mouth from the surrounding sea, it begins subdividing into more mouths and tentacles. A second polyp buds from the first, and then two or three bud from the second. Each constructs its own limestone exoskeleton. Hundreds are so closely clustered, each within its own cup, that it is soon impossible to determine which was the colonial progenitor. Each additional polyp is joined to the others by a sheet of tissue folded outward from the skeletal cup. Although a massive brain coral may eventually measure ten feet in diameter, it is made up of millions of individual polyps which share a common digestive tract so that all parts of a colony can benefit if only one part reaps a current-borne bonanza of phytoplankton.

Although some specialized corals have been found growing nearly three miles deep, and star coral thrives even in the cold waters of New England, coral growth is always most vigorous in warm seas just below the low-water mark. The reason may be the presence of symbiotic algal cells called zooxanthellae, which are found growing in the tissues of all corals where sunlight is intense. Although many corals can exist without such cells, none of the faster-growing varieties are without a significant allotment of zooxanthellae. This alga, plus the polyps and connective tissue that bind together the coral colonies, is what the parrotfishes are after when they nip off the tips of horn and finger corals and placidly grind them up to get the goodies within. Branched corals grow rapidly to compensate for the continual attrition caused by parrotfishes as well as by storm waves. Contrariwise, the rounded bulk of brain corals swells very slowly because such spherical surfaces are less susceptible to both storms and parrotfishes once the size of the colony exceeds a fish's bite.

About the only enemies the slower-growing corals have once they reach boulder size are pollution, reef subsidence, and cold water. Not many years ago, scientists from the U.S. Geological Survey took core samples from massive *Montastraea annularis* corals on Hen and Chickens Reef off the upper Florida Keys to try to determine what had killed this reef. Siltation from local dredging operations and chemical pollution may have weakened the coral, but stress bands within the annual rings of coral growth suggested that the telling blow had been struck during the winter of 1969–70 by extremely cold water flushed from Florida Bay through a tidal pass opening directly over the reef. That same winter season, hundreds of thousands of tropical fishes died throughout the upper Keys.

In a follow-up study, the Geological Survey's Harold Hudson successfully removed a ten-foot core from a large specimen of *M. annularis* and found that the coral head had begun forming about the time the Pilgrims landed at Plymouth. Various stress bands within the core were evidence of previous cold spells, and an especially pronounced stress band correlates with the great freeze of 1894, which persuaded Henry M. Flagler to extend his railroad to Miami and totally frost-free Key West.

I surface, blow water from the snorkel, and paddle on. Below me, a blue parrotfish pokes its face beneath a limestone ledge. It lays over to squeeze its humped forehead under the rock, then backs out, reverses itself, and tries again. Once more it backs out, turns over, and suddenly slides out of sight just as a spotted moray flows out from the other side of the rock.

The changing of the guard: the blue parrotfish looking for a safe place in which to secrete its protective mucous nightgown that apparently reduces odor and, hence, the fish's vulnerability when it is keeled over asleep; and the moray, supreme predator of the coral caverns, emerging to forage through the darkness for small fish, spiny lobster, and its favorite prey, octopus. Since both the eel and the parrotfish are of the same three-foot length, the parrotfish is safe from this particular eel, and the eel is always safe from parrotfishes.

But the shy moray is taking no chances. When the bulky parrotfish moves in, the eel moves out.

Morays have fanglike teeth that in some species are so long in their arched jaws, the teeth are menacingly exposed even when their mouths are closed. Some species are fiercely territorial, and the locally abundant green moray will sometimes chase or bite divers who blindly thrust their hands into the eel's home lair. Such aggressive-defensiveness and their sinuous appearance have given the moray an evil and unfair press second only to that heaped upon the circum-spect but snaggle-toothed barracuda.

Barracudas, morays, and even parrotfishes often harm man, but they do so more regularly as ciguatera-blemished food than as living creatures.

The word *ciguatera* is derived from the Spanish name for a poisonous snail, but the disease was first reported as fish toxin from the West Indies in 1555 by Peter Martyr. The symptoms are abdominal cramps, nausea, vomiting, and watery diarrhea. Sometimes the victim feels numb in his extremities, a reversal of hot and cold temperature sensation, looseness and pain in his teeth, and blindness. If the patient survives for four days, he will probably live, although one victim was ill twenty-six days and only recovered after she began taking large doses of vitamin B, B_{12}, and C.

Although the most frequently blighted fishes are barracuda, red snapper, amberjack, and grouper in that order, any of the fishes that feed on the benthic blue-green algae that are the source of the toxin can be poisonous—which is how parrotfishes, angelfishes, and other reef grazers come into the picture. Any predator which then feeds on these grazers concentrates the toxin into even more poisonous doses—which is how barracudas and morays get implicated.

Yet barracudas and morays, especially spotted morays, are eaten by people throughout the Caribbean. The fish are consumed according to dependable but unexplainable geographical codes. For example, barracuda on one side of Grand Cayman Island are considered safe and, if less than two feet long, delectable. However, barracuda from the other side of the island are not consumed. Such guidelines are not totally illogical when one considers that certain reef predators, especially barracuda and amberjack, tend to patrol limited territories within a reef for weeks or months at a time. Hence, they may be confined in or excluded from ciguatera-free zones.

Whatever the reason, thousands of tons of fish species linked to ciguatera poisoning are eaten annually by people in the Caribbean without the first case of even indigestion. On the other hand, ciguatera is a very real threat with frequently deadly consequences in those areas of the Caribbean without ciguatera-free zones and with high human populations who have no choice but to play Russian roulette with what they eat.

My feet touch bottom in a quiet cove on the other side of the park dock from where I started. The bottom is littered with dead seagrape leaves and a palm frond, while a few bits of woody material float at the surface. Among them is a small needlefish (Belonidae) pretending to be nothing alive so it will not be noticed by a predator or its prey.

I sit in the shallows and remove my mask, snorkel, and swim fins. The water is nearly the same temperature as the evening air, and I remain there, watching the western sky and waiting for the tropical sunset afterflash that rarely occurs and does not tonight. The lights in camp begin to glow brighter than the twilight, and a friend's shadow moves in front of the tent.

The sea, as always, has been refreshing, but there is something else in my contentment this evening having, perhaps, to do with the completion of my circumnavigation of the tiny island or maybe the culmination of my Atlantic odyssey. One of the ways we measure education and progress is by how well science dispels the fears and illusions of our youth. A child dreads darkness and anything unknown because he imagines that child-eating monsters are there. However, as a person or society matures, that which is mysterious becomes appealing, not appalling.

A century ago, almost all mankind regarded the sea as containing only two kinds of creatures: those worth gold as food or oil and those less than worthless because they ate the valuable creatures or ourselves. Today, however, a growing number of thoughtful writers and filmmakers are communicating the wonder of scientific discovery to the public, and an increasing number of ordinary people are taking an interest in nature and its diversity, particularly those creatures which look or act like the monsters of our childhood nightmares.

Even as recently as 1950 in his account of the *Kon-Tiki* voyage, Thor Heyerdahl dramatized the hazards he and his crew faced from sea monsters. When a huge, but quite harmless whale shark appears alongside his raft, Heyerdahl transforms this docile plankton feeder into such a hideous apparition, the reader is relieved when one of

Heyerdahl's companions, Erick Hesselberg, thrusts a harpoon "with all his giant strength down between his legs and deep into the whale shark's grisly head."

Thor Heyerdahl may be embarrassed today by some of the things he wrote more than three decades ago; derisive laughter, after all, adversely affects his credibility and his campaign to arouse people's concern for an increasingly depleted and contaminated sea. Yet why should a man, any more than a society, be embarrassed about what he or it did, built, or wrote during its callow youth? The wonder of humanity lies in our capacity both as individuals and societies to continue growing intellectually until we die. We may create follies in our youth—Fort Jeffersons of the mind as well as of brick and mortar. However, as we grow older, many individuals and some societies learn to live with nature and inevitable death and not continue denying them or trying to conquer them.

Societies seem to differ in some of the ways that corals do. Just as there are branched corals which grow rapidly to compensate for the attrition provoked by the coral's elaborate designs, there are societies whose relatively brief existences are based on the incompatibility of their wants with nature's needs. By contrast, some societies, like some corals, grow slowly and live for many hundreds of years, surviving by not competing with nature but by adjusting to its pace and dynamism. People within such societies seem to understand that our most certain immortality lies within ourselves, not within monuments.

APPENDIX

SELECTED SCIENTIFIC AND CONSERVATION ORGANIZATIONS

American Fisheries Society
5410 Grosvenor Lane
Bethesda, MD 20014
(301) 897-8616

American Littoral Society
Sandy Hook
Highlands, NJ 07732
(201) 291-0055

The American Museum
   of Natural History
Central Park West at 79th Street
New York, NY 10024
(212) 873-1300

Atlantic Center for the
   Environment
39 South Main Street
Ipswich, Massachusetts 01938
(617) 356-0038

Audubon Naturalist Society of
   the Central Atlantic States, Inc.
8940 Jones Mill Road
Washington, DC 20015
(301) 652-9188

The Conservation Foundation
1717 Massachusetts Avenue NW
Washington, DC 20036
(202) 797-4300

International Game Fish
   Association
3000 East Las Olas Boulevard
Fort Lauderdale, FL 33316
(305) 467-0161

The Izaak Walton League
   of America
Suite 806
1800 North Kent Street
Arlington, VA 22209
(703) 528-1818

Marine Mammal Program
Smithsonian Institution
NHB Stop 108
Washington, DC 20560
(202) 357-1920

National Audubon Society
950 Third Avenue
New York, NY 10022
(212) 833-3200

National Coalition for
  Marine Conservation
P.O. Box 23298
Savannah, GA 31403
(912) 234-8062

National Geographic Society
17th and M Streets NW
Washington, DC 20036
(202) 857-7000

National Wildlife Federation
1412 16th Street NW
Washington, DC 20036
(202) 797-6800

The Nature Conservancy
Suite 800
1800 North Kent Street
Arlington, VA 22209
(703) 841-5300

The Oceanic Society
Executive Offices
Stamford Marine Center
Magee Avenue
Stamford, CT 06902
(203) 327-9786

Scientific Event Alert Network
Smithsonian Institution
  (24-hour answering)
  (202) 357-1511
Telex 89599 SCINET WSH
Datagram (800) 325-6000
  ID No. 1776

Sport Fishing Institute
Suite 801
608 13th Street NW
Washington, DC 20005
(202) 737-0668

Stripers Unlimited, Inc.
P.O. Box 45
South Attleboro, MA 02703
(617) 761-7983

GLOSSARY OF FLORA AND FAUNA

(See Index for First Mention)

albatross, *Diomedea* sp.
alewife, *Pomolobus pseudoharengus*
alligator, American, *Alligator mississippiensis*
amberjack, *Seriola dumerili*
angelfish, Family Chaetodontidae
angelfish, black, *Pomocanthus areuatus*
angelfish, French, *Holacanthus ciliaris*
anglerfish, Family Lophiidae
arrowwood, *Viburnum dentatum*

barracuda, *Sphyraena* sp.
bass, common sea, *Centropristes striatus;* also, black sea bass
bass, largemouth, *Micropterus salmoides*
bass, spottail, *Sciaenops ocellatus;* also, channel bass, red drum
bass, striped, *Morone saxatilis*
batfish, shortnose, *Ogcocephalus nasutus*
bayberry, *Myrica pensylvanica*
blackbird, redwinged, *Agelaius phoeniceus*
blueberry, *Vaccinium* sp.
bluebird, eastern, *Sialia sialis*
bluefish, *Pomatomus saltatrix*
bluehead wrasse, *Thalassoma bifasciatum*
booby, red-footed, *Sula sula*
brant, Atlantic, *Branta bernicla*

broadsole, Family Soleidae
budgerigar, *Melopsittacus undulatus*
bufflehead, *Bucephala albeola*
butterfish, *Poronotus triacanthus*
butterfly, monarch, *Danaus plexippus*
buttonwood, *Conocarpus erecta*

cardinal, American, *Cardinalis cardinalis*
cardinal, red-crested, *Paroaria coronata*
carp, *Cyprinus carpio*
catfish, walking, *Clarias batrachus*
cedar, bay, *Suriana maritima*
cedar, red, *Juniperus virginiana*
cedar, saltwater, *Tamarix gallica*
cherry, wild, *Prunus serotina*
chigger, a skin-burrowing mite of the Order Acarina not to be confused with the chigger flea or chigoe, *Tunga penetrans,* more commonly found in Mexico, Central and South America
chipmunk, *Tamias striatus*
clam, black, *Arctica islandica*
clam, hard-shell, *Mercenaria mercenaria*
clam, soft-shelled, *Mya arenonia*
clam, surf, *Spisula solidissima*
cobra, *Naja* sp.
coot, American, *Fulica americana*

257

copperhead, *Agkistrodon contortrix*
coral, brain, *Colpophyllia natans*
coral, branched, *Acropora* sp.
coral, finger, *Porites* sp.
coral, star, *Astrangia danae*
coral, stinging, *Millepora* sp.
cottonmouth, *Agkistrodon piscivorus*
crab, blue, *Callinectes sapidus*
crab, china-back fiddler, *Uca pugilator*
crab, horseshoe, *Limulus polyphemus*
crab, mud fiddler, *Uca minax*
crab, salt marsh fiddler, *Uca pugnax*
crappie, *Pomoxis* sp.
crocodile, American, *Crocodylus acutus*
crow, fish, *Corvus ossifragus*
crowberry, black, *Empetrum nigrum*
curlew, long-billed, *Numenius americanus*
cusk, *Brosme brosme*
cypress, bald, *Taxodium distichum*

damselfish, Family Pomacentridae
dolphin, bottlenosed, *Tursiops truncatus*
dolphin, common, *Delphinus delphis*; also, crisscross dolphin, saddleback dolphin
dolphinfish, *Coryphaena hippurus*
dovekie, *Alle alle*
duck, black, *Anas rubripes*
duck, harlequin, *Histrionicus histrionicus*
duck, mallard, *Anas platyrhynchos*
duck, ruddy, *Oxyura jamaicenis*
duck, wood, *Aix sponsa*
dusty miller, *Artemisia stelleriana*

eagle, bald, *Haliaetus leucocephalus* southern bald eagle, *H. l. leucocephalus*
eel, American, *Anguilla rostrata*
eel, green moray, *Gymnothorax funebris*
eel, spotted moray, *Gymnothorax moringa*

eelgrass, *Zostera marina*
egret, American, *Casmerodius albus*: also Great
egret, cattle, *Bubulcus ibis*
egret, snowy, *Egretta thula*
eider, common, *Somateria mollisima*

falcon, peregrine, *Falco peregrinus*
filefish, Family Monacanthidae
flamingo, *Phoenicopterus ruber*
flounder, Gulf, *Paralichthys albigutta*
flounder, hogchoker, *Trinectus maculatus*
flounder, sundial, *Lophopsetta maculata*; also, windowpane
flounder, winter, *Pseudopleuronectes americanus*
fluke, *Paralichthys dentatus*; also summer flounder, northern fluke
fluke, four-spotted, *Paralichthys oblongus*
fluke, southern, *Paralichthys lethostigmus*
fly, deer, *Chrysops callidus*
fly, greenhead, *Tabanus nigrovitatti*
flying fish, Family Evocoetidae
fulmar, northern, *Fulmarus glacialis*

gallinule, common, *Gallinula chloropus*
gallinule, purple, *Porphyrula martinica*
gannet, *Morus bassanus*
goldeneye, *Bucephala* sp.
goldenrod, seaside, *Solidago sempervirens*
goose, Canada, *Branta canadensis*
goose, greater snow, *Chen caerulescens atlantica*
grackle, boat-tailed, *Cassidix mexicanus*
grape, wild, *Vitus labrusca*
grass, beach, *Ammophila brevigulata*
grass, reed, *Phragmites* sp.
grass, salt hay, *Spartina patens*; also, salt meadow hay, marsh hay cordgrass

grebe, Family Podicipedidae
greenbriar, *Smilax rotundifolia*
grenadier, Family Macrouridae
groundsel, *Baccharis halinifolia*
grouper, Family Serranidae
grouper, gag, *Mycteroperca microlepis*
grouper, snowy, *Epinephelus niveatus*
grunt, Family Pomadasyidae
grunt, blue-striped, *Haemulon sciurus*
guillemot, black, *Cepphus grylle*
gull, glaucous, *Larus hyperboreus*
gull, great black-backed, *Larus marinus*
gull, herring, *Larus argentatus*
gull, Iceland, *Larus glaucoides*
gull, laughing, *Larus atricilla*
gull, lesser black-backed, *Larus fuscus*

hackberry, *Celtis laevigata*
hagfish, Atlantic, *Myxine glutinosa*
hairgrass, *Deschampsia oaespitosa*
hake, *Urophycis* sp.
halibut, Family Hippoglossidae
hawk, Cooper's, *Accipiter cooperii*
hawk, sharp-shinned, *Accipiter striatus*
heather, beach, *Hudsonia tomentosa*
heron, black-crowned night, *Nycticorax nycticorax*
heron, great blue, *Ardea herodias*
heron, little blue, *Florida caerulea*
heron, Louisiana, *Hydranassa tricolor*
heron, yellow-crowned night, *Nycticorax violacea*
herring, blueback, *Pomolobus aestivalis*
herring, sea, *Clupea harengus*; also, sardine
hickory, pignut, *Carya glabra*
hickory, shagbark, *Carya ovata*
hogfish, common, *Lachnolaimus maximus*
hogfish, Spanish, *Bodianus rufus*
holly, American, *Ilex opaca*
honeysuckle, *Lonicera japonica*

hornet, bald-faced, *Vespula maculata*
horsefly, black, *Tabanus attratus*

ibis, glossy, *Plegadis falcinellus*
ibis, white, *Eudocinius albus*
Indian pipe, *Monotropa uniflora*
Irish moss, *Chondrus crispus*
ironwood, black, *Krugiodendron ferreum*

jack crevalle, *Caranx hippos*
Japanese beetle, *Popullia japonica*
joewood, *Jaquinia keyensis*
juneberry, coastal, *Amelanchier obvalis*

kingfish, northern, *Menticirrhus saxatilis*; also, king whiting
kite, Everglades, *Rostrhamus sociabilis*; also, snail kite
kittiwake, black-legged, *Rissa tridactyla*
krill, *Euphausia* sp.

ladyfish, *Elops saurus*
lavender, sea, *Tournefortia gnaphalodes*
lignum vitae, *Guaiacum sanctum*
lizard, anole, *Anolis* sp.; also, chameleon
lobster, spiny, *Panuliris argus*
locust, Family Cicadidae
lookdown, *Selene vomer*
loon, common, *Gavia immer*
looper caterpillar, Family Geometridae

mackerel, Atlantic, *Scomber scombrus*
mackerel, king, *Scomberomorus cavalla*
mackerel, Spanish, *Scomberomorus maculatus*
mahoe, sea, *Hibiscus tiliacens*
mahogany, *Swietenia mahogani*
manatee, *Trichechus manatus*
mangrove, black, *Aviceunia nitida*
mangrove, red, *Rhizophora mangle*
marlin, white, *Makaira albida*
marsh elder, *Iva frutescens*

menhaden, Atlantic, *Brevoortia tyrannus;* also, mossbunker, 'bunker, pogy, fatback
menhaden, Gulf, *Brevoortia patronus*
minnow, sheepshead, *Cyprinodon variegatus*
mockingbird, *Mimus polyglottos*
mourning dove, *Zenaida macroura*
mouse, house, *Mus musculus*
mulberry, *Morus alba*
mullet, Family Mugilidae
mummichog, *Fundulus heteroclitus;* also, bull minnow, mud minnow
murre, *Uria* sp.
mynah, hill, *Gracula religiosa*
myrtle, sea, *Baccharis halimifolia*
myrtle, wax, *Myrica cerifera*

needlefish, Family Belonidae
needlerush, black, *Juncus roemerianus*
noddy, brown, *Anous stolidus*
nutria, *Myocastor coypus*

oak, red, *Quercus rubra*
oak, Spanish, *Quercus falcata*
oak, white, *Quercus alba*
octopus, common, *Octopus vulgaris*
oldsquaw, *Clangula hyemalis*
osprey, *Pandion haliaetus*
owl, screech, *Otus asio*
owl, short-eared, *Asio flammens*
oxeye, sea, *Borrichia frutescens*
oyster, common, *Crassostrea virginica*
oyster drill, *Urosalpinx cinerea*
oyster toad, *Opsanus tau*

palm, royal, *Roystonia regia*
palmetto, saw, *Serenoa repens*
paper wasp, zebra, *Polistes exclamans*
parakeet, canary-winged, *Brotogesis versicolorus*
parakeet, monk, *Myiopsitta monachus*
parrotfish, Family Scaridae
parrotfish, blue, *Scarus coeruleus*
parrotfish, midnight, *Scarus coelestinus*

penguin, Emperor, *Aptenodytes forsteri*
pepper, Brazilian, *Schinus terebinthefolius*
perch, sand, *Diplectrum formosum*
perch, white, *Morone americana*
perch, yellow, *Perca flavescens*
permit, *Trachinotus falcatus*
persimmon, *Diospyros virginiana*
petrel, band-rumped storm, *Oceanodroma castro*
petrel, South Trinidad, *Pterodroma arminjoniana*
petrel, white-faced storm, *Pelagodroma marina*
pickerel, redfin, *Esox americanus*
pine, Australian, *Casuarina* sp.
pine, loblolly, *Pinus taeda*
pine, Norfolk Island, *Araucaria excelsa*
pine, pitch, *Pinus rigida*
pine, slash, *Pinus elliottii*
pipefish, northern, *Synnathus fuseus*
piranha, *Serrasalmus* sp.
pitcher plant, *Sarracenia purpurea*
plover, black-bellied, *Pluvialis squatarola*
plover, golden, *Pluvialis dominica*
poison ivy, *Rhus radicans*
porcupine fish, Family Diodontidae
porgy, northern, *Stenotomus chrysops;* also, scup
porkfish, *Anisotremus virginicus*
porpoise, common, *Phocoena phocoena;* also, harbor porpoise
prickly pear, *Opuntia humifera*
puffer, northern, *Sphaeroides maculatus*
puffin, *Fratercula arctica*

quahog, *Mercenaria mercenaria*
quahog, ocean, *Arctica islandica*
quail, bobwhite, *Colinus virginianus*

rail, black, *Laterallus jamaicensis*
rail, clapper, *Rallus longirostris;* also, marsh hen
rail, sora, *Porzana carolina*
rail, Virginia, *Rallus limicola*

rail, yellow, *Coturnicops
noveboracensis*
rat, Norway, *Rattus norveticus*
robin, *Turdus migratorius*
robin, sea, *Prionotus* sp.
rock beauty, *Holacanthus tricolor*

salmon, Atlantic, *Salmo salar*
saltwort, *Salicornia* sp.; also,
glasswort
sand dab, Family Pleuronectidae
sand perch, *Diplectrum formosum*
sandpiper, purple, *Calidris
maritima*
sand spur, *Cenchrus* sp.
sardine, *Clupea harengus*
sassafras, *Sassafras albidum*
scaup, greater, *Aythya marila*
scoter, surf, *Melanitta perspicillata*
scoter, white-winged, *Melanitta
deglandi*
sea bass, Family Serranidae
sea duck, Family Aythyinae
seagrape, *Coccoloba uvifera*
seal, gray, *Halichoerus grypus*
seal, harbor, *Phoca vitulina*
sea lettuce, *ulva lactuca*
sea star, *Asterias* sp.
sea urchin, green,
*Strongylocentrotus
droebachiensis*
sergeant major, *Abudefduf saxatilis*
shad, American, *Alosa sapidissima*
shadbush, *Amelanchier obvalis*
shark, blacktip, *Carcharhinus
limbatus*
shark, blue, *Prionace glauca*
shark, brown, *Carcharhinus
milberti*; also, sandbar shark
shark, cookie-cutter, *Isistius
phitodus*
shark, great white, *Carcharodon
carcharias*
shark, lemon, *Negaprion
brevriostris*
shark, mako, *Isurus oxyrhinchus*
shark, sand tiger, *Carcharias
taurus*
shark, smooth dogfish, *Mustelus
canis*
shark, spiny dogfish, *Squalus
acanthias*

shark, whale, *Rhincodon typus*
shearwater, Audubon's, *Puffinus
therminieri*
shearwater, Cory's, *Puffinus
diomedea*
shearwater, greater, *Puffinus gravis*
shearwater, little, *Puffinus
assimilus*
shearwater, Manx, *Puffinus
puffinus*
sheepshead, *Archosargus
probatocephalus*
silverside, Atlantic, *Menidia
menidia*
silverside, tidewater, *Menidia
beryllina*
skimmer, black, *Rynchops niger*
skua, great, *Catharacta skua*
skua, south polar, *Catharacta
maccormicki*
slippery dick, *Halichoeres
bivittatus*
smelt, *Osmerus mordax*
snake, hognose, *Heterodon
platyrhinos*
snapper, gray, *Lutjanus griseus*;
also, mangrove snapper
snapper, lane, *Lutjanus synagris*
snapper, mutton, *Lutjanus analis*
snapper, schoolmaster, *Lutjanus
apodus*
snapper, yellowtail, *Ocyurus
chrysurus*
snook, *Centropomus undecimalis*
sole, Family Achiridae
sparrow, English, *Passer
domesticus*; also, house sparrow
sparrow, Java, *Padda oryzivora*
sparrow, song, *Melospiza melodia*
sponge, red fire, *Tedania ignis*
spruce, white, *Picea glauca*
squid, long-finned, *Loligo pealei*
squid, short-finned, *Illex
illecebrosus*; also, boreal squid
starling, *Sturnus vulgaris*
stickleback, four-spine, *Apeltes
quadracus*
stickleback, three-spine,
Gasterosteus aculeatus
stingray, Family Dasyatidae
sturgeon, Atlantic, *Acipenser
oxyrhynchus*

sumac, nonpoisonous, *Rhus glabra*
sunfish, ocean, *Mola mola*
swordfish, broadbill, *Xiphias
gladius*

tamarind, *Lysilome bahamensis*
tautog, *Tautoga onitis*
tern, Arctic, *Sterna paradisaea*
tern, black, *Chlidonias niger*
tern, bridled, *Sterna anaethetus*
tern, Caspian, *Sterna caspia*
tern, common, *Sterna hirundo*
tern, elegant, *Sterna elegans*
tern, Forster's, *Sterna forsteri*
tern, gull-billed, *Gelochelidon
nilotica*
tern, little, *Sterna albifrons*
tern, noddy, *Anous stolidus*
tern, roseate, *Sterna dougalli*
tern, royal, *Sterna maxima*
tern, sandwich, *Sterna
sandvicensis*
tern, sooty, *Sterna fuscata*
tilefish, *Lopholatilus
chamaeleonticeps*
toad, giant marine, *Bufo marinus*
tonguefish, Family Cynoglossidae,
Symphurus plagiusa
trout, brook, *Salvelinius fontinalis*
trout, brown, *Salmo trutta*
trout, silver, *Cynoscion nothus*;
also, white trout
trout, spotted sea, *Cynoscion
nebulosus*; also, speckled trout,
winter trout
tuna, bluefin, *Thunnus thynnus*
tuna, yellowfin, *Thunnus albacares*
turnstone, ruddy, *Arenaria
interpres*
turtle, eastern box, *Terrapene
carolina carolina*
turtle, leatherback, *Dermochelys
coriacea*
turtle, loggerhead, *Caretta caretta*

Virginia creeper, *Partherrocissus
quinquefolia*; also, woodbine

walrus, *Odobenus rosmarus*
warbler, yellow-rumped, *Dendroica
coronata*; also, myrtle warbler
wax myrtle, *Myrica pensylvanica*

waxwings, *Bombycilla* sp.
weakfish, *Cynoscion regalis*; also,
gray trout, summer trout,
squeteague, tiderunner
whale, Arctic bowhead, *Balaena
mysticetus*
whale, Blainville's beaked,
Mesoplodon densirostris; also
dense-beaked whale
whale, blue, *Balaenoptera
musculus*
whale, Bryde's, *Balaenoptera edeni*
whale, Cuvier's beaked, *Ziphius
cavirostris*; also, goosebeaked
whale
whale, dwarf sperm, *Kogia simus*
whale, finback, *Balaenoptera
physalus*
whale, Gervais' beaked,
Mesoplodon europaeus; also,
Gulf Stream beaked whale
whale, gray, *Eschricthius
(robustus) gibbosus* [Atlantic
race or subspecies is extinct]
whale, Gray's beaked,
Mesoplodon grayi; also,
Camperdown whale
whale, humpback, *Megaptera
novaeangliae*
whale, killer, *Orcinus orca*
whale, minke, *Balaenoptera
acutorostrata*
whale, northern bottlenose,
Hyperoodon ampullatus
whale, pigmy sperm, *Kogia
breviceps*
whale, pilot, *Globicephala
melaena*; also, blackfish
whale, right, *Eubalaena glacialis
glacialis*
whale, sei, *Balaenoptera borealis*
whale, Sowerby's beaked,
Mesoplodon bidens; also, North
Sea beaked whale
whale, sperm, *Physeter catodon*
whale, True's beaked,
Mesoplodon mirus
whiff, Family Pleuronectidae
whimbrel, *Numenius phaeopus*;
also, Hudsonian curlew
willet, *Catoptrophorus
semipalmatus*

woodcock, *Philohela minor*
wrasse, Family Labridae
wrasse, hump-headed Maori,
  Cheilinus undulatus
wrasse blenny, *Hemiemblemaria
  simulus*

wren, Carolina, *Thryothorus
  ludovicianus*

yellowlegs, greater, *Tringa
  melaneleuca*
yew, Japanese, *Taxus cuspidata*

BIBLIOGRAPHY

Ackerman, Bill. *Handbook of Fishes of the Atlantic Seaboard.* Washington, D.C.: The American Publishing Co., 1951.
Abbott, R. Tucker. *How to Know the American Marine Shells.* New York: The New American Library, 1961.
————. *Sea Shells of the World.* New York: Golden Press, 1962.
Allen, Dennis M.; J. P. Clymer; and S. S. Herman. *Fishes of the Hereford Inlet Estuary—Southern New Jersey.* Bethlehem, Pa.: The Wetlands Institute and Lehigh University, 1978.
Allen, Joel Asaph. *History of North American Pinnipeds.* Washington, D.C.: U.S. Government Printing Office, 1880.
Alpers, Anthony. *Dolphins, The Myth and the Mammal.* Boston: Houghton Mifflin Co., 1961.
Amos, William H. *The Life of the Seashore.* New York: McGraw-Hill Book Co., 1966.
Andrews, Roy Chapman. *Under a Lucky Star, A Lifetime of Adventure.* New York: The Viking Press, 1943.
————. *Whale Hunting with Gun and Camera.* New York: D. Appleton and Co., 1916.
Angeletti, Sergio. *Sea Shells: How to Identify and Collect Them.* New York: Golden Press, 1974.
Bailey, Reeve M., committee chairman. *A List of Common and Scientific Names of Fishes from the United States and Canada.* Washington, D.C.: American Fisheries Society, 1970.
Barbour, Michael G.; Robert B. Craig; Frank R. Drysdale; and Michael T. Ghiselin. *Coastal Ecology.* Berkeley: University of California Press, 1973.
Barker, Will. *Familiar Insects of America.* New York: Harper & Brothers, 1960.
Bates, Marston. *The Forest and the Sea.* New York: Vintage Books, 1970.
Beebe, William. *Jungle Peace.* New York: The Modern Library, 1920.
————, and John Tee-Van. *Field Book of the Shore Fishes of Bermuda.* New York: G. P. Putnam's Sons, 1933.

Bennett, D. W. *Fish Stories*. Highlands, N.J.: American Littoral Society, 1979.

———, *202 Questions for the Endangered Coastal Zone*. Highlands, N.J.: American Littoral Society, 1970.

Benson, Norman G., ed. *A Century of Fisheries in North America*. Washington, D.C.: American Fisheries Society, 1970.

Beston, Henry. *The Outermost House*. New York: Ballantine Books, 1956.

Birmingham, Stephen. *The Right People*. Boston: Little, Brown and Co., 1968.

Böhlke, James E., and Charles C. G. Chaplin. *Fishes of the Bahamas and Adjacent Tropical Waters*. Wynnewood, Pa.: Livingston Publishing Co., 1968.

Bond, James. *Birds of the West Indies*. 3d American ed. Boston: Houghton Mifflin Co., 1971.

Boyle, Robert E. *The Hudson River*. New York: W. W. Norton & Co., 1969.

Breder, Charles M., Jr. *Field Book of Marine Fishes of .the Atlantic Coast*. New York: G. P. Putnam's Sons, 1929.

Brewington, M. V. *Chesapeake Bay, A Pictorial Maritime History*. New York: Bonanza Books, 1953.

Brockman, C. Frank. *Trees of North America*. New York: Golden Press, 1968.

Brower, Kenneth. *Wake of the Whale*. New York: Friends of the Earth, 1979.

Browkaw, Howard P., ed. *Wildlife and America*. Washington, D.C.: Council on Environmental Quality, U.S. Government Printing Office, 1978.

Burgess, Robert H. *This Was Chesapeake Bay*. Cambridge, Md.: Cornell Maritime Press, 1963.

Burror, Donald J., and Richard E. White. *A Field Guide to the Insects*. Boston: Houghton Mifflin Co., 1970.

Burt, William H., and Richard P. Grossenheider. *A Field Guide to the Mammals*. Boston: Houghton Mifflin Co., 1964.

Butcher, Russell D. *Field Guide to Acadia National Park, Maine*. New York: Reader's Digest Press, 1977.

Carey, George. *A Faraway Time and Place, Lore of the Eastern Shore*. Washington, D.C.: Robert B. Luce, 1971.

Carr, Archie. *So Excellent a Fishe, A Natural History of Sea Turtles*. Garden City, N.Y.: The Natural History Press, 1967.

———. *The Windward Road*. Tallahassee: University Presses of Florida, 1979 reissue.

Carrington, Richard. *A Biography of the Sea*. New York: Basic Books, 1960.

Carson, Rachel. *The Edge of the Sea*. Illustrated by Bob Hines. Boston: Houghton Mifflin Co., 1955.

———. *The Sea Around Us*. New York: Oxford University Press, 1951.

———. *Silent Spring*. Boston: Houghton Mifflin Co., 1962.

Casey, John G. *Anglers' Guide to Sharks of the Northeastern United States, Maine to Chesapeake Bay*. Washington, D.C.: Bureau of Sport Fisheries and Wildlife, April 1964.

Chapman, Frank M. *Handbook of Birds of Eastern North America*. New York: D. Appleton and Co., 1907.

————. *What Bird Is That?* New York: D. Appleton and Co., 1920.
Clark, John. *Coastal Ecosystems.* Washington, D.C.: The Conservation Foundation, 1974.
————. *Fish & Man.* Highlands, N.J.: American Littoral Society, 1962.
————. *Shark Frenzy.* New York: Grosset & Dunlap, 1975.
Clifford, Harold B. *Charlie York, Maine Coast Fisherman.* Camden, Maine: International Marine Publishing Co., 1974.
Coffey, David J. *Dolphins, Whales and Porpoises: An Encyclopedia of Sea Mammals.* New York: Macmillan Publishing Co., 1977.
Cole, John N. *Striper.* Boston: Little, Brown and Co., 1978.
Conant, Roger. *A Field Guide to Reptiles and Amphibians of Eastern North America.* Boston: Houghton Mifflin Co., 1958.
Cramp, Stanley; W. R. P. Bourne; and David Saunders. *The Seabirds of Britain and Ireland.* New York: Taplinger Publishing Co., 1974.
Crowder, William. *A Naturalist at the Seashore.* New York: The Century Company, 1928.
Culliney, John L. *The Forests of the Sea.* San Francisco: Sierra Club Books, 1976.
Curtis, Brian. *The Life Story of the Fish.* New York: Dover Publications, 1949.
Dibner, Bern. *The Atlantic Cable.* Norwalk, Conn.: Burndy Library, 1959.
Dowden, Anne Ophelia. *The Secret Life of the Flowers.* New York: The Odyssey Press, 1964.
Duncan, Wilbur H., and Leonard E. Foote. *Wildflowers of the Southeastern United States.* Athens: The University of Georgia Press, 1975.
Earle, Swepson. *The Chesapeake Bay Country.* New York: Weathervane Books, 1923.
Elliott, William. *Carolina Sports by Land and Water.* New York: Arno Press, 1967.
Ellis, Richard. *The Book of Sharks.* New York: Grosset & Dunlap, 1976.
Elmhirst, Richard. *The Naturalist at the Sea-Shore.* London: Adam and Charles Black, 1913.
Evans, Howard Ensign. *Wasp Farm.* Garden City, N.Y.: Doubleday & Co., Anchor Press, 1973.
Falorp, Nelson P. *Cape May to Montauk.* New York: The Viking Press, 1973.
Farb, Peter. *Face of North America.* New York: Harper & Row, 1963.
Fisher, James, and R. M. Lockley. *Sea-Birds.* Boston: Houghton Mifflin Co., 1954.
Frost, S. W. *Insect Life and Insect Natural History.* 2d rev. ed. New York: Dover Publications, 1959.
Frye, John. *The Men All Singing, The Story of Menhaden Fishing.* Virginia Beach, Va.: Downing Company, 1978.
Gantz, Charlotte Orr. *A Naturalist in Southern Florida.* Coral Gables, Fla.: University of Miami Press, 1971.
Gates, David Alan. *Seasons of the Salt Marsh.* Old Greenwich, Conn.: The Chatham Press, 1975.
George, Jean Craighead. *Everglades Wildguide.* Washington, D.C.: National Park Service, 1972.
Gibbons, Boyd. *Wye Island.* Baltimore: The Johns Hopkins University Press, 1977.

Goode, G. Brown. *A History of the Menhaden*. New York: Orange Judd Co., 1880.

———. *American Fishes*. Boston: L. C. Page & Co., 1887.

———. *The Fisheries and Fishery Industries of the United States*. Washington, D.C.: U.S. Government Printing Office, 1887.

Gordon, Bernard Ludwig. *The Secret Lives of Fishes*. New York: Grosset & Dunlap, 1977.

Gosner, Kenneth L. *A Field Guide to the Atlantic Seashore*. New York: Houghton Mifflin Co., 1979.

Goulding, F. R. *The Young Marooners on the Florida Coast*. New York: Dodd, Mead & Co., 1887.

Graetz, Karl E. *Seacoast Plants of the Carolinas*. Raleigh, N.C.: Soil Conservation Service, February 1973.

Graham, Frank, Jr. *Where the Place Called Morning Lies*. New York: The Viking Press, 1973.

Greenberg, Idaz and Jerry. *Waterproof Guide to Corals and Fishes of Florida, the Bahamas and the Caribbean*. Miami: Seahawk Press, 1977.

Griffin, Donald R. *Bird Migration*. Garden City, N.Y.: Doubleday & Co., 1964.

Hall, Henry Marion. *A Gathering of Shore Birds*. Edited with additions by Roland C. Clement. New York: The Devin-Adair Co., 1960.

Hallock, Charles, ed. *Camp Life in Florida*. New York: Forest and Stream Publishing Co., 1876.

———. *The Sportsman's Gazetteer and General Guide*. New York: Orange Judd Co., 1878.

Halstead, Bruce. *Dangerous Marine Animals*. Cambridge, Md.: Cornell Maritime Press, 1959.

Hancock, James, and Hugh Elliott. *The Herons of the World*. New York: Harper & Row, 1978.

Hanley, Wayne. *Natural History in America*. New York: Quadrangle/ The New York Times Book Co., 1977.

Harrison, Richard J., and Judith E. King. *Marine Mammals*. 2d ed. London: Hutchinson & Co., 1980.

Hay, John. *The Run*. New York: W. W. Norton & Co., 1979.

Heintzelman, Donald S. *A World Guide to Whales, Dolphins, and Porpoises*. Tulsa, Okla.: Winchester Press, 1981.

Herald, Earl S. *Living Fishes of the World*. Rev. ed. Garden City, N.Y.: Doubleday & Co., 1962.

Heyerdahl, Thor. *Kon-Tiki*. Chicago: Rand McNally & Co., 1950.

Hickin, Norman. *Beachcombing for Beginners*. London: David & Charles Co., 1975.

Huth, Hans. *Nature and the American*. Berkeley: University of California Press, 1957.

Idyll, C. P. *Abyss*. New York: Thomas Y. Crowell Co., 1976.

Jacobson, Morris K., and William K. Emerson. *Shells from Cape Cod to Cape May*. New York: Dover Publications, 1971.

Jensen, Albert C. *The Cod*. New York: Thomas Y. Crowell Co., 1972.

Johnsgard, Paul A. *The Plovers, Sandpipers, and Snipes of the World*. Lincoln: University of Nebraska Press, 1981.

Jordan, David Starr. *A Guide to the Study of Fishes*. Vols. I and II. New York: Henry Holt and Co., 1905.

Joseph, James; Witold Klawe; and Pat Murphy. *Tuna and Billfish.* La Jolla, Calif.: Inter-American Tropical Tuna Commission, 1980.
Katona, Steven; David Richardson; and Robin Hazard. *A Field Guide to the Whales and Seals of the Gulf of Maine.* Bar Harbor, Maine: College of the Atlantic, 1977.
Klingel, Gilbert C. *The Bay.* New York: Dodd, Mead & Co., 1951.
Klots, Alexander B. *A Field Guide to the Butterflies.* Boston: Houghton Mifflin Co., 1951.
Kopper, Philip. *The Wild Edge.* New York: Penguin Books, 1981.
La Monte, Francesca. *North American Game Fishes.* New York: Doubleday & Co., 1946.
Lanham, Url. *The Fishes.* New York: Columbia University Press, 1962.
Lanyon, Wesley E. *Biology of Birds.* Garden City, N.Y.: The Natural History Press, 1963.
Leatherwood, Stephen; David K. Caldwell; and Howard E. Winn. *Whales, Dolphins, and Porpoises of the Western North Atlantic.* Seattle, Wash.: National Oceanographic and Atmospheric Administration, August 1976.
Leonard, Jonathan Norton. *Atlantic Beaches.* New York: Time-Life Books, 1972.
Lincoln, Frederick C. *Migration of Birds.* Rev. ed. Illustrated by Bob Hines. Washington, D.C.: U.S. Fish and Wildlife Service, 1979.
Lindbergh, Anne Morrow. *Gift from the Sea.* New York: Pantheon Books, 1955.
Lippson, Alice Jane, ed. *The Chesapeake Bay in Maryland: An Atlas of Natural Resources.* Baltimore: The Johns Hopkins University Press, 1973.
List, Ilka Katherine. *Questions and Answers About Seashore Life.* New York: Four Winds Press, 1970.
Lucy, Jon. *Handle With Care! Mid-Atlantic Marine Animals that Demand Your Respect.* Gloucester Point, Va.: Virginia Institute of Marine Science, n.d.
Lunt, Dudley Cammett. *Taylors Gut in the Delaware State.* New York: Alfred A. Knopf, 1968.
———. *Thousand Acre Marsh.* New York: The Macmillan Co., 1959.
Lutz, Frank E. *Field Book of Insects.* 3d ed. New York: G. P. Putnam's Sons, 1948.
McCarthy, Joe. "The Man Who Invented Miami Beach." *American Heritage* 28, no. 1 (December 1975).
McClane, A. J., ed. *McClane's New Standard Fishing Encyclopedia.* New York: Holt, Rinehart and Winston, 1974.
MacCord, Howard A., Sr., and William Jack Hranicky. *A Basic Guide to Virginia Prehistoric Projectile Points.* Richmond: Archeological Society of Virginia, 1979.
McCormick, Harold W., and Tom Allen. *Shadows in the Sea, The Sharks, Skates and Rays.* Philadelphia: Chilton Book Co., 1963.
Marsh, George Perkins. *Man and Nature.* Cambridge, Mass.: Harvard University Press, Belknap Press, 1965.
Matthiessen, F. O., ed. *The Oxford Book of American Verse.* New York: Oxford University Press, 1950.
Matthiessen, Peter. *Wildlife in America.* Illustrated by Bob Hines. New York: The Viking Press, 1959.

————. *The Wind Birds.* New York: The Viking Press, 1973.
Meanley, Brooke. *Birds and Marshes of the Chesapeake Bay Country.* Cambridge, Md.: Tidewater Publishers, 1975.
————. *Birdlife at Chincoteague and the Virginia Barrier Islands.* Centreville, Md.: Tidewater Publishers, 1981.
Meyer, Alfred, ed. *The Magnificent Foragers.* Washington, D.C.: Smithsonian Exposition Books, 1978.
Migdalski, Edward C. *Angler's Guide to the Salt Water Game Fishes.* New York: The Ronald Press Co., 1958.
————, and George S. Fichter. *The Fresh and Salt Water Fishes of the World.* New York: Alfred A. Knopf, 1976.
Millus, Donald. *A Contemplative Fishing Guide to the Grand Strand.* Lexington, S.C.: The Sandlapper Store, 1977.
Mitchell, E. D., ed. *Review of Biology and Fisheries for Smaller Cetaceans.* Ottawa: Journal of The Fisheries Research Board of Canada 32, no. 7 (July 1975).
Mitchell, Edward. *Porpoise, Dolphin and Small Whale Fisheries of the World.* International Union for Conservation of Nature and Natural Resources, Morges, Switzerland, 1975.
Morgan, Ann Haven. *Field Book of Ponds and Streams.* New York: G. P. Putnam's Sons, 1930.
Moriarty, Christopher. *Eels.* New York: Universe Books, 1978.
Morison, Samuel Eliot. *Spring Tides.* Boston: Houghton Mifflin Co., 1975.
————. *The Story of Mount Desert Island.* Boston: Little, Brown and Co., 1960.
Morris, Percy A. *A Field Guide to the Shells.* Boston: Houghton Mifflin Co., 1951.
Murphy, Robert Cushman. *Oceanic Birds of South America.* Vols. I and II. New York: The Macmillan Co., 1936.
Nash, Roderick, ed. *The American Environment: Readings in the History of Conservation.* 2d ed. Reading, Mass.: Addison-Wesley Publishing Co., 1976.
————. *Wilderness and the American Mind.* Rev. ed. New Haven, Conn.: Yale University Press, 1973.
Nelson, Joseph S. *Fishes of the World.* London: John Wiley & Sons, 1976.
Netboy, Anthony. *Salmon, The World's Most Harassed Fish.* Tulsa, Okla.: Winchester Press, 1980.
————. *The Atlantic Salmon, A Vanishing Species?* Boston: Houghton Mifflin Co., 1968.
Niemeyer, Virginia Berry, and Dorothy A. Martin. *A Guide to the Identification of Marine Plants and Invertebrate Animals of Tidewater Virginia.* Gloucester Point, Va.: Virginia Institute of Marine Science, 1967.
Norman, J. R., and F. C. Fraser, *Field Book of Giant Fishes.* New York: G. P. Putnam's Sons, 1949.
————. *Giant Fishes, Whales and Dolphins.* New York: W. W. Norton & Co., 1938.
Norris, Kenneth S., ed. *Whales, Dolphins, and Porpoises.* Berkeley: University of California Press, 1966.
Nuttall, Thomas. *A Popular Handbook of the Birds of the United States and Canada.* Boston: Little, Brown and Co., 1911.

Ogburn, Charlton, Jr. *The Winter Beach*. New York: William Morrow & Co., Inc., 1966.

Perlmutter, Alfred. *Guide to Marine Fishes*. New York: Bramhall House, 1961.

Peterson, Roger Tory. *A Field Guide to the Birds*. 4th ed. Boston: Houghton Mifflin Co., 1980.

——, and Margaret McKenny. *A Field Guide to Wildflowers*. Boston: Houghton Mifflin Co., 1968.

Petrides, George A. *A Field Guide to Trees and Shrubs*. Boston: Houghton Mifflin Co., 1972.

Ray, Carleton, and Elgin Ciampi. *The Underwater Guide to Marine Life*. New York: A. S. Barnes and Co., 1956.

Rebel, Thomas P. *Sea Turtles*. Rev. ed. Coral Gables, Fla.: University of Miami Press, 1974.

Reiger, George. *Profiles in Saltwater Angling*. Englewood Cliffs, N.J.: Prentice-Hall, 1973.

——. *The Audubon Society Book of Marine Wildlife*. With photo captions by Les Line. New York: Harry N. Abrams Publishers, 1979.

——. *The Wings of Dawn*. New York: Stein and Day, 1980.

Richardson, Wyman. *The House on Nauset Marsh*. New York: W. W. Norton & Co., 1955.

Ripley, S. Dillon. *Rails of the World*. Boston: David R. Godine Publisher, 1977.

Robbins, Chandler S.; Bertel Bruun; and Herbert S. Zim. *Birds of North America*. New York: Golden Press, 1966.

Roberts, Mervin F. *The Tidemarsh Guide*. New York: E. P. Dutton, 1979.

* Ross, Malcolm. *The Cape Fear*. New York: Holt, Rinehart and Winston, 1965.

Rounsefell, George A. *Ecology, Utilization, and Management of Maine Fisheries*. St. Louis, Mo.: C. V. Mosby Co., 1975.

Rowan, William. *The Riddle of Migration*. Baltimore: The Williams & Wilkins Co., 1931.

Saila, Saul B., ed. *Coastal and Offshore Environmental Inventory: Cape Hatteras to Nantucket Shoals*. Kingston: University of Rhode Island, 1973.

Samuel, Arthur Michael. *The Herring*. London: John Murray, 1918.

Samuels, Edward A. *Our Northern and Eastern Birds*. New York: R. Worthington, 1883.

Sanderson, Glen C., ed. *Management of Migratory Shore and Upland Game Birds in North America*. Washington, D.C.: International Association of Fish and Wildlife Agencies, 1977.

* Other books covering rivers that run to the Atlantic in the monumental Rivers of America Series edited by Carl Carmer are *The Brandywine* by Henry Seidel Canby, *The Connecticut* by Walter Hard, *The Delaware* by Harry Emerson Wildes, *The Housatonic* by Chard Powers Smith, *The Hudson* by Carl Carmer, *The James* by Blair Niles, *The Kennebec* by Robert P. Tristram Coffin, *The Merrimack* by Raymond P. Holden, *The Potomac* by Frederick Gutheim, *River of the Carolinas: The Santee* by Henry Savage, Jr., *Rivers of the Eastern Shore* by Hulbert Footner, *The St. Croix* by James Taylor Dunn, *The St. Lawrence* by Henry Beston, *Salt Rivers of the Massachusetts Shore* by Henry F. Howe, *The Savannah* by Thomas L. Stokes, *The Susquehanna* by Carl Carmer, *Twin Rivers: The Raritan and the Passaic* by Harry Emerson Wildes.

Saunders, David. *Sea Birds*. New York: Bantam Books, 1974.
Scheffer, Victor B. *A Natural History of Marine Mammals*. New York: Charles Scribner's Sons, 1976.
————. *Seals, Sea Lions, and Walruses*. Stanford, Calif.: Stanford University Press, 1958.
————. *The Year of the Whale*. New York: Charles Scribner's Sons, 1969.
Schevill, William E. *The Whale Problem*. Cambridge, Mass.: Harvard University Press, 1974.
Schoenbaum, Thomas J. *Islands, Capes, and Sounds, The North Carolina Coast*. Winston-Salem, N.C.: John F. Blair, Publisher, 1982.
Schultz, Leonard P., with Edith M. Stern. *The Ways of Fishes*. New York: D. Van Nostrand Co., 1948.
Schwartz, Frank J. *Sharks of North Carolina and Adjacent Waters*. Morehead City: University of North Carolina, 1975.
Shannon, Howard J. *The Book of the Seashore*. Garden City, N.Y.: Doubleday, Doran & Co., 1935.
Shapiro, Sidney, ed. *Our Changing Fisheries*. Illustrated by Bob Hines. Washington, D.C.: U.S. Government Printing Office, 1971.
Sharpe, Grant W. *A Guide to Acadia National Park and the Nearby Coast of Maine*. New York: Golden Press, 1968.
Sherwood, Arthur W. *Understanding the Chesapeake*. Cambridge, Md.: Tidewater Publishers, 1973.
Silberhorn, Gene M. *Tidal Wetland Plants of Virginia*. Gloucester Point, Va.: Virginia Institute of Marine Science, 1976.
Smiley, Nixon. *Yesterday's Miami*. 2d ed. Miami: E. A. Seeman Publishing Co., 1974.
Spoczynska, Joy O. I. *An Age of Fishes*. New York: Charles Scribner's Sons, 1976.
Sprunt, Alexander, Jr. *North American Birds of Prey*. New York: Bonanza Books, 1955.
Sterling, Dorothy. *The Outer Lands: A Natural History Guide to Cape Cod, Martha's Vineyard, Nantucket, Block Island and Long Island*. Garden City, N.Y.: Doubleday & Co., Anchor Press, 1974.
————. *Our Cape Cod Salt Marshes*. Orleans, Mass.: Association for the Preservation of Cape Cod, n.d.
Swan, Lester A., and Charles S. Papp. *The Common Insects of North America*. New York: Harper & Row, 1972.
Teal, John and Mildred. *Life and Death of the Salt Marsh*. Boston: Little, Brown and Co., 1969.
Tebeau, Charlton W. *A History of Florida*. Coral Gables, Fla.: University of Miami Press, 1971.
————. *Man in the Everglades*. Rev. ed. Coral Gables, Fla.: University of Miami Press, 1968.
Thoreau, Henry David. *Cape Cod*. New York: Bramball House, 1951.
Tryckare, Tre, and E. Cagner. *The Lore of Sportfishing*. New York: Crown Publishers, 1976.
————. *The Whale*. New York: Simon and Schuster, 1968.
Verrill, A. Hyatt. *Shell Collector's Handbook*. New York: G. P. Putnam's Sons, 1950.
Walker, Michael, ed. *Sport Fishing, USA*. Illustrated by Bob Hines. Washington, D.C.: U.S. Bureau of Sport Fisheries and Wildlife, U.S. Government Printing Office, 1971.

Warner, William W. *Beautiful Swimmers*. Boston: Little, Brown and Co., 1976.

Waters, John F. *The Mysterious Eel*. New York: Hastings House, 1973.

Wennersten, John R. *The Oyster Wars of Chesapeake Bay*. Centreville, Md.: Cornell Maritime Press, 1981.

Wheeler, Alwyne. *Fishes of the World, An Illustrated Dictionary*. New York: Macmillan Publishing Co., 1975.

Windhorn, Stan, and Wright Langley. *Yesterday's Florida Keys*. Miami: E. A. Seeman Publishing Co., 1974.

Zim, Herbert S., and Hurst H. Shoemaker. *Fishes*. New York: Simon and Schuster, 1956.

————, and Alexander C. Martin. *Trees, A Guide to Familiar American Trees*. New York: Simon and Schuster, 1952.

Zinn, Donald J. *The Handbook for Beach Strollers from Maine to Cape Hatteras*. Chester, Conn.: The Pequot Press, 1975.

INDEX

eagle, *continued*
  southern bald, 126
Edge of the Sea, The (Carson), 10
eel, 107, 108, 123
  American, 173
  green moray, 248, 251
  spotted moray, 250-52
eelgrass, 46-47, 207
egret, 194-95
  American, 196, 200
  cattle, 198-99, 206
  common, 194
  snowy, 194, 196, 199-200
  see also heron
eider, common, 140, 169
eiderdown, 100
Electra (Euripides), 161
Elenkin, Alexander, 26
Elliott, William, 191-93, 200
Endangered Species Act, 142, 157
Environmental Defense Fund, 50
Environmental Protection Agency, 35
Euripides, 161

Fabulous Hoosier (Fisher), 227
falcon, peregrine, 137, 170, 173, 229
Federal Energy Regulatory Commission, 37
fern, Christmas, 182
Field, Cyrus W., 87
Field Book of Ponds and Streams (Morgan), 43
Field Guide to the Birds (Peterson), 139
filefish, 73
Firestone, Harvey S., 228
Fish & Man (Clark), 81-82
Fish and Wildlife Service, U.S., 49, 57, 93, 133
Fisher, Carl Graham, 226-29
Fisher, Jane, 227
Fishery Conservation and Management Act (1976), 76
Fishes of the Hereford Inlet Estuary (Allen, Clymer, and Herman), 105
Flagler, Henry Morrison, 223-26, 229, 250
flamingo, 140, 220
Flanagan, Kevin, 54

Fleischmann, Julius L., 228
Florida, 219-53
  beach restoration in, 238-39
  first railroads in, 219, 222-26
  fishing in, 233-39
  Indians in, 220-21, 223
  mangroves in, 231-33, 236
  pollution of, 237-38
  tourism developed in, 221-29
flounder, 53, 184-87
  ambicoloration of, 186
  Gulf, 185
  hogchoker, 108, 185
  right-handed vs. left-handed, 185
  southern, 181
  summer, 106
  sundial, 185-86
  winter, 89, 202
fluke, 106, 110, 184
  four-spotted, 185
  northern, 185, 186
  southern, 185
fly, greenhead, 45-46
flying fish, 72
Fort Hancock, N.J., 9
Fort Jefferson, Fla., 240-50
Frye, John, 10
fulmar, northern, 174-76
Fulton Fish Market, N.Y., 128

gallinule:
  common, 211
  purple, 211
gannet, 174, 197
Gardiners Island, N.Y., 51
Gardner, Keith, 97
Gateway National Recreation Area, N.Y., 9, 88-91
Geological Survey, U.S., 250
Georges Bank, Mass., 19, 20-22
Georgia, marshes in, *see* marshes, in Georgia
Gettysburg, Battle of, 84
glasswort, 207
Godfrey, Paul J., 165-67
goldeneye, 133
goldenrod, seaside, 84
Gonyaulax tamarensis, 32-34
Goode, George Brown, 10, 103-4
goose:
  Canada, 93-95, 123, 164
  greater snow, 93-95, 96, 197

puffer, northern, 106-7
puffin, 133, 176-78, 179
pupfish, 106
purse seining, 74-75

quahog, 51-52, 123
quail, 49-50
  bobwhite, 233

rabbit, 98
raccoon, 230
rail:
  black, 211
  clapper, 194, 211-12
  sora, 211
  Virginia, 211
  yellow, 211, 215
Randall, Burton, 122
rat, Norway, 227
red tides, 30-33
Revolutionary War:
  Sandy Hook in, 86
Ship Harbor in, 28
Richardson, Elliot L., 47
Richardson, Wyman, 46-47, 63
Rickenbacker, Eddie, 227
Right Rigger!, 10
roanoke, 123-24
Robbins, Chandler S., 179
robin, 84, 183
robin, sea, 111
rock beauty, 235
Rockefeller, John D., 224
Rogers, Will, 228
Roney, N. B. T., 227
Roosevelt, Franklin D., 241
Roosevelt, Theodore, 138
Ruffin, Edmund, 189
Russell Dam, 208
Rutgers University, 46

St. Augustine, Fla., 223
Salicornia, 207
salmon, 37
  Atlantic, 101-2, 133, 203
  Pacific, 24
salt meadow hay, 206-7
Salt Water Sportsman, 11
saltwort, 207
sand dab, 184
sandpiper, purple, 169-70
sand spur, 233

Sandy Hook, N.J., 84-88
  dunes on, 87-88
  lighthouse on, 85-86
  military activities on, 84
Santee-Cooper power project, 193
Santee River, 192, 193-94
sardine, 38-41
sassafras albidum, 98
Savannah, Ga., 202-3
sawfly, 43-44
Scarburgh, Edmund, 116-17
scaup, greater, 58, 85
Schwendener, Simon, 26
Science, 10
Science News, 10
Scientific American, 10
scoter, surf, 30
Scotian Shelf, oil drilling on, 19
Scribner's Monthly, 87
Scripps Institution of Oceanog-
    raphy, Climate Research
    Group of, 26-27
sculpin, 67
sea anemone, 246, 249
sea duck, 107-8
seagrape, 224, 229, 233
seal:
  gray, 70, 120
  harbor, 70, 120
sea lettuce, 180, 207
sea star, 117-18
sea urchin, 244
  green, 41
sergeant major, 245-46
Severn River, 108
shad, 37, 38, 109, 123
  American, 101-2
shadbush, 100-101
shark, 82, 109-13, 133
  blacktip, 215
  bronze whaler, 216
  brown, 111-12, 113
  bull, 216
  cookie-cutter, 216
  fishing for, 109-13
  great white, 152
  lemon, 215-18
  mako, 68, 69
  oceanic whitetip, 216
  sand tiger, 110, 113, 216
  spiny dogfish, 54-55
  tagging of, 82, 112-13